SIEGFRIED SASSOON DIARIES

1923–1925

S. S. at Garsington, 1924

SIEGFRIED SASSOON
DIARIES
1923–1925

Edited and introduced by
RUPERT HART-DAVIS

ff
faber and faber
LONDON · BOSTON

First published in 1985
by Faber and Faber Limited
3 Queen Square London WC1N 3AU

Typeset by Speedspools, Edinburgh
Printed in Great Britain by
Redwood Burn Ltd, Trowbridge, Wiltshire
All rights reserved

Selections from
COLLECTED POEMS OF SIEGFRIED SASSOON
Copyright 1936, 1946, 1948 by Siegfried Sassoon.
Reprinted by permission of Viking Penguin Inc.
Photograph of Siegfried Sassoon reproduced by kind permission of
Mrs Igor Vinogradoff

Library of Congress Cataloging in Publication Data

Sassoon Siegfried, 1886-1967.
Siegfried Sassoon diaries, 1923-1925.

1. Sassoon, Siegfried, 1886-1967—Diaries.
2. Poets, English—20th century—Biography.
I. Hart-Davis, Rupert, 1907-   II. Title.
PR6037.A86Z4725 1984   821'.912 [B]   84-13539

ISBN 0-571-13322-3

British Library Cataloguing in Publication Data

Sassoon, Siegfried
Siegfried Sassoon diaries 1923-1925.
1. Sassoon, Siegfried—Biography   2. Poets,
English—20th century—Biography
I. Title   II. Hart-Davis, Rupert
821'.912   PR6037.A86Z/

ISBN 0-571-13322-3

CONTENTS

INTRODUCTION

In 1931 and 1932 Siegfried Sassoon amused himself by making fair copies of what seemed to him the most interesting passages in his earlier diaries, from January 1923 to May 1924 and from May to November 1925. Thereafter he presumably destroyed those original diaries, since they were missing from the collection when he died.

Most of the text of this volume is therefore taken from the fair copies, and the only passages which come from the original diaries are from the end of May to October 1924 and from 23 November to 31 December 1925. But the entries for two days (15 and 19 May 1924) escaped destruction. From them and from a few other passages, such as his meetings with Edmund Gosse, which he fair-copied from contemporary notebooks, it seems clear that he made few changes in the fair copies, except for the omission of hurtful passages about his family and occasional improvements of grammar or syntax. In a note he recorded that he had removed all reference to 'affairs of the heart'.

Introduction

As before I have included poems where they occur in the diaries: those that carry no note of publication are printed here for the first time. To all Siegfried's footnotes I have added his initials: the others are mine. I have again extended all the abbreviations which he used to save space.

I am grateful for help received from Paul Chipchase, Mrs Enid Fry, Mr Michael Halls of King's College Cambridge, Joan Littlejohn of the Royal College of Music, Raymond Mander and Joe Mitchenson, Henry Maxwell, Ernest and Joyce Mehew, Canon P. R. Rounds, Mark Stevenson, Oliver Stonor, and Mrs Igor Vinogradoff.

For permission to print extracts from letters I thank Mr P. N. Furbank for E. M. Forster, and Mr Raglan Squire for J. C. Squire; and Messrs Faber & Faber and the Viking Press for permission to reprint Siegfried's published poems.

Marske-in-Swaledale   RUPERT HART-DAVIS
August 1984

BIOGRAPHICAL TABLE

1886	September 8	Siegfried Sassoon born at Weirleigh, near Paddock Wood in Kent, the second son of Alfred Sassoon and Theresa, née Thornycroft
1902–4		At Marlborough College
1905–6		At Clare College, Cambridge
1906–14		Lived mostly at home, hunting, playing cricket and writing poems, which he had privately printed in small editions
1914	May–August	Living in Raymond Buildings, Gray's Inn
	August 3	Enlisted as trooper in Sussex Yeomanry
1915	Spring	In hospital with broken arm
	May	Commissioned in Royal Welch Fusiliers
	November 24	Joined First Battalion R.W.F. in France

Biographical Table

1916	April 20	To Fourth Army School at Flixécourt for four-week course
	June	Awarded Military Cross for gallantry in action
	August 2	Invalided home with trench fever
		In hospital at Somerville College, Oxford
		Convalescent at Weirleigh
	December 4	Reported to Regimental Depot at Litherland, near Liverpool
1917	February 16	Arrived at Infantry Base Depot, Rouen
	February 18–27	In 25 Stationary Hospital, Rouen, with German measles
	March 11	Joined Second Battalion R.W.F. on the Somme front
	April 16	Wounded in shoulder
	April 20	In hospital at Denmark Hill
	May 8	*The Old Huntsman* published
	May 12–June 4	In convalescent home at Chapelwood Manor, Nutley, Sussex
	June 20	Attended Medical Board at Liverpool. Sent to Craiglockhart War Hospital, near Edinburgh, where he was a patient of W. H. R. Rivers and met Wilfred Owen
	July 30	His statement against the continuation of the war read out in House of Commons and reported in *The Times* next day
	November 26	Passed fit for General Service
	December 11	Reported back to Litherland
1918	January 7	Posted to Limerick
	February 8	Posted to Palestine with Twenty-Fifth Battalion R.W.F.
	May 9	Battalion arrived in France
	June 27	*Counter-Attack* published
	July 13	Wounded in head; to American Red Cross Hospital, 98 Lancaster Gate, London

Biographical Table

	August 20	To convalescent home at Lennel House, near Coldstream in Berwickshire. Thereafter on indefinite sick-leave
	November	First visit to Thomas Hardy
1919	February	Lived briefly in Oxford
	March 12	Officially retired from Army
	March	Appointed Literary Editor of the Socialist *Daily Herald*
	June	*Picture Show* issued
	October 30	*War Poems* published
1920	January–August	Reading his poems in America
	August	Moved into 54 Tufton Street, London S.W.1
1922	July–December	Travels on the Continent

1923

1923

━━━⊷◉⊶━━━

January 11 (54 Tufton Street)[1]
Lunched at Marlborough Club with Gosse.[2] Edmund Blunden[3]
was the third; this being his first meeting with E.G., whose
manner was somehow different from what it would have been
at 17 Hanover Terrace, owing to his entertaining us at 'the
Marlborough'. (E.G. pronounces *Marl* . . . as marl'—not mawl,
creating an impression that *marl* is the aristocratic pronuncia-
tion, just as old-fashioned ladies say *'ain't* you'.) Anyhow the
club atmosphere added a sort of extra mellowness to his manner,
like a coat of varnish to a fine old picture. It was one of E.G's
'special occasions' and he made it entirely delightful. All the
amenities were scrupulously observed, and G. is an artist in
amenities, both social and literary. E.B. made no mistakes and
was admirable in his naturalness and tact. His refinement,

[1] Where S.S. had rented a room since 1920.
[2] Edmund Gosse (1849–1928). Critic, biographer and man of letters. Knighted
1925. S.S. first met him in 1909. See *The Weald of Youth*.
[3] Poet and man of letters (1896–1974). S.S. first met him in 1919. See *Siegfried's
Journey*.

dignity and modesty are inherent, not acquired. It was G's immediate recognition of these qualities which gave him such pleasure. I felt myself E.B's sponsor—a very crude and clumsy one! It was as if I were a large dog; occasionally G. gave me an affectionate pat, and when I emitted an irrelevant bark or made some incongruous canine gesture such behaviour was received as an engaging pleasantry—not to be treated seriously. They discussed Leigh Hunt. After lunch we talked about Hardy. G. urged B. to cultivate *rhyme*, and objected to his rhyming 'was' with 'cross' or 'loss'—'a vulgar rhyme', he called it. E.B. was wearing a new soft tweed suit, roomily cut, of a rough light-greyish material. E.G. said afterwards 'he looked like a dear little chinchilla'. As an example of B's unaffected candour, when we were going downstairs at the end, G. asked B. which day he comes up to London (for his *Athenaeum* work). 'On Fridays,' said B.

E.G. (with beaming urbanity) 'So *this* is a special expedition?'

B. 'No. I can always change the day if I want to.' I couldn't have said that to G. He looked slightly surprised, but I am sure he appreciated the candour.[1]

March 8 (Cicely Hill House, Cirencester) (staying with the Norman Loders[2])

Two days spent at Cheltenham Races (National Hunt Meeting). After watching racing and listening to earnest discussions about the form of horses, I go up to bed very glad to read a few pages of George Moore's *Ave*. Race-meetings are a wholesome contrast to the intellectual life; they convert fine literature into a serene paradise of escape! Not that I feel any active dislike for the sporting excesses of my fellow-countrymen. But I feel 'a bit of an outsider' when I am strolling round the Cheltenham Enclosure, conscious of being somewhat different to the crowds who throng there.

At a literary and artistic party, however, I feel definitely ill

---

[1] I remember, when E.B. was in Japan, showing E.G. a letter from him, in which he referred to 'good old Gosse'. E.G. being sensitive about old age, made me doubt the safety of showing this, but it was a triumph. 'Good old Gosse,' he beamed, adding 'Good old Blunden.' S.S.

[2] Pre-war hunting friends of S.S. See *Diaries 1920–1922*.

at ease. I dislike a 'Phoenix Society'[1] audience, as a whole, more than the assembled members of the Cheltenham Race Club. The races are only a smart bean-feast, and the serious business involved (betting and killing time) does not include intellectual issues. At a 'literary gathering' I am, supposedly, in my own professional environment, for the people are interested in the things which concern my serious existence. But most of them only chatter about 'the arts', in the same way as the empty-headed 'sporting folk' chatter about racing and hunting. In one place I am a critic of the conversation; in the other I am merely a half-amused spectator.

The crowd at Cheltenham—automatically oblivious to any ideas outside Sport—was only a fraction of the herd which bullocks its way through a segment of a century. How small is the fraction which strives to infuse *thought* into the whole heavy lump of contemporary humanity! To-day I watched famous cross-country riders. In ten years there will be a fresh gang of them, equally conspicuous.

March 13

To-day I rode Higham Destiny in the Open Race at the Beaufort Point-to-Point. There were twenty-two starters. Going to the post my mare was very excited, bucking and yawing, going sideways through the spectators, and giving me an uncomfortable time. She is (as Norman Loder remarked sagely) 'very highly strung'! I can't say I felt very confident while she bounded across a stubble-field under a dark lowering sky that looked like a heavy rain-storm impending. But the excitement was exhilarating. At the post everyone seemed to be pushing and shoving and turning round while the Starter made ineffective attempts to get the unruly riders into some sort of line. Finally he allowed us to go, regardless of further formalities. I had ranged my mare alongside Geoffrey Pease, who uneasily asked 'whether she jumped straight'. 'I'll take damned good care she does,' I muttered indomitably, and a few moments later we were hurtling down to the first fence, which I jumped among the first half-dozen. As usual in Open Races there

---

[1] A subscription society which put on productions of Elizabethan and Restoration plays for one or two performances each.

were some very wild riders, and I was thankful when I was over the first four fences and the field was getting strung out. Little Eric P—, on his £500 Waving Pin, fell off at the third fence, though the horse only blundered slightly. (With a good jockey this horse would have won the race.) Soon afterwards Captain 'Fruity' Metcalfe,[1] on the Prince of Wales's Australian steeple-chaser Kinlark, created a diversion by leading two or three others in the wrong direction, thereby losing about a hundred lengths from the leaders. My mare had settled down and was going easily and jumping well. At the water (seventh fence) two horses collided with me in the air and the mare was almost knocked off her feet, but went on gallantly. As I jumped the eleventh fence I heard Phyllis Loder's voice shout 'Go on, Sig!'

The voice seemed to come from a long way off, but pleased me. At the thirteenth fence—an awkward one on a bank, with an old cart-road and a ditch on the take-off side—a man just in front fell and his horse rolled head over heels, and I had to pull across to the left to avoid being brought down by landing on him. (Rather a clever bit of riding, I thought.) There was a nice long stretch of grass before the next fence, so I counted the horses in front of me. There were seven, so I wasn't doing badly, but the race was being run very fast and the course was sticky after last night's rain. Higham Destiny seemed to be 'dying away' a bit; I hit her twice and she responded with a spurt and jumped four more fences nicely. I was then four fences from the finish and the leaders were racing away from me, so I circumspectly pulled up and jogged blissfully back to the paddock, to be welcomed by Norman and Phyllis, who thought it 'a very good show'. No one expected the mare to do more, as she has only been in work for three weeks, after being laid up with her poisoned knee. (Five weeks ago Norman said there was no chance of her running at all this year.) Geoffrey Pease was leading at the last fence, but was beaten by three lengths by K. L. Gibson (who is riding in the Grand National next week). A horse called Piano Player was second.

[1] Edward Dudley Metcalfe (d.1957), A.D.C. and close friend of the Prince of Wales.

March 14

I slept badly last night. Awake till 3 a.m. and then dreamt that I threw my poems into the sea! (It was the copy of *Picture Show*,[1] limited edition, into which I have pasted my recent poems out of magazines.)When I'd done it, I at once felt that I'd made an awful mistake, and plunged into the water to rescue the book, but found myself being carried away by a strong current (my 'water-phobia'?). The dream fizzled out in my regaining the shore without the book. I suppose the dream expressed a conflict between athletic and intellectual interests!

March 18 (*54* Tufton Street)

Norman drove me to Kemble Junction this afternoon, but the 1.15 train proved to be a weekday one, and for the next hour I was the only occupant of the station, except for a large rook, who walked about on the 'down' platform for several minutes and then flapped away into the dry cold sunlight. A loitering train conveyed me to Paddington by 5 o'clock, while I read the first hundred pages of a book on Tennyson by Harold Nicolson.[2]

I found this house empty, except for Edward Shanks[3] (who has a tiny room here and uses it one or two nights a week). He was just going out. 'The very man I want!' he exclaimed, and borrowed ten shillings.

I dined with the Asquiths at 44 Bedford Square. A dozen people at the table. I sat between Viola Tree[4] and Jelly D'Arányi[5] (the violinist). Lady Desborough sat opposite me, with J. M. Keynes beside her, and Lady Hartington (who has a charming face) next to Keynes. Viola Tree tried Bob Nichols[6] as a conversational opening, but I soon realised that she doesn't know him well or take any interest in him. So we lapsed into laboured talk about the theatre. Jelly D'Arányi tried Robert Graves and

---

[1] Thirty-four poems by S.S., privately printed in an edition of 200 copies in 1919. An unlimited edition, containing seven further poems, was published by E. P. Dutton in New York in 1920.

[2] Which S.S. reviewed in the *Daily Herald* on 28 March.

[3] Poet (1892–1953). Assistant Editor of the *London Mercury* 1919–22.

[4] Actress and singer (1884–1938).

[5] Hungarian violinist (1893–1966).

[6] Robert Nichols, poet (1893–1944) whom S.S. had met with Robbie Ross in 1917. See *Diaries 1920–22*.

Garsington[1] (the last time I met her was in 1916 at Garsington, when Robert Graves was there with me). But I didn't want to discuss R.G.

When the ladies had vanished I sat beside Mr Asquith, who was listening to Keynes talking about the election of a new Fellow at King's. I managed to converse with the flushed and silver-haired statesman, by asking if he'd seen Nicolson's *Tennyson*. (Mr A. being, of course, a staunch Tennysonian.) He gave me an account of his meeting with Tennyson at Professor Jowett's in the Seventies. No doubt the story will appear in his Memoirs.[2]

After that there was a party, and about twenty people arrived. Someone played the piano, and J.D. played the violin, and Viola Tree and Betty Pollock[3] tried to be amusing with mimicries. Margot, as usual, was very 'natural' and demon-strative, and completely in control of the social situation. But I came away feeling that I'd been too self-conscious and awkward to have enjoyed the evening. Walked to Trafalgar Square, where I got into a taxi and found two shillings and one penny on the seat. Gave it to the driver, who probably thought I was drunk when I told him I'd found it in his conveyance.

March 21 (Cicely Hill House)

Posterity will be impatient to learn how I 'got on' in the Cotswold Open Race. But my race-riding doesn't seem to provide many thrills. I jumped the last fence twenty lengths behind the winner and finished fifth (out of eight). It was raining hard when I awoke this morning. While shaving I caught a glimpse of Higham Destiny, pacing sedately down the road in the downpour, rugged and hooded, for the 10.30 train to Cheltenham. Later in the morning the Loders departed for Liverpool, full of regrets that they couldn't 'see me ride'. (But the National will be better value, I surmise!)

Motored to the races with Geoffrey Pease and Myles Thompson. Walked round the course, which wasn't very 'big'.

[1] The home near Oxford of Philip and Ottoline Morrell.
[2] Only a brief mention, without details in Vol. I of Asquith's *Memoirs and Reflections* (1928).
[3] Actress and mimic (1898–1970).

I then inserted my legs into my smart new boots and breeches, feeling slightly forlorn without Norman to look after my preliminaries. Discreetly remote from the crowd and the bawling bookies, I held my mare's highly-strung head while her devoted little groom saddled her and fastened many straps, adjusting the weight-cloth, etc. I felt a shade more nervous than last time, but was riding 'in colours', which always gives rather a jolly professional feeling. Nice Mary Gibson (wife of K.L.G. who is riding in the National on Friday) was the only one of my sporting acquaintances who discovered me. She gave me a cheery send-off, but I missed Phyllis and Norman at the moment of departure, when the saddle felt slippery and my heart was in my mouth, and the mare was bounding along sideways.

As usual, all nervousness evaporated the moment we were off, and I was conscious of nothing except a fixed resolve to make the most of my mare and keep her from falling. (She is rather a chancy jumper.) The course was rather heavy after the rain, which is a handicap for lightly-built Higham Destiny. She always seemed to be going as fast as she could, but I could never get nearer than five lengths behind Myles Thompson, who made the pace all the way round (and looked rather a 'passenger'). But it was a hopeless affair. The mare does her living best, but doesn't seem fast enough to win an Open Race, even if she were quite fit. Wheeler (the groom) didn't seem to be disappointed. He merely said 'A gallop like that does a horse a lot of good', adding 'She jumped the fence at the bottom fine', and began rubbing her down. Then he led her away to Cheltenham, and I went back to the dressing-tents, passing the admiring crowd round Myles's horse Enniscorthy, who won by half-a-length (and feeling rather disillusioned about the racing which I'd looked forward to so eagerly all the winter). Geoffrey Pease won the Farmers' Race easily, on Actress. One or two people smiled at me and said 'Had a good ride?' without wanting an answer. And that was all. I still have a slight chance of winning the V.W.H. Lightweight Race on April 11, but if Enniscorthy runs I can't hope to do better than last year, when I was a bad second on good old Lady Jill. To-day was my eighteenth race (on horses *owned* by me). I have never fallen, and the Beaufort was the first time I've failed to finish the course. I have won four; three seconds; three thirds—which proves that I am not an absolute mug at it.

March 27

'I get more pleasure from my horses than from anything else!' I remarked this evening, when Phyllis had been saying 'What a pity it is Mr Turner[1] doesn't play any games!' Riding about in Gloucestershire on a fine spring day and feeling healthy, certainly that is a pleasant way of spending one's time. And when my chestnut mare sails over the top twig of a big fence and gallops along a stretch of sound old turf I am happier than I am when I am huddled in a five-and-ninepenny seat in Queen's Hall indulging my emotional day-dreams—yes, I am! Some day, when I have 'settled down' and come into a fortune, I will buy a little manor house in a good hunting country and keep three or four 'nailing good performers', and play on a grand piano in a room full of books, with a window looking on to an old-fashioned garden full of warbling birds and mossy apple-trees. When I am forty-nine I will begin to look for that house, and when I am in it I will write wise books.

April 11

An unsuccessful day! We started late—Phyllis never has any idea of time, and was upstairs powdering her nose while Norman and I were waiting for her in desperation.

Left here at 1—my race being at 2, and the distance thirteen miles. Then we got in an enormous queue of cars approaching the course (a huge crowd had come to see the Prince ride) and I had to get out and run across two fields carrying my kitbag. I got to the weighing-tent at 1.45. Luckily I'd changed before starting, so I managed to get down to the post with half-a-minute to spare. To get 'to the post' one goes down a very steep slope; my stirrup-leathers were unequal lengths—one much too short—and I never felt less like riding a race. Thirteen started, and more by luck than judgment I got away well and jumped the first fence with the first three. At the third fence—

[1] W. J. Turner (1889–1946). Australian poet and music critic, S.S's landlord in Tufton Street.

the water—Geoffrey Pease, on Enniscorthy, took off much too soon and landed in the water. I looked round and saw him standing by his horse's head, and thought 'Now I've got a better chance of winning.' After that all went well for a time. The others dropped back, and I found myself going along a few lengths behind the Prince of Wales, J. B. Powell and Nigel Worthington. The going was terribly sticky, but Higham Destiny jumped every fence perfectly. At the fence where they turn into the last half-mile (straight), Powell fell and I was close behind the P. of W. and Worthington, with four fences to jump. Another horse came up to me, and I felt the mare dying away. Geoffrey Pease passed me, though very tired with making up lost ground. Then old Nisbet on his grey (who beat me last year) passed me. Going at the last fence I knew that Higham Destiny was 'stone-cold', but didn't want to pull up. The result was that she landed in the ditch on the far side and lay on the ground for about ten minutes with a gaping crowd round her. I was afraid she'd broken her back, but she was only completely 'blown', and finally struggled to her feet and walked away with her ears cocked, none the worse. She is a gallant little animal, but nothing like as fast as I used to think. Norman and Phyllis had come down to the fence, and we toddled up the hill to the paddock, behind the mare led by the groom—a forlorn little procession. The mare falling like that made me realise that there is something rather brutal about racing.

The rest of the afternoon was disastrous. Geoffrey Pease had lost £50 backing Enniscorthy. In the Open Race he rode Palm Ring and lost some more. (He fell at the last fence, but wouldn't have won.) Worst of all, poor Dick Allan broke his horse's back in the Heavyweight Race. Rain came on early in the afternoon, and the place was a welter of mud and cars trying to get away, with wheels slipping on the greasy field.

My failures with Higham Destiny make me realise that racing isn't as important as poetry. Supposing she'd turned out to be really fast and I'd won to-day (as I might have done, for I know I rode her all right), should I be any happier?

April 15 (Garsington)

April 12 was the wettest day for weeks, and the King and Queen visited Cirencester, planted trees at the Agricultural College, lunched with the Bathursts,[1] and retired at 3. Hundreds of schoolchildren were given a flag to wave and a bun to munch, and all the local patriotic organisations paraded to catch colds and cheer.

Next day the hounds met in Cirencester Park. Finding at once, they ran through the woods with a great cry and went away to Edgworth and Miserden. They slipped the field, and only Lord Bathurst (who never jumps a fence) and the second whip were with them.

Norman and I were careering round the country looking for them, when I gave my shin and ankle an awful bruising in a gateway. Rode about for some time, in considerable pain, and got home soaked through, to find that I'd got a nasty hole in my leg.[2] Came here yesterday, and am staying in bed. Stanley Spencer (the painter)[3] is staying here. Nice little chap, and a genius, but very exhausting as he talks incessantly.

April 18

Spring is making rapid progress outside my windows. Watching the tall yews which form two sides of a court (with the high grey gateposts facing the house-front which contains my two windows) I listen to a twittering and warbling world of gently swaying green. All the cold freshness of spring is in the air. Socrates (the pug) snores on my bed, and the walls of my room are friendly with small old-fashioned pictures (by W. Turner of Oxford[4]).

May 4 (Garsington)

I have now delayed here for three weeks of compulsory idleness, and my leg is not quite healed up.

[1] The seventh Earl Bathurst (1864–1943), Master of the Vale of White Horse Foxhounds. Lady Bathurst was a daughter of Lord Glenesk.
[2] *This was my last day's hunting until January 1931.* S.S.
[3] 1891–1959. R.A. 1950. Knighted 1959.
[4] William Turner (1789–1862).

It might have been expected that a few lines of verse would have shaped themselves. But no. In vain I stroll between yew hedges, eyeing the apple-blossom and the wavering shadows on orchard grass. Primavera produces no poetic feelings in me. The confused cloudy masses of my mental existence remain shapeless. I am indeed the most muddle-headed of men. Snatches of desultory reading refresh me, but bring no intellectual activity. I seem to have formed a habit of refusing to attempt verse-writing unless I am sure I have a subject. I can no longer persuade myself to embark on meditative or rhapsodic meanderings on the fluid element of language—those little voyages once round the bay and back again, which fill so many trim volumes of verse. Marooned on the island of my journal, I contemplate infinity.

May 13 (54 Tufton Street)

Sixth day here since I left Garsington. Feeling low-spirited and headachy. Drank half a bottle of white wine at the Reform and read 150 pages of *Men Like Gods* by H. G. Wells. I can't understand Turner thinking the book *bad*. H.G's idea of Utopia (rather a garden-suburb world) isn't altogether to my taste, but the fresh and hopeful vigour of the book roused my enthusiasm, and made me long to escape into a cleaner and more civilised Future. Turner says 'Wells is no more use to me. I used to read everything he'd written, but I'm beyond him now.' He has reviewed *Men Like Gods* contemptuously in the *Daily Herald*. H.G.W. (evidently thinking that the *Herald* reaches a public which needs his prophesyings) wrote two savage letters (to the *Herald*) wiping the floor with Turner. Anyhow I came home tonight feeling much more alive (though with pains behind the eyes). In the background of my mind there is always the dramatised thought of the ME who never gets a chance to function freely, and H.G's book made me conscious of being imprisoned in a pathological inferno. Can I ever liberate myself and write something which can be of service to this un-Utopian Age? To-morrow I shall be the same melancholy moper, killing time and brooding over my inactivity.

May 14

Finished H.G's book this evening. Enjoyed the last part as good exciting stuff. The characterisation (except in the protagonist, Barnstaple — a sort of H. W. Massingham[1]) is journalistic. Winston and Eddie Marsh[2] recognisable and vindictively done. As a work of imagination it is thin, but his immense vitality carries him through. It is a great propagandist pamphlet for young people who need to be taught that they must work for the improvement of the world.

May 21 (Whit Monday)

Weather milder at last. Feeling less melancholy than I've done since I left Garsington, so I rang up the Gosses and asked myself for tea. Was invited to dinner and went. Max Beerbohm and his wife, Sickert,[3] and Maurice Baring[4] there. Also Mrs Chalmers Mitchell[5] and Miss Darling (daughter of the Judge). I'd met the Beerbohms once before, in 1916 (also at Gosse's). Sat between Mrs Max and Mrs C. M. (who knew Pater, Mark Pattison, and Jowett). In spite of introspection, solitude, and 'feeling middle-aged', I feel young when I 'go out', and I find myself talking very fast (and not very distinctly). Max was not talkative, but quite charming. I shared a taxi back to Jermyn Street with them (they are staying with the William Nicholsons[6]). When saying good-night, I felt impelled to say, with a bashful air, 'I think you are one of the best authors.' 'How delightful of you,' was the appropriate reply, and it was duly forthcoming. (My remark was gospel truth.) Sickert was rather silent, while E.G. sparkled. Baring giggled a good deal, as usual.

After writing the above entry I remembered that Mrs

---

[1] Liberal journalist (1860–1924). Editor of the *Nation* 1907–23.
[2] Edward Marsh (1872–1953), civil servant, translator, patron of poets and painters. See *The Weald of Youth*.
[3] Walter Richard Sickert (1860–1942), painter.
[4] Poet, novelist, diplomat and man of letters (1874–1946).
[5] Lilian, wife of Peter Chalmers Mitchell (1864–1945). He was Secretary to the Zoological Society 1908–35, and was knighted in 1929.
[6] William Nicholson (1872–1949), painter, knighted 1936, and his second wife Edie, daughter of Sir Lionel Phillips and widow of John Stuart-Worpley.

Chalmers Mitchell spoke affectionately about Robbie Ross,[1] and told me a story about how he chivalrously escorted a beggar-woman across Piccadilly during an Air Raid. He led her across to the Ritz arches; pieces of anti-aircraft shell were falling, and Robbie gravely *put up his umbrella* while they crossed the street. I am sure he was wearing his top-hat. 'Impostors always wear silk-hats' he used to say.

May 22

Letter from Norman Loder saying that Higham Destiny is sold for £140. But this doesn't help much, as I owe N.L. £183 for keep of my two horses last winter. Lady Jill's rheumatism is now so bad that she will have to be 'put down'. I can't afford to buy another horse this year, or to hunt at all even if I had one. And Turner has lost his *Daily Herald* job (£4 a week) and may be in financial straits by the autumn. I am half-inclined to go abroad next winter. The Loder-hunting habit is too much of a tax on my vitality. Last winter the hunting definitely interfered with my writing, though it kept my muscles good, and I am very fond of the Loders. But I can get no detachment of mind or continuity of thought when I am always being wrenched from one environment to another. And I have to be so terribly 'bright' when I get there!

May 24

Lunched with Mother at her club. Listened to the usual recital of her antagonism (unavoidable) toward my sister-in-law.[2] It is an impossible situation for Mother, having my brother and his family in her house (for the last two and a half years!) but she wrecks her own peace of mind by failing ever to get free from trivial domestic details and the exasperations which she to some extent *creates*. How fine she is, and how pathetic!

---

[1] Robert Baldwin Ross (1869–1918). Literary journalist and art critic. Faithful friend of Oscar Wilde. S.S. had first met him at the Gosses' in 1915. See *Siegfried's Journey*.

[2] S.S's elder brother, Michael Thornycroft Sassoon (1884–1969), married Violet Mildred Stroud in 1907.

May 26 (The Wharf, Sutton Courtenay[1])

Am here for the week-end! Arrived about 7, feeling town-jaded and weak-eyed (after eighteen days at Tufton Street). Walter Rummel[2] (pianist) on the train, so I had to share a taxi with him. He is a long-haired, pallid, velvet-collared sham-Bohemian. When we arrived, he hurried into the house so as to avoid paying his share of the taxi (which seemed to me significant). This place seems to exist for bridge.[3] Rummel and I were the only two not playing this evening (in a party of fourteen). A stockbroker named Smith is evidently here solely because he is 'a crack card-player at the Portland Club'. An M.P. who has made a fortune in Peruvian Copper Mines is, I imagine, here as a possible supporter of Asquithian party-politics. Lady Coats, a kindly heavyweight dowager. Lady Bradford, lady-in-waiting to the Queen, smart, sporting, and heavily rouged. Mrs Geoffrey Howard, friendly, fair-haired, and hard-looking (daughter of Lord Methuen). Mrs Marshall Roberts, youngish (American?), has a large album which she illustrates—castles and house-party signatures—that album is a microcosm of boredom, sport, and good living.

May 27

Loafed about alone most of the day. Rummel played the piano (at the Mill House—a sort of annexe to The Wharf) before lunch, and Margot gave a description of Holy Week at Seville, which she'd seen this year, and gave a Spanish dance!

At lunch she talked to me about Gosse, accusing him of treachery, because he praised her *Autobiography* in manuscript and was much less enthusiastic when he reviewed it. After lunch I was hiding in my room, but was turned out by the butler (Clouder, a great character-part) who burst in with some assistants, to rectify some electric-light apparatus which had gone wrong and had its *fons et origo* behind my bed. An east-wind day; too much rich food. Everyone playing bridge after

---

[1] The country house of Mr and Mrs Asquith.
[2] Anglo-German pianist (1887–1953).
[3] One might almost suspect that Mr Asquith appointed Bridges Poet Laureate on the strength of his *name*! S.S.

dinner except Puffin[1] and me and Sylvester Gates.[2] (Rummel left after tea.) Last night I dreamt about a book called *Making Good* by Senator Stung B. Confusion—rather a good name!

May 28

Mr and Mrs Asquith drove me up to town. I was feeling bilious, and the swaying of the car made me feel quite sick. They dropped me at the Marble Arch. At one time I really thought I should be sick.

May 31

To Max Exhibition.[3] Rather cruel one of O. and S. Sitwell.

June 1

Went to 40 Half Moon Street 5.15. (Burton's[4] birthday, which I'd forgotten, but I didn't tell her I'd come by chance!) O. Sitwell opened the door! He seemed nervous, but assumed *sang froid* demeanour. 'How *are* you?' etc. I was grim, and asked how he liked his Max caricature. He said it made him look too thin. (An attempt at a joke.) I asked if he thought it a good criticism, which was unkind and confused him a bit. He left soon after.

June 2

The last four weeks have been like March. In to-day's *Nation* there is a sneering review of Bob Nichols's *Fantastica*[5] (which I've read, with a great effort) by O. Sitwell. O.S. seems incapable of any generous appreciation of anyone except his own family and intimates. Everything he writes leaves an impression of *spite* against everyone who doesn't flatter him.

---

[1] Anthony Asquith (1902–68), film director. Youngest son of the Prime Minister.
[2] Barrister and banker (1901–72).
[3] Of caricatures by Max Beerbohm at the Leicester Galleries.
[4] Nellie Burton, proprietress of 40 Half Moon Street, where she let rooms to single gentlemen. S.S's friend Robbie Ross spent his last years there.
[5] A volume of stories (1923).

June 4

Going through old letters, I discovered a press-cutting of a generous letter Bob Nichols wrote to the *New Witness* (September 1919) in defence of O. Sitwell (who had been attacked by C. K. Scott Moncrieff[1]). Sent it to O.S. without comment.

June 6 (Derby Day. Grey and drizzly.)

Went to hear Robert Graves read his play *John Kemp's Wager* to Frederic Austin[2] at Apple Tree Yard.[3] Amusing but not dramatic. Nancy very distant and went away at once.

After dinner I returned to Apple Tree Yard and talked (alone) to R.G. for two hours. He is as stimulating as ever, and I take up my talk with him as though we hadn't been apart for months. He complains that he has too much domestic work to do, but his productivity seems to prove that the life agrees with him. Nancy and her father returned from Gay's *Polly* at 11.15. N. was grumpy (because I avoid going to Islip, I suppose). What a contrast R.G. is to O.S.! He has all the humanity (and humility) which O. lacks. There is nothing mean or malicious about R.G. A happy evening. While R. discoursed, I sat puffing my pipe and gazing at the superb 'Popomack' fruit which William Nicholson has made for Turner's play.[4] (He is designing the scenery.)

June 8

Cool grey windy weather. Walking by the Serpentine about 3.15, I caught sight of Henry Head[5] on the sky-line, tripping along in his baggy blue suit and looking more like an ex-sea-captain than a famous scientist. This was very pleasant, as I was feeling lonely and the afternoon had no objective. (Fifteen minutes before I'd met S. Sitwell in St James's Square. He bore

[1] Translator of Proust (1889–1930).

[2] Baritone and composer (1872–1952). Arranged the music for the revival of *The Beggar's Opera* in 1920 and *Polly* in 1922.

[3] The London home of William Nicholson. His daughter, Nancy, was married to Graves.

[4] *The Man who ate the Popomack.*

[5] Neurologist (1861–1940). Knighted 1927. After W. H. R. Rivers the chief father-figure in S.S's life.

down on me and flashed past with a basilisk stare. The rapidity and precision of his gait caused me to assume, mentally, the physical semblance of a decrepit clubman.) Henry Head made me feel a callow youngster again. We walked and talked (about de la Mare's new book *The Riddle*[1]), back to Montagu Square for tea. H.H. left at 4.30, for a consultation.

Talking to Ruth Head I began to think aloud, or talk behaviouristically, expressing my recent revulsion against hunting and being involved in the intellectual limitations of the Loders. Mrs Head talked about a young friend who had gone to live to Freiburg, and this made me crave to go away abroad and get mental detachment.

June 12

Last night I read D. H. Lawrence's remarkable tale 'The Fox'[2] which carried me on till 4.15 a.m. It was daylight when I switched off the light, and the strange pallor of dawn was on the walls, and my blotting-pad was a patch of phosphorescent white. (It was a cold white dawn.) Standing in the middle of the room, wrought up by the emotion of D.H.L's strange genius and the queer unreality of the early morning, I seemed to be looking at my little white room for the first time; and it was as if I were saying good-bye to it also.

Turner's play at the Savoy in the afternoon. Sat in a box with Nicholson and Sir Edwin Lutyens.[3] L. greeted me with 'You don't look like a Parsee. Are you rich?' I said I was neither. His outspokenness seemed rather buffoonish. The play went splendidly. (The first performance of the Sitwells' *Façade* was at Aeolian Hall the same afternoon.)

June 14

Recreations[4] arrived from the binders (at Oxford) this morning. (Edition of eighty copies.) After lunch I was choosing the

---

[1] Which S.S. reviewed in the *Daily Herald* on 6 June.
[2] Published in 1923 in a volume containing also 'The Ladybird' and 'The Captain's Doll'.
[3] Leading architect (1869–1944). Knighted 1918, O.M. 1942.
[4] A privately printed volume of S.S's poems.

right size of envelope in the Reform Club library, and encountered E. M. Forster. (Hadn't seen him for five months.) Went to London Library and *New Statesman* office with him as he had jobs to do there. Then to Max exhibition, and back here for tea. Lent him my 1921–22 journal—rather a rash thing to do—and gave him one of the five large-paper copies of *Recreations*. Talked about D. H. Lawrence. E.M.F. likes 'The Fox', but thinks 'The Captain's Doll' badly constructed and containing irrelevant material. He said : 'The problem of this age is to combine freedom of soul with the necessity to know people intimately.' (Or words to that effect.) This, he thinks, is what makes D.H.L's work confused and not quite satisfactory. I was so pleased and excited by seeing him that I got the time of day mixed up. I'd engaged myself to dine with my pre-war friend Charles Wiggin and his wife. When I got there in my dinner-jacket, they'd only just returned from the polo at Hurlingham or somewhere, and I found that I was an hour early. Of course they attributed this to my being a poet! Charles has a heart of gold, but the dinner-party (ten of us) was not a good sequel to Forster's conversation. Nothing but hunting, racing, and polo, with sherry, champagne, port and brandy to wash it down. I left at 11, just as they were settling down to play poker. I am a 'freak' among such well-washed and good-natured Philistines.

June 19

Went to Bray on Saturday. Only Schuster[1] and Anzie[2] there. Weather chilly and grey. Returning this morning (driven by Anzie in the Rolls) we met the Ascot procession of limousines and char-à-bancs—the social extremes of stupidity. This afternoon I went to see Duse[3] in *Ghosts*. Ralph Hodgson[4] sends a

---

[1] Frank Schuster (1840–1928), wealthy music-lover and giver of parties. See *Diaries 1920–1922*.

[2] Nickname of Leslie Wylde, a New Zealand friend and protégé of Schuster's.

[3] Eleonora Duse (1859–1924), great Italian actress. James Agate wrote of her portrayal of Mrs Alving in Ibsen's *Ghosts*: 'To see the Italian actress move, draped as she always is like a queen, is a whole folio in ecstasy, her play of hands about face and robe a revelation.'

[4] Poet (1871–1962).

message by Delphine[1] that I am one of the living writers who has an individual vocabulary. He thinks my method of issuing my poems right. E. M. Forster writes, about my Journal:

> The Journal's great work, and I could discuss the writer and his judgments endlessly, were that my point. But how are you to transfer its qualities into a story? Some dodge is required, and I can't think what it is. You are not (at present) a story-writer, but why not? I wish I could tell you. I can only advise you to try again. Sit down, invent (drearily) characters and a plot. Sit down again and begin to write out same. Possibly the whole thing will come alive during the second sitting. The method of your 1921 story has been a failure—distinction, power, liveliness, all got side-tracked. So I can only suggest that you try an entirely new method and do not await the visiting of 'inspiration'. If it fails we must try something else, for certainly the stuff is inside you—indeed it is 'out' in your journal.

June 25

To-night Turner gave me a ticket for *Tristan*. I missed Act I (missing an Act always increases one's enjoyment of Wagner) and left at Isolde's entrance in the last Act. I found myself feeling violently antagonistic to the Wagnerian tradition of *Love*! Surely it is an utterly obsolete notion of romantic passion. The spectacle of that corpulent couple galumphing about in their ocean of melodious eroticism appeared grotesque. And the audience! What do those old women with skimpy white hair feel as they sit for hours drowning in the Wagnerian ocean? What a colossal joke Wagner played on cultured humanity! When the lights were turned up after Act II, the faces, young and old, wore a drugged look. They had been witnessing one of 'the world's supreme love-dramas'. How many of them ever ask themselves whether *love* is like that now or was like that in Tristan's time?

During the interval I met Schuster, fashionably attired and steering his course toward Melba's box.[2] He was in raptures over the performance until a well-known and wine-flushed critic

[1] Mrs W. J. Turner.
[2] Australian soprano prima donna (1859–1931). Created D.B.E. 1927.

asserted 'that Tristan had been singing very much out of tune
and that Isolde was no great shakes either'. Schuster hedged, by
exclaiming, 'But you aren't old enough, my dear Toye,[1] to
remember the Bayreuth performances when *both* of them sang
out of tune during the whole of the love-duet!' Schuster's method
of keeping the game alive is to try and persuade himself that
everything in life is a superb performance. (Much better than
pulling a long face and grumbling, which he does when food
and weather aren't good.)

Lying in bed this morning I was thinking about methods of
disciplining myself to enjoy life quietly—feeding the mind and
getting the better of animalisms. Suddenly I wondered whether
one *can* change one's natural way of living. How terrible, I
thought, if it is all self-deception and I am essentially unamen-
able to self-discipline! Of course I can't change my character (or
those of Turner, O. Sitwell, and R. Nichols). Can I influence my
life 'on large lines' any more than Schuster can influence the
weather?

My former brother-officer V. Pinto[2] writes me a rather
pedantic letter from Paris—about *Recreations*. 'As poetry,
although some of it is exquisite art, it lacks something. A faith,
a passion—that was what made the Shakespeares and the
Donnes. We seem incapable of it now. You had it for a moment
during the war, but now there is only a fine technique and the
languid interest of a half-amused spectator.' I don't blame him
for arriving at this conclusion. But I am certain that I have never
been less languid or uninterested than I am now. Pinto, however, is a professor, and has just *re-written* his life of Sir Charles
Sedley.[3] He is obsessed by the idea that the Elizabethans were
the climax of English Literature. Linguistically, they probably
were. But the next few hundred years may discover new
continents of European intelligence. Professors are apt to regard
their own age as a 'dark one'. I am a spark sailing up from the
bonfire of 1914–1918. And I am desirous of believing that I am
a bright spark from the cultural conflagration!

[1] Francis Toye (1883–1964), music critic and author.
[2] Vivian de Sola Pinto (1895–1969), poet, critic and Professor of English
Literature. He had been S.S's second-in-command on the Western Front.
[3] Courtier and poet (1639–1701).

June 27

After dinner I went to 40 Half Moon Street and sat till after mid-night with Roderick Meiklejohn[1] and three others who'd been dining with him at Brooks's Club. They'd all drunk a little too much, and were continuing to do so. A. T. Bartholomew[2] (who spends his life in the University Library at Cambridge) told me that I need to fall in love. R. Temple[3] (press-agent for the Savoy Hotel) was consuming Corona-Coronas with prodigal abandon. Roderick was lamenting that he'd not been born a Roman Senator in the Age of Nero (instead of being the son of an Aberdeen professor). Roderick's career as a Treasury official seems to have produced a philosophy of autumnal despair. There is, for him, no such thing as the future, and the present is an event to be deplored. Only the past is to be applauded. He venerates Virgil, Dante, Cervantes, Milton, etc. To-night he exclaimed (refilling his glass with Spanish brandy), 'I *respect* Christ. He drank. And he was a great wit.' After that I left. Out in the street a prostitute begged me to be a sport and give her her cab-fare back to Clapham.

June 28

Arnold Bennett gracefully acknowledges *Recreations* (I've given away nearly fifty copies so far) but goes on to say 'Dare I ask when you intend to emerge from what I call "the carping school"? I want something more benevolent, more sublime, and more ideally beautiful. Osbert *is* emerging from it. I think his *Out of the Flame*[4] shows development.' etc. This reference to O.S. in connection with my own book irritated me, and I lay in bed improvising spiteful repartees for dear old A.B. (on his yacht). There is no doubt that I'm paying heavily for my

---

[1] 1876–1962. Senior Treasury Official. Knighted 1931.

[2] 1882–1933. Worked in the Cambridge University Library from 1900 until his death, ending as Under-Librarian.

[3] Richmond Temple (1893–1958), one of the first and most successful of public relations consultants, was a director of the Savoy Hotel Company from 1922 to 1938, then a director of the Dorchester Hotel. He was also adviser to British Railways and to the London Tin Corporation. Among his literary friends were the Sitwells and Arnold Bennett, to whom he gave much detailed information for Bennett's hotel-novel *Imperial Palace* (1930). Its hero Evelyn Orcham was in part based on Temple.

[4] Osbert Sitwell's second volume of poems (1923).

eighteen-months-old feud with O.S. Scarcely a day passes without my being reminded of him. People often mention him in conversation, usually without knowing that I've quarrelled with him.

Replying to A.B. I wrote, after an amiable opening, 'I probably caught the carping disease in 1919, from your friend O.S. whose poems you have been reading. If, as you suggest, he is freeing himself from his vicious habit of mockery and mischievousness, it is a good thing for him.' How futile all this ill-feeling is! At present O.S. is the only person toward whom I nourish such self-lacerating sensations. Mutual friends say 'Why do you take Osbert so seriously?' I reply 'I do not insult people by treating them as a joke.'

Meanwhile O. practises passive resistance, sending me amiable messages by Meiklejohn. He 'does not want to attack any of my friends' etc.

It is all very silly, but I can't see myself reconciled. O.S. is associated in my mind with a very bad period of my life immediately after the war when I was unwell and nervy.

I take things too *literally* and overdo the effort to tidy everything up (including my friends). This tidiness has resulted in my producing an unusually tidy little collection of verses. I loathe the idea of becoming a finicky *petit maître* sort of writer. I'd much rather be exuberant and sumptuous and slightly chaotic. When I was a boy I had a mania for cricket-statistics. Now I am in danger of a different sort of mental rigidity. What I want is a flexible simplicity of life which would be reflected in my writing.

Dining at Harold Laski's[1] this evening I found myself inveighing against 'the vulgarity of the age'. I was exalting my own behaviour in seeking anonymity and avoidance of publicity and so on. Such gestures are quite genuine, but they are almost morbidly self-conscious, and no better than the publicity gestures of Bob Nichols, in his prefaces. I suppose, at the back of all this smothering of my natural impulsiveness and love of success, there is my grievance against society for refusing to allow me to write freely. 'If they won't allow me to print my emotional stuff I'll only dole them out my constipated midnight-oil stuff!' The letters I've received about *Recreations* represent a sort of success

[1] Left-wing political theorist and university teacher (1893–1950).

but rather a dreary one. W. H. Davies[1] has 'thoroughly enjoyed' the book. R. Hodgson thinks I could 'do anything, given the spell'. Lytton Strachey has 'enjoyed reading them very much, but wishes I could produce something with still more of myself in it'. John Masefield likes them better on the whole than anything I've done, but feels that I do not give myself a free hand. Edmund Gosse finds them 'charming and musical'. Eddie Marsh calls it 'a delightful little book'. And R. Graves hails it as 'an important achievement'. (I asked T. Hardy not to worry himself with writing about the book.) But there is something lulling and dangerous about their acknowledgments of the 'charm' etc. They have to be polite. I would prefer them to be puzzled and excited. But how can I possibly produce A.B's benevolent, sublime, and ideally beautiful book in less than a lifetime?

June 29

I 'entertained' my brother to lunch at the Reform. He entertained me for three hours, chattering about local happenings at Matfield and talking a lot about a book by Henry Ford, the cheap-car manufacturer, who is one of his heroes. 'Great chap, Henry.' After lunch I tried in vain to shake him off. I had a note for David Cecil,[2] and stuck to my intention of leaving it at 21 Arlington Street, though feeling a sort of snobbishness in doing so while my brother was with me. So we stumped up there, and he asked who lived in the large mansion. I replied 'A man named Salisbury', adding that I knew his son. (I only know him slightly.) It was absurd, but I felt unable to enunciate '*Lord* Salisbury'. I suppose, if it had been Buckingham Palace, I'd have said 'A man named Windsor'.

June 30 (Fitzwilliam Street, Cambridge)

Last night H. G. Wells joined me as I was beginning my dinner at the Reform. He ordered a bottle of champagne (which he divided, to a fraction of an inch). He gave me a complete account of Harry Cust's editorship of the *Pall Mall Gazette*— thirty years ago—very amusing. He described J. M. Keynes as

[1] Poet (1871–1940).
[2] Lord David Cecil (b.1902), biographer and man of letters. Younger son of the fourth Marquess of Salisbury.

'a man who believes himself to have been brilliant but was really only opportune'. Belloc (who went round America lecturing against H.G. last winter) came and sat at the next table. When H.G. got up to depart, Belloc snorted and prepared to cut him. H.G. strolled across and slapped him on the back, exclaiming 'Why, Belloc, you're getting fat!' Belloc could say nothing. H.G. remarked to me 'It's a great advantage, when dealing with pompous people, to be a cad!'

I might have done the same thing to Osbert (who isn't pompous, however, and always gets the best of me in warfare) for the Sitwells were dining with Meiklejohn and I unexpectedly caught O's light-blue eye as I walked past their embrasured table. Taken unawares, I forgot to scowl, but abstained from smiling.

Upstairs H.G. gave me a detailed account of his recent 'nerve-shock'. This was an unpleasant episode at his flat in Queen Anne's Mansions, when a crazy Austrian woman called and tried to cut her throat. The evening papers got hold of the story, of course.

H.G's narrative (evidently intended to be 'passed on') began, 'I am not a good man. I have a wife for whom I have a deep respect. And a mistress for whom I have a deep affection.' As he pointed out, people who disliked him will now fabricate a new myth about the monstrous wickedness of his life. These confidences, plus the champagne, caused *me* to talk rather indiscreetly.

H.G. left at 9.15, and the Sitwells came into the smoking-room with Meiklejohn. I felt embarrassed and went outside. Soon afterwards they all walked past me. Seeing O. filled me with hostility. (I feel neutral about S. Sitwell.) O. made things worse by leaving (with the hall-porter) a 'funny' postcard for me. It was a photograph of the late Princess Christian,[1] inscribed 'To remind you of a noble and suffering life'. This banter infuriated me.

At Tufton Street I found the Hodgsons talking to the Turners. They discussed H.G.W. Turner said 'The young intellectuals ought to destroy H.G. because he has ceased to be any use to them.' Hodgson defended H.G., though he 'cannot read him'. He agreed with me that H.G. is still a great power for creating

[1] The third daughter of Queen Victoria (born 1846) had died on 9 June 1923.

an enlightened public opinion. Turner also thinks that 'Shaw has ceased to be any use'. But he can't suggest any substitutes for Wells and Shaw.

The day had been too 'crowded with incident', and I was awake till 5.30 a.m. I got to Cambridge at 4 in fine weather (the sun veiled by thin clouds). I am staying with Cyril Tom-kinson[1] (a little parson who was introduced to me by R. Nichols, and also knew Rivers[2]).

I decided to avoid seeing him till dinner-time, as I felt the worse for wear. After strolling about the Backs, I went into the Fellows' Garden at Pembroke and sat there unhappily from 6 to 7. In a newspaper shop I'd bought a vulgar postcard of two cockatoos in bed, one of them saying 'Shall we ask mother to stay with us?' This I sent to O. Sitwell, about whom I was still in an internal tantrum. (The card was a reference to Max's caricature of O. and S. with parrots on their fists saying 'Well done, Osbert' and 'Well done, Sacheverell'.) Contemptible bad taste on my part of course. So I sat in the pleasant garden, tearing myself to tatters and wishing I hadn't sent the card, while enjoying the idea of paining O.S.

Then I discovered that I'd been locked into the garden, and I had to get over the twelve-foot wall by a ladder, which I found by a tool-shed. I pulled it up after me and let it down into Free School Lane, and then threw it back over the wall, to the astonishment of a passing don.

This evening has been quite pleasant, but C.T. makes me too voluble and communicative, for he has a great knack of drawing people out. This is my first visit to Cambridge since Rivers's funeral a year ago. How ironic that I should have celebrated my return by perpetrating that mean and spiteful postcard affair. The memory of Rivers rebukes me. But I excuse myself by thinking that I am fighting O.S. with his own weapons. I mentioned the squabble, but not the postcard, to C.T.

---

[1] 1886–1968. Curate of Little St Mary's, Cambridge, 1923–30. Later vicar of various parishes.

[2] W. H. R. Rivers (1864–1922), psychologist and anthropologist, had been S.S's doctor at Craiglockhart War Hospital, and became his chief father-figure. See *Sherston's Progress, Siegfried's Journey* and *Diaries 1920–1922*.

July 3

Returned from Cambridge this morning. Yesterday was
pleasant and included an expedition to Grantchester, where we
had tea in the orchard and sat until the shadows were long. This
evening has been a blank, as David Cecil failed to appear for
dinner at the Reform. I waited an hour and then rang up 'Salisbury's house' and was told that D.C. had gone to the country. I
felt rather aggrieved that he should have behaved so casually,
after seeming so anxious to dine with me.

What a disappointing man Elgar is! When I met him a week
or two ago I told him I was sending him a copy of *Recreations*
and mentioned that there is a reference to his Concerto in the
piece called 'Philharmonic'.[1] To-day he writes. 'Many thanks
for the book. I cannot quite follow you through it all. I gather
from the "Philharmonic" that you most judiciously fled from
the Concerto. I am sorry you don't like it. Yrs (scribble) E.E.'
I replied 'Dear Sir Edward, Let me reassure you (in case my
admiration is of any value to you) that I have heard the Violin
Concerto eleven times, and its beauty has moved me to an
increasing degree. Why should I have sent you my book if it
contained a sneer at your music? And how could I have sent it
to you unless I admired your work? You surprise me. I merely
wished to show my gratitude. Yours sincerely.' But Elgar is
always behaving like that. He is on the look-out for affronts, and
probably thinks that all the 'younger generation' despises his
music.[2]

Returning here, I found, of course, a valentine from O.S., in
the form of two 'birthday cards' of equal vulgarity to mine, with
an equally mocking inscription. He always gets the last word
and scores off me. He writes: 'It *was* nice hearing from you
again. I sent you H.R.H. Princess Christian in order that the
Memory of a Gracious Presence might cheer and uplift you on
this earthly pilgrimage.' This sort of thing is likely to poison
me. As Head says, when you hate people you put yourself in
their power. I don't hate O.S. I merely 'resent his attitude
toward life'! He and his sister make a hobby of provoking
squabbles, in print, with their critics and adversaries. They seem
to spend half their time writing to the papers about themselves.

[1] First published in the *London Mercury* April 1921.
[2] My letter produced a charming reply, so all was well. S.S.

To ease my mind, I have written O. a very decent letter, explaining how he exasperates and disappoints me. But I don't want to return to the 1919–21 relationship (which largely consisted in his reading his poems aloud to me and ignoring the fact that I am a writer). I suppose I am too 'earnest and serious' for him. His hostility to Turner made it impossible for me to be friendly. In future I shall try to avoid him politely. Quarrelling actively is too harassing. But it seems as if one part of me really enjoys nourishing ill-feeling against people I am inwardly fond of (or *have* been).

July 5

Yesterday I received an untidy scribble of eight pages from O.S. in which he tries to be candid and avoids levity. The letter has relieved my mind, though I still feel no inclination to see O.

To-day has been the first really hot day of this grey summer. Phyllis Loder wired, asking me to lunch, and called for me at the Reform. I feel quite pleased at being 'called for' by such a lovely creature. It isn't often that I am 'seen about with a beautiful lady'.

We lunched at Jules in Jermyn Street, sat in the Park (by Park Lane) and she caught the 3.15 back to Cirencester. I broke the news that I shall not hunt next winter. She had a cold and wasn't at her best. I hadn't seen her since April 15. She left me with a strong feeling of the futility of her existence. She might be such a brilliant creature if she mixed with intelligent people. After I'd seen her into the train I had an impression of some tragic element in our encounter. I visualised her, in the hot glare of this afternoon, in her dark flimsy dress and round black hat, rather jaded and nervy, saying that London always gives her a headache. 'Don't you long to be in the country?' she asked, and it seemed as if I might never see her again, and look back afterwards on that final meeting, seeing in it a foreboding of tragedy. I felt that there ought to be a railway accident to her train, or that she must be starting some mortal illness! This is the kind of thing which passes for premonition of disaster.[1]

[1] In a sense it *was*. I saw her again a fortnight later, but not again since then. In April 1927 her only child died suddenly. Three months ago I met her sister-in-law who said 'Norman seems to be interested in nothing now. Phyllis didn't seem

July 6

Tea at 17 Hanover Terrace. I went there to ask Gosse to support the civil-list pension appeal for Charlotte Mew.[1] He agreed to do so, though not sharing the high opinions expressed by Hardy, de la Mare, and Masefield. (The appeal was inaugurated by S. C. Cockerell,[2] who came to see me at Tufton Street before I went to see E.G.—who isn't very well-disposed toward S.C.C.)

July 6 and 7 (90 in the shade both days)

On Friday night Ralph Hodgson was at Tufton Street (he seldom misses coming there on Fridays). Louis and Jean Untermeyer[3] dined with me and I took them to Tufton Street. Gertler[4] and the Morrells there also. R.H. didn't want to meet the Ms and wouldn't talk until they'd all gone. Then he stayed till 2 a.m. I never saw him so excited. He was on his favourite subjects, War, The Future of the World, etc. (How tedious it sounds, but how wonderfully he talks!) He said 'Science has destroyed God; we have got to make another God who will be able to withstand Science.' 'Bunyan must have been as great as any man has been.' Muriel (Hodgson) kept tiresomely saying— 'Ralph' (she pronounces the *l* in Ralph) 'we *must* go home now', but R.H. obstinately refused, saying 'I feel as if I might never see these people again.' He was 'above' his usual self—talking louder and with more violent emphasis. Strange, that such a man should come to the house I live in. Stranger still that I should so often come in and go upstairs to sit alone because I don't feel like talking to anyone.

---

to mind John's death (the little boy) as much as Norman.' I knew what that signified. Phyllis isn't the sort that shows it when hurt. I can imagine her reckless gaiety, in public. Going harder than ever to hounds, and dancing herself haggard at Hunt Balls. S.S.

[1] Poet (1869–1928).

[2] Sydney Cockerell (1867–1962). Director of the Fitzwilliam Museum, Cambridge, 1908–37. Knighted 1934.

[3] Louis Untermeyer (1885–1977), American author and editor. His wife Jean was a poet.

[4] Mark Gertler (1891–1939), painter.

July 8 (Coombe, near Woodstock) (staying with the Hamo Thornycrofts[1])

This entry in my diary is an example of inadequate and unskilful diarising. But, when all is said and done, leading a good life is more important than keeping a good diary, and in this case there were extenuating circumstances. One was the heat-wave, which lasted from July 5 to 16. Also one must be alone to write a diary well—alone *mentally*, I mean. Uncle Hamo was a man whose temperament, I think, was against excessive analysis. Do a good day's work; don't be reclusive (he warned me against my tendency to reclusiveness when I was at Cambridge); go to bed in good time and get up early. That was his rule of life, and it served him well.

Anyhow I didn't find it possible to do more than scribble more than a page and a half during the visit, which lasted from Saturday evening till Tuesday morning.

It was a happy visit; and it was delightful to see Uncle Hamo in the house he had built (out of the framework of an old farmhouse). I'd not been there before, and I haven't been there since.[2] After the war I'd neglected him (as one always does neglect relations). I dined twice at his flat in Finchley Road (Marlborough Mansions—a name coincidence, because Coombe is on the edge of Blenheim Park). Otherwise I only saw him a few times at his studio in Melbury Road.

At Coombe I was introduced to 'broadcasting'. Uncle H. had a wireless, very elaborate and good—he always liked playing with anything engineerish or scientific. I can remember the almost reverential way in which he manipulated and listened to the apparatus (installed by his son, who is an electrical engineer). Uncle Hamo also enjoyed being a sort of Squire of the village. He was essentially a countryman. He loved and respected everything countrified. He was a man whose whole personality was a rebuke to anything dishonest or undignified or mean. Refinement and simplicity shone from him. He was never 'on his dignity', and could be astonishingly 'jolly' at the age of seventy-three (he was born in 1850).

On the Monday morning of that visit he took me down to the Evenlode, where he had a canoe. (He had always loved swim-

---

[1] H.T. was S.S's mother's brother (1850–1925). R.A. Sculptor. Knighted 1917.
[2] My Aunt Agatha still lives there. Uncle Hamo died in December 1925. S.S.

ming and boating beyond anything else.) We navigated the
reed-choked and willow-cumbered little river with high gusto,
Uncle H. getting out and wading a lot. He would have played
any boyish game on that river, pretending we were explorers in
America etc. Youthfulness and a wholesome love of outdoor life
were still strong in him. That evening after dinner he and I and
Aunt Agatha walked into Blenheim Park. The weather was
abnormally sultry (there was a terrific thunderstorm in London
that night) and the Park felt very strange as we walked under
the ancient trees to look at High Lodge, a haunted-looking
house, used by a keeper. High Lodge was where the poet Lord
Rochester died.[1] On our way home, at 10.30, Uncle H. knocked
at the village inn, and was surreptitiously admitted by the landlord, who served us ('out of hours') with some very special beer.
(Or 'ale' as Uncle H. preferred it to be called.) In a diminutive
panelled parlour, under the rays of an oil-lamp, we discussed (I
noted) 'fires in furniture repositories', the landlord being an
ex-fireman. 'Come and see us again, old man,' was Uncle
Hamo's farewell to me on Tuesday morning.[2]

The last letter written by H.T. (to my aunt Mrs Donaldson)
was characteristic of him. He was being kept in bed, because of
the arterial trouble in his leg, but wrote very cheerfully, describ-
ing a delicious country lunch he'd just had — 'a fine Oxfordshire
capon, etc.' His enjoyment of food etc was all part of his grateful
acceptance of the kindly fruits of the earth — as different to the
self-indulgence of the gourmet as an honest home-made loaf is
different from smart hotel food.

July 10 (Harnham, Weybridge)
After lunch I came here to stay a couple of nights with E. M.
Forster and his mother. E.M.F. met me at the top of the station-
steps, wistful and attenuated, in a wide-brimmed black Italian
hat. I was bubbling over with 'things to tell him'; he always
makes me into a chatterbox. After tea the climate became super-

[1] John Wilmot, Earl of Rochester (1647–80).
[2] Alas! that I never did (though I contrived that he paid the Poet Laureate a visit,
  in the summer of 1925, reviving an old acquaintanceship. He and Bridges had a
  certain affinity of character—perhaps it was that both of them were countrymen,
  lovers of classical music, and well-bred in an 'old fashioned' way). S.S.

sultry and we gaped like penguins in the tiny garden behind the
low-windowed brick villa (roomy, comfortable, and Victorian-
furnished). During tea I ate strawberries and conversed in
sprightly style (mostly about my career as a club cricketer in
Kent—the Forsters once lived at Tunbridge Wells). Mrs F. is
a charming, dumpy, white-haired old lady of sixty-eight. She
has the same face as E.M.F. but a more condensed nose and
chin. Very chatty, she puts me quite at my ease. Behind her
chair in the dining-room hangs a Turneresque classical painting
by her great-uncle (Whichelo).[1] The picture belonged to H.
Festing-Jones,[2] who stayed here this year, and gave it her.
Before dinner there was a heavy thunder-shower, which failed to
clear the air.

At 9.30, the rain having ceased, E.M.F. and I went for a walk
by the River Wey. In the sultry twilight the river created a
double world in which reflection and reality were indistinguish-
able. Upside-down was the same as right-way-up. Neither sky
nor water moved, and the looming masses and smoky remoteness of riverside trees hung tranced in a stillness under which we
flitted like bats, or like our own vague musings as we hovered
along the tow-path, staring into the sultry dusk. Shadow melted
into shadow; all was painted in subaqueous neutral tones, and
the stars were veiled by an imperceptible mistiness. A mile
away a line of poplars pointed skyward. 'It's like the life after
death,' I suggested, diffidently. My conventional comment
failed to satisfy Forster, whose subdued voice, mingling with
the unearthly twilight stillness, syllabled a few sayings which
have since vanished into the mazes of my forgetfulness.

July 16 (Belle Vue, Stansfield)

Last Wednesday Forster and I made an expedition to Ashley
Park, Walton-on-Thames. Now 'to let', it is the house where
my father was born and spent his childhood and adolescence. I'd
never seen it before. (And shall never see it again, because it
has since been pulled down, and the park built over.) It was
built by Cardinal Wolsey. My grandfather affixed a heavy coat

[1] C. J. M. Whichelo (d.1865).
[2] 1851–1928. Author, close friend, executor and biographer of Samuel Butler.
Nicknamed Enrico.

of arms above one of the doors, but I observed that it was such a shoddy piece of work that already (after only seventy years) it is sagging outwards, as if protesting that it was too hastily concocted by the Heralds' College. My uncle Joseph (whom I saw only twice) lived there till he died, two or three years ago.[1] On Thursday morning E.M.F. and I journeyed to London. There were four Sandhurst cadets in our carriage. Separately we 'sized them up', and came to similar conclusions about their characters (which I've since forgotten entirely). Thursday and Friday were tropically torrid.

I came here on Saturday, by a sauntering train which missed its connection at Saffron Walden and caused me to have lunch there. Blunden and Mary B. met me at Clare Station with a white pony in a governess cart. We called at the local printer's for a parcel, which contained a small edition of E.B's poem *Old Homes* (for private circulation). This morning is cool, breezy, and green. Sun-baked Suffolk has been superficially sprinkled by showers, and I also am feeling refreshed.

It is difficult to diarise in rural surroundings. Late at night in London a page of introspection or daylight-description soaks on to the paper easily enough. But down here, in silver-green East Anglia, I am indolent-minded, and the mapping out of my delicious colloquies with Edmund seems to be continually postponed until briskness of brain shall speed the pen and illuminate mistiness.

This morning, when I was writing my page, Edmund popped his birdlike head in at the door (a most welcome interruption) and called me downstairs.

The little tub-cart and white pony joggled us up and down hill for a few miles of rural remoteness, to Gifford's Hall, where we lunched with Mr Fass. (Mary drove, dressed in her silks and fine array.) Gifford's Hall is a timbered and moated masterpiece with lozenge-paned windows, fine panellings, and beamed ceilings. Mr Fass is a middle-aged bachelor, pink-skinned, and sandy-grey-haired, grey-eyed, and full of cultivated social and antiquarian chat. Gifford's Hall (where he spends the summer months fostering local traditions, herbaceous borders, and rustic recreations) is only twelve miles from Newmarket Heath, so there was an authentic ring in his casual reference to some

[1] A reclusive bibliophile (1855–1918).

notorious event which occurred 'two Cesarewitches ago'. He'd been reading Creevey's Memoirs last night; evidently he enjoys Memoirs more than modernities. A charming host, and a delightful expedition.

On July 18 I returned to London. Too busy talking to E.B. to record any of it.

July 21–22

Stayed at Cirencester. Rather a sad visit. On Sunday I bicycled several miles to Williamstrip, to see my old mare Lady Jill who has carried me so well since 1920. It was good-bye; her rheumatism is so bad that she must be 'put down'. She was hobbling about in a field, with several other 'summering' hunters, a cripple among the active ones—a miserable episode. Phyllis was out all day playing in a tennis-tournament, and Norman was out playing golf. I played cricket on the lawn with little John (aged eight). Returned to London on Monday afternoon, which was grey and rainy. I little knew that I should not see them again—not for eight years anyhow, and that seems unlikely enough in 1931. Nor did I dream that John would die in 1927.

The Loders moved to Ettington, near Stratford-on-Avon, that autumn, taking with them my saddles, bridles, hunting-clothes etc. I suppose they still keep them.

July 25 (Came Rectory)

Came to Dorchester with Blunden by the train arriving 9.40. On our way from the station we called at Max Gate for ten minutes. Hardy came down from his study and was quite gay and alert and saw us out to the gate.

E.B. and I are staying here as paying guests, and have our meals in a separate room. After half-an-hour's talk with the parson (the Reverend W. Godber) and his wife in 'the study', we retired. I am now in my bedroom, the room in which William Barnes[1] died (a month before I was born). The parson's talk was stereotyped. He is a sporting type (or would be if he could afford it) and was a padre in the Great War. He

[1] Dorset poet (1800–86).

talks about 'the lads in France', 'the 1914 spirit', and the decline of the old-fashioned (hat-touching?) agricultural labourer.

July 27

Tea at Max Gate yesterday and to-day revealed T.H. as charming and alert as ever. It is good to watch him talking while little Blunden listens, intent, respectful, and bird-like.

July 28

A grey, soaking morning of wind-slanted rain. I stare out at the narrow lawn and the beeches, and the occasional gigs and motors that pass the gate. E.B. is busy in his room, concocting a review of R. Graves's new poem[1] for *The Times Literary Supplement*. The wind blusters among dark green boughs from a featureless white sky. A straggling pile of flapping rooks crosses the opaque pallor, travelling into the wind.

I ought to feel satisfied. E.B. is here, backed by our four years of flawless friendship, to discuss poetry and cricket, and the last war, and the next one. Half-a-mile away T.H. is busy in his study, finishing the one-act play about Tristram and Iseult which he has written for the Dorchester Players[2] ('but I have stipulated that they mustn't perform it in London'). He has offered to read it to us. (Florence H. says 'Reading is not one of T.H's strong points'.) Rain-drops fall in white streaks from the thatch of Barnes's old Rectory. The postman has brought the mid-day post, but the letter I was waiting for has not arrived.

Tea at Max Gate. Lady Stacie there, a descendant of R. B. Sheridan—and a fashionable lady, formerly a great beauty. She gushed to T.H. about his novels at the tea-table. He shut her up by saying 'I am not interested in my novels. I haven't written one for more than thirty years.' 6–7.30 in golden weather E.B. and I bicycled to Upper Bockhampton, as E.B. hadn't yet seen T.H's birthplace. After dinner T. E. Lawrence turned up (from

---

[1] *The Feather Bed*, published in a limited edition by Leonard and Virginia Woolf from Richmond. E.B's anonymous review appeared in the *T.L.S.* on 23 August.
[2] *The Famous Tragedy of the Queen of Cornwall*, 1923.

the Tank Corps camp near Wool). He rang the bell, left a message with the maid that he would come to lunch tomorrow, and departed. I dashed out and caught him as he went through the gate. He looked well—a queer little figure in dark motor-overalls, his brown and grimy face framed in a fur-lined cap.

He had a passenger waiting in his side-car, and only stayed a minute.

July 30

T.E.L. arrived yesterday at 1 and stayed with us till 6.30. Tea at Max Gate. In the evening E.B. and I made copious notes of the conversation between T.H. and T.E.L., so I am absolved from effort, and perhaps E.B. will amplify the notes some day. To-day we went to Weymouth for lunch, and had our usual tea at Max Gate.

August 1 (54 Tufton Street)

We left Came Rectory at 9.15 this morning. Called at Max Gate to say good-bye. T.H., as usual, looked rather doleful as I drove away. I think he has a great liking for E.B. also. What a blessing little B. is!

August 3–11 (Staying at King's, Cambridge, with R. Wood.[1])

August 24 (Weirleigh)

I am not at my best when I return to this house where I lived almost continuously from December 1906 (when I quitted Cambridge after four futile terms) to September 1913. Those were my years of arrested development, when I got into a groove of minor poetry and sport—a groove from which the war extracted me. (I always feel that I am seven years younger than my age.) When I've been here since the war, I've found my former lazy-mindedness returning to a certain extent. The atmosphere of Weirleigh is intellectually enervating. My attitude to it is retrospective. Nothing takes the place of my old

[1] Richardson Wood, American journalist and town-planner.

idle existence, which survives in the unreadable remnants of my adolescently acquired library, and the junk manuscripts and letters which lurk in the drawers of writing-tables. My only activity since I came here on August 20 has been rummaging among these relics. I have destroyed the last of my juvenile manuscripts (mostly cliché sonnets) and carried a mass of letters up to Tufton Street. (I went there for the day on Wednesday.) I also carried up to town three first editions of Drinkwater, which I sold to Sotheran's for £10! There was, also, a first edition of *A Shropshire Lad*, which belonged to Robbie Ross. I didn't intend to sell that, naturally, but I showed it to R. Temple in the Union Club, and mentioned that I am short of money. R.T. offered to 'take care of it' for me, and handed me a £10 note, which I accepted unwillingly.[1]

Mother has become keen on broadcasting, but I prefer to make my own music, on an old upright in the studio. I also roll the tennis-court (the one which has recovered from the war). The lawns here have become the Hyde Park of numerous rabbits and the whole garden looks neglected. An invalid jackdaw inhabits a hutch on the old 'best' tennis-lawn, which became a hayfield during the war and remains unshaven. What hours I used to spend in manicuring that expanse of turf! The jackdaw was brought from Twirton by my eldest nephew. (My brother and his family are now at St Leonards until September 3, which makes it possible for me to stay here.)

I have brought the Tufton Street kitten here, as the Turners are away. He will probably stay here permanently. His antics have provided a continuous topic of conversation with Mother (who always apologises for having no conversation, though she is one of the chattiest people I know).

August 27

A pleasant little 'outing' with Mother to-day. How the rural distances diminish in these days! In the old days Cranbrook was a 'far cry' in pony-cart or dog-cart. To-day, in the new motor-bus, we were hurried nearly ten miles in half-an-hour.

[1] In 1930 I saw the book in Dulau's catalogue, price £100! Afterwards, an American wrote to me from Cincinnati, asking for 'the history of the book'. I did not reply, and felt much annoyed. S.S.

We went to lunch with Irvine and Agnes Stirling, a middle-aged brother and sister, in a charming old house on the edge of Glassenbury Park (reputed to be the oldest Park in Kent). The weather was richly golden between rain-storms, and it was fine when we alighted at one of the gates into the park. Irvine met us there, and conducted us the half mile to his house. He is a taciturn member of the Athenaeum Club, almost eccentric in his reclusiveness. (He is a Chancery Court barrister.) Though short-sighted, he is much addicted to rabbit-shooting, and while we toddled across the park, under dripping ancient oaks, his utterances were almost wholly addressed to a young black retriever which refused to pace sedately at his heels in the prescribed manner. Miss Stirling is extremely chatty, like a bright little bird. We stayed till five o'clock, and I did my best to be 'an agreeable rattle'. I am very fond of houses which smell of log-fires. When old Sir James (the Judge)[1] was alive, I often stayed with the Stirlings for dances, and the house they lived in then had a large old hall where there was always a huge log burning. Irvine's house is likewise log-smoke-scented.

October 1 (54 Tufton Street. Except for two week-ends, I've been here all September.)[2]

R. Hodgson was here to tea yesterday. He described T. S. Eliot's *The Waste Land* as 'literary leg-pulling', which comforted me. Before dinner to-day I saw the Turners off at Victoria. They have gone to Florence for ten weeks (as paying guests with the Aldous Huxleys). After a lot of uncertainty, and people 'coming to look at the house', (during which I realised that I didn't want to go away and had nowhere to go) a climax came when a woman agreed to rent the house on condition that the wall between my bedroom and sitting-room was knocked down. This was too much for me, and I had a 'bright idea'. Why hadn't it struck me before? I said to Turner, 'Shall I rent the house?' So I am paying him £5 a week for it.

[1] A lord justice in the Court of Appeal (1836–1916). His daughter Marjorie Forster (1887–1976) was a childhood and lifelong friend of S.S. See *Diaries 1920–1922*.

[2] 'Savoy Dinner, given by the Savoy to a few journalists and Sassoon and me, to introduce (privately) the new "Savoy Orpheans" the wonder-band.' (Arnold Bennett's *Journal*, 29 September 1923.)

(To which, I suppose, must be added the £65-a-year interest on the £1300 I lent him to buy it with—interest of which he has never been able to pay me a penny.)[1] So I am getting the house rather cheap—the only disadvantage being that Shanks has a bedroom in it (for which he pays Turner a pound a week). But Shanks only sleeps here a couple of nights a week.

Dear Delphine's last remark to me was, 'I think you ought to get someone to sleep at Tufton Street. I'm nervous of your being alone there.' (This remark was caused by last week's burglary, when the house was broken into while we were all out at a concert; the burglars took all D's little valuables, and a lot of Turner's and my clothes.)

October 5

The Turners have been gone five days, and I cannot conceal the fact that I am genuinely enjoying 'having the house to myself'. For the first time since I have lived here I am able to sit at Turner's writing-desk, recording my great thoughts after fumbling amiably through the first movement of a Mozart piano concerto (which I heard at Queen's Hall this evening).

Musing, in the gallery at the concert, I decided to publish my *Recreations* next autumn. That will be exactly five years after my last volume (*War Poems*, October 1919, very few of which were new ones).

I also decided to call my *next* book (love and lyrical poems) *The Heart's Journey*, and publish it in October 1926 (after my fortieth birthday).[2]

I say that I am enjoying the absence of the Turners. But I am looking forward to surprising them on their return, by a general brightening and smartening of this room. The dinginess of their sofa has always depressed me. To-day I bought (for twenty-three shillings at Heal's) a golden cover for the sofa, which now looks very bright. Turner is not tidy, and the room already has an unwonted air of unslovenliness, due to my having cleared up various refuse. He is the sort of man who keeps old envelopes on his table for weeks, and has a new sheet of blotting-paper only

---

[1] Neither interest nor capital was ever repaid. S.S.
[2] *Satirical Poems* was published in April 1926, *The Heart's Journey* in August 1928. S.S.

about twice a year. But I am cat-like in my enjoyment of neatness. Mentally I am over-meticulous about small details. Yet I am a very illogical reasoner.

October 6

How delightful to be sitting here, fortified against all intruders! If anyone rings the bell I needn't open the door, and Mrs Binks the comic domestic only comes for half the day. Roderick Meiklejohn sends me a postcard showing Dante's tomb. He is at Ravenna, fairly revelling in thoughts of Dante, who is one of his favourite names in literature, though he speaks very little Italian.

Lunching at the Reform I found myself surrounded by members of the Garrick Club (who are using the Reform this month). Henry Ainley[1] was at my table, conversing suavely in a plumpty mellow voice. How conceited successful actors look! Sir Squire Bancroft[2] came and caressed him with congratulations on his performance in *Hassan*[3] (which is set for a six months' run at His Majesty's). Bancroft would pass for an ill-preserved man of sixty. (He is eighty.) But these Garrickites, with their voluminous chatter and convivial names, are a cheerful contrast to the parchment-souled, procedure-bound lawyers, politicians and civil servants who predominate at the Reform (their ranks reinforced by well-nourished bridge-playing business men). As someone says, 'Business men do so well because they've only themselves to compete against.' After lunch I went to an exhibition of French paintings and drawings at the Leicester Galleries. I saw Will Rothenstein,[4] who asked me to give him a copy of *Recreations* — gilding the pill by mentioning that 'Max was most enthusiastic and read several aloud to me'. This pleased me, as Max hasn't acknowledged the copy I sent him. I never quite liked Rothenstein, when I sat to him. E. M. Forster agrees. He was 'sitting' last week, and said he 'disliked R's "pi" talk'.

[1] Leading actor (1879–1945).
[2] Actor-manager (1841–1926).
[3] By James Elroy Flecker (1884–1915).
[4] Artist and writer (1872–1945). Principal of the Royal College of Art 1920–35. Knighted 1931.

Posting him a copy (one of the last dozen) I console myself by thinking that he will talk about it, and help to create subterranean interest in my 'new work'.

W.R.   'Have you seen Sassoon's new poems?'
Someone   'No. I haven't heard about them.'
W.R.   'They're splendid!'
Someone   'Where can I get them?'
W.R.   'You can't.' (Adding) 'But he gave ME a copy. Max thinks them superb.'

October 12

Mother wrote yesterday 'I am so cross about your clothes being stolen, and trust you got a ready-made overcoat at once, though I know such a coat would not be at all nice.' To-day I went to try on my new thick suit and overcoat. I asked Morris (the bald, spectacled, and obese little Jewish sartorial expert) whether any of his customers wear corsets. He replied, 'A few conceited young men, sir.' 'The ones with the squeaky voices, I suppose?' said I. He smiled. 'You writers have to know a lot about human nature, I expect, sir.'

October 13

Slept badly last night, and failed to enjoy Queen's Hall this afternoon. Holst's[1] *Planets* sounded meretricious, and Mozart's E flat violin concerto bored me.

E. M. Forster came here for tea and stayed one and a half hours. He seemed in good spirits, though he is feeling disheartened about his almost completed novel (*A Passage to India*). After dining alone (mildly enjoying Laurence Housman's reconstruction of a conversation with Oscar Wilde in 1899[2]) I returned here feeling dreary. However the evening paper announces that the Hon. N. C. Rothschild has cut his throat, so I am better off than Nathaniel R. (who was the world's greatest authority on Fleas).

[1] Gustav Holst (1874–1934).
[2] *Echo de Paris* (1923).

October 15

Six nights in the last eleven I have been able to work at poetry, which proves that living here alone is beneficial for my work. I must try and produce as much as possible before the Turners return (and hope that they'll go away again *next* winter!). Shanks here to-night.

October 24

Up till 5.45 a.m., writing fifty-six lines of colloquial verse (called 'A Ramble in Relativity'), probably futile, about what I'd be like in twenty years if I could get there and see. (Afterwards tore it up.) This evening I dined with Walter Taylor[1] (11 Oxford Square). The de la Mares, the Morrells, and Mark Gertler were there.

De la M., who wore a white tie and a black waistcoat, looked rather like a tired but distinguished butler. At dinner, J. M. Murry[2] and his new magazine the *Adelphi* were discussed. De la Mare defended Murry's exhibitions of his own emotions. I found myself talking very loud, getting excited, and accusing Murry of 'exploiting his emotions for journalistic purposes'. I didn't go there to argue and exhibit my prejudice against Murry (which dates from his attack on my war-poems in the *Nation* four and a half years ago). I went there for a pleasant evening; and it seems a horrible one when I look back on it. Drank claret and champagne, which made matters worse. Gertler also shouted, and so did Philip Morrell. Walter Taylor (blinking through his glasses like the sheep in *Alice in Wonderland*) only spoke once during the meal. Gertler was saying that he 'blushed all over when he remembered the things he used to say when he was younger'. Taylor turned his mild, spectacled face, and said, in his low-pitched voice, 'Do you ever blush about the things you say now?' Everyone at the table, except Mrs de la Mare and Taylor, seemed over-eager to reveal their most private feelings. I must also except de la Mare, who, as usual, encouraged these 'self-revelations'. He is insatiably curious about other people's mind-processes. While we were on the subject of Murry 'making people feel uncomfortable', I thought

[1] Painter in watercolour (1860–1943). Great friend of W. R. Sickert.
[2] John Middleton Murry (1889–1957), critic. Husband of Katherine Mansfield.

how I'd done much the same with some of my war-poems. And when we were upstairs, de la M. remarked quietly, 'You know, Siegfried, *you* made some people feel rather uncomfortable during the war.'

D. H. Lawrence was also discussed at great length, Ottoline leading the talk. The dinner was an intellectual nightmare. I came home feeling shattered and ashamed of myself. (After dinner T. S. Eliot came in for an hour, but I was unable to follow his talk with de la Mare, as I was conversing aimlessly with Ottoline.)

I have since written a few lines to de la M. regretting my violence about Murry, which has relieved me slightly.

Sat up till 5 a.m. composing a (fairly good?) sonnet.

October 26

Yesterday was uneventful. Stayed in bed till 3. Played Wagner till dinner-time. Back here by 10. Read some musical textbooks of Turner's (on conducting etc.) but felt incapable of writing, even in this diary. Between 1 and 3 a.m. I revived, and wrote a fourteen-line poem, which still seems quite pleasant.

> Song, be my soul; set forth the fairest part
> Of all that moved harmonious through my heart;
> And gather me to your arms; for we must go
> To childhood's garden when the moon is low
> And over the leaf-shadow-latticed grass
> The whispering wraiths of my dead selves repass.
>
> Soul, be my song; return arrayed in white;
> Lead home the loves that I have wronged and slain:
> Bring back the summer dawns that banished night
> With distant-warbling bird-notes after rain . . .
> Time's way-worn traveller I. And you, O song,
> O soul, my Paradise laid waste so long.[1]

These 'idyllic poems' all derive from old days in the garden at Weirleigh (which is also the background of all my dreams, both pleasant and unpleasant). This evening the broadcasting people write for permission to broadcast 'Everyone Sang' on

[1] Published in *The Heart's Journey*.

Armistice Day. This pleases me, though I talk about 'despising broadcasting'. It will gratify Mother immensely. To-day I again stayed in bed till 3. Talked to E. M. Forster at the club 8.30–11. I always end by telling him all my secrets, which never seem to bore him, strange to say. He said, 'My theory is that one only gets the beneficial results of great passion after it has died,' adding, 'Every time I've been in love I have got nothing but good from it in the end. But I don't want to be in love like that again—not at present, anyhow.' He doubted whether it is possible to love *intensely* more than two or three times, quoting some Frenchman who said that love is only intense when it is 'involuntary'. My own feelings lately support E.M.F's 'theory'. O what a relief if I am to be spared any more severe lacerations from 'being in love'! A detached and benevolent amorist—that is what I should enjoy being.

I have written 325 lines of verse since October 3. These little jets of emotion, pumped up in the small hours, seem to be all I can manage. I long for something sustained, with noble architectural qualities!

November 5

A dark day, but I didn't go out till after 4, so it didn't matter. I usually have my breakfast–lunch at 2.30. Mrs Binks looks after me very well, and produces fried soles and milk puddings —the sort of food I prefer. It is a great relief to be able to have meals in the house. To-day I ate my lunch while consuming the contents of a vast envelope from Tokyo—a letter of forty-five closely written pages, from Bob Nichols, and probably the longest letter I shall ever receive. It is all about himself, and written on a boat, going from California to Japan. The word-cascades of his convey very little to my brain. The sentences go past like low-flying rain-clouds, amorphous and colourless, with suggestions of brandishing forms but no definite design. Half-way through, he gets on to the subject of the press-notices of his last book, and comes to earth at last. (His remarks are evidently aimed at O. Sitwell, who made fun of him in the *Nation*.)

But Osbert, if R.N. did meet him at a party, would get the better of him. He would 'creep from the room'! But R.N. does seem 'bigger' than O.S.—in spite of the bunkum of confused philosophies which he lets off in letters to his familiar friends. This evening I avoided the Reform, as I knew I should meet Meiklejohn, who has just returned from Italy, and has been at Florence and Amalfi with the Sitwells (though I'd like to hear about them, at an appropriate moment).

November 6

I'd asked the Hodgsons to come here this evening. They were here 9.30–12.15. Everything neat and tidy for the little 'party'. Mooster's bowl of water under the piano. (Mooster is H's famous brown bull-terrier.) I was slightly nervous about sustaining a long conversation with R.H., as I'd never talked to him alone before. Mrs H. is a background for R.H., rather than a third person, though she talks a lot if she is allowed to! The evening was a success. R.H. very pleased about my poem being broadcast. 'You must take it as an honour to Poetry.' He urged me to 'say' it myself, adding 'You will regret it afterwards if it is badly done.' Should I? And would it be well done if I 'said' it? Somehow the idea of a million listeners to my lyric doesn't appeal to my imagination as it ought to. We discussed Bob Nichols. 'He has genius,' said R.H. 'and he is (with the exception of James Stephens[1] and A.E.[2]) the only man who is obviously *a bard*.' H. had been to Oxford to spend a day with Bridges. 'The day went like lightning,' he said. He was much impressed by R.B's youthful flexibility of mind—'like a man of thirty'.

R.H. has the most *religious* mind I know. By that I mean that he is passionately concerned about *goodness*. Poetry is the central point of his religion. 'I believe in the divinity of poets.' ('But the coming and going of the "spell"—by which he means afflatus—is a thing beyond explanation.') As usual, we agreed about the false atmosphere in which modern poets exist—bandied about between publishers and reviewers, and unable to assert their 'prophetic aloofness'. At the end he became transcendental-speculative-biological-mystical (about the chemical effects of prayer) and I was unable to compete.

Earlier in the evening we were talking about disgruntled

[1] Irish poet (1882–1950).
[2] Pen-name of George William Russell, Irish poet (1867–1935).

poets who have outlived their first fame. He mentioned William Watson,[1] of whose rhetorical sonorities he said, 'A giant like James Thomson[2] knew how to handle that sort of vocabulary.' I was surprised to hear the author of *The City of Dreadful Night* named as a giant. Probably one could find traces of J.T's influence in R.H's early work. I've never been able to penetrate J.T's poetry.

MY MEMOIRS

When I was a child, old Queen Victoria reigned
And country doctors drove about in gigs
While Doctor Grace played cricket and remained
Supreme. Fat farmers haggled and complained,
And Kentish hop-pickers were housed like pigs.

Summer was bright and dry in '93.
In '92 those months were mostly wet.
What '91 was like, I quite forget,
And 1890 is a blank for me.
In 1894, I think, I met
Mischance when jumping off a laurel tree.

The local gentlefolk who came to call
Of safety bicycles knew nothing at all,
Had seen Sir Henry Irving in *Macbeth*,
Danced *The Blue Danube* at the County Ball,
And mourned for 'dear Lord Tennyson's sad death'.

These are my Recollections, tersely told,
Up to the time when I was eight years old.
Have patience, reader, if you find them tame:
In sixty years they will not seem the same.[3]

---

[1] Poet (1858–1935). Knighted 1917.
[2] Poet (1834–82).
[3] This is of interest to me, as it was the first time I saw the '90's as having 'period' attractiveness. It was, in fact, the beginning of the autobiographical prose which broke through three years later. I wrote it after an evening with Ralph Hodgson, and gave him the only copy I made from my notebook. His conversation probably caused my new awareness of the period feeling of the '90's. S.S.

November 9

Weather cold, rainy, and foggy. Saw no one yesterday. To-day has been too social. My great-aunt Mozelle[1] came to tea and stayed two hours. Her father was born in 1791 and died in Bombay when she was nine years old (in 1864). He never came to England, and 'only spoke' Arabic, Hebrew, and Hindustani! Poor Aunt M. is a very harassing companion. When not asking questions such as 'Is Galsworthy a clever man?' (never waiting for an answer) she says 'You *are* fond of me, aren't you.' I am gentle with her and do my best, but she always leaves me grinding my teeth with nerves!

Dining at 120 Maida Vale (alone with Enrico Festing-Jones) was very soothing. (How could such a wise, gentle, intelligent, humorous, and sympathetic man fail to be soothing?)

Back here at midnight. Soon afterwards E. Shanks came in, very tipsy, from a party at the Poetry Book Shop! When he comes in, he fetches two enormous bottles of beer from the kitchen, places them on the shelf above the fireplace, and stands there sipping and exuding literary gossip. To-night I resolutely refused to allow him to wreck my 'evening', and played Bach firmly while he unsteadily tipped beer into his glass (and then into himself). He was so drunk that he soon fell asleep by the fire. At 1.30 I suggested that he'd better stagger to bed, which he did. It *is* a bit tiresome to have a tipsy man, for whom one feels a pronounced antipathy, dumping himself in one's room, for which one is paying £5 a week in the hope of being undisturbed. I can always avoid Shanks by going up to my own room, but I have got to like this one and feel averse to using my own.

November 11

This afternoon a messenger-boy came from Miss Fogerty,[2] asking me to go and hear her reciting my poems at the B.B.C. (She recited 'Aftermath' and 'Everyone Sang'.) I went, thread-

---

[1] Mozelle Sassoon, a lifelong invalid, was in fact S.S's first cousin once removed, though he referred to her as his great-aunt. See *The Weald of Youth*.

[2] Founder and Principal of the Central School of Speech Training and Dramatic Art (1866–1945). S.S. had been to her for elocution lessons before his American tour.

ing the Armistice Day crowds, by Westminster Abbey. The Unknown Warrior and Cenotaph queues were abnormally long. As I walked down to Savoy Hill from the Strand, thousands of starlings were shrilling from the leafless trees in the twilight, by the Savoy Chapel. I was feeling pleased at my poems being given national publicity. The B.B.C. had just given Mr Baldwin's 'address from the plinth of Nelson's Column', which was being followed by a concert by a Territorial Brass Band (with my poems to finish up with). I got into the room in time to hear a military march called 'King of the Isles'. The small room looked rather ludicrous with the khaki-clad musicians squeezed in, supervised by two suave men in smart morning-coats. Miss F. spoke the poems finely; I sat in a fat arm-chair, and my eyes filled with tears. Then everyone crowded out. The band were in a hurry for their tea, and as I was being pushed along the narrow passage, one of them trod my shoe off by the heel.

November 16

Dined with Anzie Wylde at Old Queen Street. Some 'expert' business men have interested him in the floating of a company for exploiting the entire anatomy of sharks (New Zealand ones). He was full of the scheme, which will, it is hoped, prove, by profits and products, that the shark is one of man's most useful friends. I spend a lot of time reading *Seven Pillars of Wisdom* (lent me by T.E.L.).[1]

November 19

Dined with Schuster and went to a party at Lady Colefax's.[2] Was introduced to Lady Sandwich, but got nothing to eat. Only stayed an hour. Why are high-class parties so dreary?

November 22

I remarked to E. M. Forster recently: 'I really must give up keeping a diary; it begins to look like a vice.' But somehow I've

[1] One of eight copies which Lawrence had printed by the *Oxford Times* for private circulation.
[2] Relentless London hostess (died 1950).

got a feeling that I am getting my roots deeper in the soil, through these recordings. I now have to remind myself every day that my period of unmolested piano-playing, and using the only nice (though dark) room in this poky house, is soon to be ended. I must revert, before long, to my routine of club-lunches and sitting upstairs listening to the Turners playing my piano. I feel like a cuckoo in a linnet's nest, anxious to elbow them out of it. But I must re-adapt myself, and try to continue verse-production (though the quality of my 500 lines since October 3 is not reassuring, being either too noble or too quizzical).

November 26

Bitter frost and dense fog. Letter from T.E.L. asking how I like his book. 'Is any of it worth while? I mean worth hanging on, either to do better, or to recollect that past work in a kind of peace?' (Rather a self-conscious way of expressing himself? And surely he *must* know that his book is all right.) Wrote a longish reply, saying how much I admire *Seven Pillars*. T.E.L. is a queer figure in the landscape of my thoughts. His book has impressed him on me as one of the most intensely real minds in my experience. He is an ascetic. And his attitudes are superb, the way he hacks his way down to reality, never sparing himself. My admiration for him grows steadily as I plough through his double-columns of small print, which are like a physical experience.

November 28

Am still trying to make the most of (and prepare for the shattering of) my solitude. No doubt I shall soon get used to the old conditions, but at present I genuinely shudder at the thought of turning out of this room and not being able to play the piano in peace. Lately I have, not for the first time, actually thought, rather cravingly, of having a house of my own. But I can't afford it, and can't leave the Turners in the lurch either. I must be grateful for these two months of nocturnal cerebration. Finished *Riceyman Steps*[1] this evening. Excellent book.

[1] By Arnold Bennett (1923).

November 30

Shanks came in late (about 1.30) tonight and caught me reading *Seven Pillars* (which I'd hitherto concealed from him, as I was told not to show it to anyone or discuss it). Shanks, of course, was very keen to have a look at it, so I read him a few extracts, as evidence of T.E.L.'s asceticism of mind. (Shanks met him once, and asserts that he said that 'a white man ought to be King of Mesopotamia', which caused Shanks to regard him as ambitiously inclined.)

December 1

I am feeling so calm and domesticated that the fact must be recorded, to balance my dreary and disgruntled entries. O, my almost ideal existence! I sit among the urbane flames of four candles; a companionable wind mumbles around the roof; the kettle cuckoos softly on the hob. At my elbow, with a half-empty cup of tea, are *Seven Pillars* and the new edition of Doughty's *Arabia Deserta*.[1] After sitting up till 6 a.m. this morning (to finish forty half-ironical lines) I slept till 4.30 p.m. Made a meal at 6 (grilled turbot, cabinet pudding, and coffee; Mrs Binks knows my ways to a nicety, and regrets the return of the Turners almost as much as I do). Played Bach and thought about nothing special till 9. Then walked across Westminster Bridge and back by Waterloo Bridge and the Strand. Ate some cod's roe sandwiches and cold rice pudding at 11. Then pored over maps of Arabia for an hour. Then played Bach, who makes other composers seem like writers of popular fiction.

Walking along the Embankment by Charing Cross, I thought how, until lately, I used to think in terms of the chronology of my own life. (Like sitting in a stuffy little room at the top of a tower.) I wanted to be of use to people who will live after I'm dead, but I scarcely thought about the people who'd already tried and failed (to be of use). As I stood on the Embankment the walls of my tower seemed to collapse outwards, letting in the night-sky and the rumours and moving lights of the city around me. The sense of freedom and development which one experiences at such a moment cannot be recovered in words or articulate thoughts, but such moments leave an effect on one's mind.

[1] With an introduction by T. E. Lawrence.

December 9

Up earlier than usual. Lunched at 2 (awake till 6 a.m.; was awake till 7 a.m. two days last week). Reading Proust all the afternoon ('Swann in Love' again after a year's interval). A queer contrast to *Seven Pillars*. It sent me back to Debussy, whereas *Seven Pillars* tied me to Bach. Dined at the Reform, reading Aldous Huxley's *Antic Hay* till 10.45. I hate it, but am interested in his style-tricks and portraits. (Bob Nichols is in it, a full-length caricature.) Hadn't any notion what I'd do on getting home, and felt rather invertebrate after Huxley's smart priapic writing. (I brought the book home, in case I felt inclined for more dust and ashes.) Proust had made me feel rather stale about *Seven Pillars* (which I've finished and started again!). Before I'd been home five minutes, there came a ring at the door. (I was busy rekindling the fire.) Who could it be? The Turners home again? (They were expected on Guy Fawkes Day, but postponed the event.) The bell had been rung by the last person I'd expected. Standing under the porch, in a new soft grey hat and light-coloured overcoat, with a large paper parcel under his arm, was a small man, whom I at once recognised. It was the author of *Seven Pillars of Wisdom*! My brain flared up sky-high. The one man I'd have selected—in fact the one man I've been craving to talk to for weeks! T.E.L. is up for a week-end's leave. General Trenchard (Air Force)[1] had sent for him. He is staying in Romney Street, a hundred and fifty yards from here. (He wrote his book there in 1919–20 and said he often saw me walking about, 'looking like death'.)

In his usual calm and restrained way, he placed himself on the orange-covered sofa, and inspected Henry Lamb's 'Lytton Strachey' oil-sketch (which I bought recently). Much excited I blundered about the room, emitting disjointed ejaculations. He stayed two and a half hours, while I blurted out questions and assertions, mainly about his book and his present health and existent prospects. I reassured him about the merits of his book, and got his permission for E. M. Forster to read it. He told me that Kipling read it and disapproved strongly. T.E.L. has been a private for nearly two years. He was quite broken down after finishing his book, and saw no way of earning his

[1] Later Marshal of the Royal Air Force. Known as 'Father of the R.A.F.' Created Viscount 1930, O.M. 1951.

living in a way which would satisfy his scruples. The army life
suits him, though he hates the absence of solitude. 'Rowton
House without the cubicles', he called it. The two years have
been a rest for mind and nerves. As he wrote in his book, 'better
to seek some mental death, a slow wasting of the brain to sink
it below these puzzlements'. But he 'lies awake at night a great
deal, thinking, and gets up every morning with it (his book) on
his mind'. When he finished the final draft, he believed that he'd
failed completely. He referred to 'the donnish style in which it
is written'. I pointed out the excellence of his paragraph method,
'like stanzas in an epic'.

How delightful to have the little man (my hero) sitting there
(he is perfectly proportioned except for a slight skimpiness
about the shoulders). He never smokes, but drank two cups of
tea and delicately nibbled some shortbread and a sponge cake,
while I puffed my pipe and jabbered and gestured at him from
the fireplace. I felt enormous and protective, as if he had worn
himself out by his exploits. (While reading his book I saw him
as an infallible superman, and myself as an invertebrate
shambler.) I never saw a man with a straighter look in his eyes.
He was 'offered the governorship of the Falkland Islands'. (Where
are they?) He said he 'hasn't a bean, and doesn't want to live
away from England'. (The only money he has is 'tied up in fifty
modern pictures and a piece of land which he can't sell'.) His All
Souls fellowship (£200 a year) is conditional on his doing
research work, to which he is averse. His nerves are better, but
still bad. (He can't stand *being driven* in a car or going by train
at night, though he can drive himself at sixty miles an hour in
his side-car.)

December 12

Awake till 8.30 this morning, and asleep most of the day. The
Turners arrived at 5.30, just as I was getting up! So far, their
return has cheered me. Turner is looking very well, and very
pleased at having finished a 'social comedy' and a farce, to his
own satisfaction. Mild, still weather. From midnight till 2.30 I
walked the deserted streets, along the Embankment to St
Paul's, which loomed sublime. Then round by Smithfield

Market, an interior white glare of pink carcasses hung on hooks—a very carnivorous vision. Home along Holborn Chancery Lane, and the Strand. Clocks strike five now.

December 13

No sleep at all last night. I feel cheapish.

E. M. Forster writes (of the eighty-four lines I sent him hopefully) 'I like the last part of the Bach one very much.[1] The early part (and most of the other poem) seems to me somehow gluey. One sticks one's nose into each separate word, particularly the adjectives, to smell out the joke or whatever the quality is. Do you think there is anything in this? I don' object to the glue as long as I feel you are experimenting, but i clogs wings. The tempo (haw, better word!) of *Recreations* and all your later work is certainly on the adagio side of andante. F's criticism about gluey adjectives is helpful (though painful) I feel very much depressed about my ten weeks' work. So I wen to the club and drank white wine and brandy till I felt dizzy and stupefied. My heart was like lead. Yet I've enjoyed writing those six hundred lines which now seem useless.

December 20 (I have given my diary a week's rest)

After writing my December 13 entry, I embarked on another sleepless night, and got so fed up that I arose at 5 a.m. and sallied forth for a day in the country. (The first time since September 17, except for an afternoon at Richmond, that I've been more than three miles from Tufton Street.)

At Victoria I got a 7.15 train to Redhill, where I had breakfast. Walked to Dorking, in glorious weather, the country looking exquisitely fresh to my town-tired eyes. After a good lunch I stumped to Leatherhead, and got on to a bus. Back by 5.15. Dined with the Gosses. E.G. very sprightly, but I could hardly keep my eyes open at the end, and fell asleep in the taxi which brought me home. Hodgson was here, arguing with

[1] 'Sheldonian Soliloquy', first published in the *Nation* on 27 May 1922, then in *Recreations*.

Turner, so I joined them, and wasn't in bed till 1.30—a very long day.

Turner has broached the question of selling this house and getting a larger one. I have felt very languid lately, but have been more social, dining with Schuster and (twice) with Berners.[1]

December 23

My ninety-eighth successive night here. Tomorrow I go away for a week, to Garsington and Faringdon. This evening a tidying-up destructiveness seized me, after retrospective ruminations by the fire. I got out my manuscripts and burnt almost all the verse I've written since February. I smiled grimly as it flickered up the chimney. Cautious people would rebuke me. But I do know when a poem succeeds as a whole, and none of these did that. They were bunglings and echoes of the past, and ingenious exercises in locution. I feel pleasantly lightened by their departure. I have no intention of hanging such millstones round my neck. I have tried and failed. Probably I have failed because I tried so hard. The only thing which matters is that I *have* failed. Yet my mind is full of poetry unexpressed. Stored, too, with observation.

Perhaps 1924 will bring a few decent poems. But if it doesn't, I shall feel as I do now (sitting here, a year nearer my tomb-stone) that I will be satisfied with nothing less than the quintessence of all that is best in me. Such a resolution is bound to gain its reward.

December 24–27 at Garsington. Then with Berners at Faring-don House till January 2. Went to tea with Bridges on December 31.

---

[1] Gerald, fourteenth Lord Berners (1883–1950), composer, painter, writer. See *Diaries 1920–1922*.

1924

1924

January 4 (54 Tufton Street)
Feeling unwell and depressed since I left Faringdon, which was
a very pleasant visit. E. M. Forster writes rapturously about
Seven Pillars, of which he has read about a quarter. A feature of
Tufton Street lately is a permanent 'fair' on the waste ground
which is waiting to be built on, after the demolition of some
squalid houses. Every night the steam hurdy-gurdy organ blares
out blatant hoots and waltz-tunes till midnight. It has just
stopped, and I only hear the muffled talking in the room below,
where Turner is in conversational conflict with Gertler and
Ottoline. Delphine's treble voice is never audible; her remarks
are rare, though always to the point. Turner's voice has a
querulous cadence and seems to go on interminably. Probably
he is uttering the wildest and most challenging statements, as
usual.

Ought I to review the past year and prognosticate on the new
one? Well, 1923 is in ruins, and I can't say that it is a noble or
picturesque ruin, though its outlines appear to be less confused
than in some of its precursors. I must have written nearly 1500
lines of verse in 1923, many of them with infinite toil and

dictionary consultation. Most of those lines have perished, and no doubt they deserve their fate. The emotional ones were mainly conventional and full of the 'abstractions' which modernists condemn so severely. In such pieces I revert to pre-war mental habits, using clichés of minor poetry. The remainder were those 'pirouettings' (as E.M.F. calls them) which were written to swell the pages of *Recreations*. In this vein I seem to have reached an impasse of over-elaboration, linguistic extravagance, and self-conscious ironic sophistication—exercises in ingenuity. While at Faringdon I recovered the simpler mode in some lines called 'Primitive Ritual'—inspired by *The Golden Bough*. Such blank verse, rich but not too singular, seems worth doing, though the Faringdon lines will probably turn out to be 'chimney-fodder'.

> Look eastward with your mindsight. Hear the moan
> Of pluvial dirge subsiding. Through the gate
> Of memory wrought with shapes of Stygian gods,
> Behold the rifted gloom of ancient dawn.
>
> Pallor, uplifting on the fluctuant veils
> Of morning, indicates a glimmering world
> Of superstitious settlements,—dim clusters
> Of matin-silvered roofs. Emerging men
> Blunder once more through daylight. Vaguely stands
> The slow-unfolding crude-remembered scene
> With jabber and jargon,—cumulative crowds
> Gathering for celebration of the spring.
>
> Wonder awakes them to the chill green earth:
> Strangeness surrounds them, setting forth to mount
> The sacrificial slope whose ominous pine
> Signals against low-burning lakes of light.
>
> Harsh-brained they go; their thoughts would speed the spring
> And banish winter whose retreating snows
> Streak the grave hills with white. Dimly they vision
> The sacrifice in purple pride of flowers,
> Who bear along with them in stiff parade
> The image of Adonis robed in red.

Fierce flutes for dead Adonis weave their wail:
Shrill flutes wind upward from the watery plain
With invocations of juvescent green.
'*Adon!*' they cry. For him their lips implore
New life, and fill with foliage all the air.

From mindsight fades the morn-ensanguined myth:
Thronged arms are lifted; looming clouds catch fire
To crown the frenzied rite whose clash recedes
Beyond the gradual darkening of those gates
Huge-wrought with twisted limbs of fabulous gods.[1]

January 6

Hodgson was here last night. I took him upstairs to show him
the coloured drawing 'In a Café' by William Roberts[2] (a nightmare which I bought for £*35* in the autumn, at the instigation
of Eric Kennington, who wrote saying that Roberts was 'almost
starving'). R.H. admired its power, but admitted that Birket
Foster[3] is more to his taste! I reminded him of what he said
about my other Roberts drawing (a war scene). 'Twenty-five
years ago that drawing was humanly impossible. No human
mind could have conceived it.' But Birket Foster expresses for
him (and for me) the 'Sunday evening ecstasy' which he has felt
when hearing church-bells across green meadows.

Downstairs, with Turner, he was eloquent about the 'new
world' to which he 'can never belong'. He said, 'I feel a
passionate desire to be twenty-three tomorrow! Then I'd belong
to this new world which is beginning, with its "television" and
heaven knows what else.' He asserted (I don't agree) that the
cinema should supersede the theatre. Turner denied this, saying
that the cinema 'can never be an art-medium any more than
photography can be—except, perhaps, in connection with
operatic music'. Then R.H. said, 'We ourselves may live to see a
world in which every child will be born to a life of *security*, a life
in which riches will have ceased to possess any meaning, since

---

[1] Published in the *New Statesman* 2 February 1924, and in the privately printed
Lingual Exercises for Advanced Vocabularians (1925).
[2] Early Vorticist artist (1895–1980). Had been an official war artist.
[3] Water-colour artist and illustrator (1825–99).

lack of security is the only thing which fosters the acquisitive instinct in men. In time they will learn to feel ashamed of exploiting their fellow-creatures and thereby becoming millionaires.'

He said (while I sat with mouth and eyes open) 'The (controlled) release of the atom will be followed by the release of the human mind. It will be done by something akin to what we call "prayer".' Turner read an extract from an article (in the *Spectator*) on 'Supernatural Science' and remarked, 'If you are so intensely aware of the new world, and long to be part of it, you *do* belong to it.' 'The old religions have failed, and Science must invent a new one,' said Hodgson. It seems wicked that he can't put his talk on paper. Perhaps he does, but I fear it all goes up in pipe-smoke and passes away with cups of tea. To reproduce the style of his talks here would be a literary achievement. I enjoy him most when he is homely and anecdotal. He is most a poet when he speaks of the past. When I told him that I'd been at Faringdon, he mentioned 'a pre-historic footpath on the downs above Wantage', and gave us his idea of what life was like when all the valleys were swamps full of plunging monsters, and the druids sat up on the hills. R.H. has been prowling among the excavations in St James's Park, picking up Cromwellian clay pipes.

January 13

A quiet day, which ended noisily (most of the noise was made by myself talking about myself to Virginia and Leonard Woolf). I have wanted to meet V.W. since last April, when I read *Jacob's Room* at Garsington. But I felt that the Woolfs belong to a rarefied intellectual atmosphere in which I should be ill at ease. I went to Paradise Road, Richmond, this evening, intending to be discreet and observantly detached. But the evening was a gossipy affair, very pleasant and unconstrained. V.W. drew me out adroitly, and I became garrulous. (Did I *bore* them once or twice?) Leonard Woolf seemed reticent and rather weary; anyhow my presence reduced him to comparative muteness. V.W. is a very fastidious lady, and looked lovely (in a lavender silk dress). She has very slender hands and a face for a miniature painter. We gossiped about the obvious names—Hardy, Gosse, Wells, Bennett, Lady Colefax, Middleton Murry, T. S. Eliot, Robert Graves, Aldous Huxley etc. But the evening became more and more a monologue by me. I feel now as if I'd been 'showing-off', behaving like I used to do five years ago, when appearing at 'first meetings' with well-known authors. Talking in the self-explanatory style which one adopts (or indulges in) with new people who are sympathetic. Telling them about my 'commentative readings' in America, my family history, and so on. In fact, saying things I've undoubtedly said before, with an air of producing them spontaneously. Perhaps my loquaciousness was only a symptom of shyness and anxiety to keep things going. Thank heaven, I avoided giving my 'war-experiences' turn. (Though I did touch on Craiglockhart Hospital, in connection with Wilfred Owen.) They agreed with me about the modern vulgarisation of fine literature by the commercialism of publishers; and urged me to publish a book with the Hogarth Press. I dallied with the idea of a small volume of 'scraps of prose', vaguely visualising selections from my journal, which I feel now to be quite impracticable. We dined in their kitchen, which was pleasant and cosy. Ottoline told me that 'Virginia is very inhuman', but I found her charming. But I am now wondering whether I can ever repeat my tour-de-force of 'creating a delightful impression'.

Talking about T. S. Eliot, V.W. said that the right way to treat him is to pull his leg, 'Old Tom' him, and so on; 'otherwise he behaves with such absurd formality and primness; he's rather an old prig, really, and needs to be chaffed out of it.' She also spoke of 'poor old Aldous', and evidently thinks his writings unimportant. This gratified me, as I'm getting fed up with being told that T.S.E. is the most important modern poet, and that Huxley is first-rate.

January 22

Wet day. Stayed in bed till 4 p.m. (after being up till 5 a.m., working at epigrammatic biographies in verse,[1] a device which needs nothing but the *Dictionary of National Biography* to

[1] Four of these appeared as 'Miniatures' in the *New Statesman* on 21 November 1925, and six more as 'Six Biographies' in the *Nation & Athenaeum* on 13 March 1926. All ten are now reprinted in the Appendix on pp. 309–12.

sustain it). Ramsay MacDonald is the first Labour Prime Minister. Lenin is dead.

January 23

Worked till 6 a.m. at my miniature biographies (which I call 'The Triumphs of Oblivion') and got to the end of Vol. III of the *D.N.B.*

January 26

Last night I dreamt about T. Hardy. (I can't remember dreaming about him before.) We were alone on a ship, in some sort of crisis. Walking along the deck, I took his hand and said, 'I do like being here with you.' Afterwards we were having breakfast together in the small smoking-room at Weirleigh. (I've never had breakfast in that room.) I had put a plate of bacon down by the fire to keep it hot for him. Then he came trotting in, very cheerful and rubbing his hands, and we ate our breakfast very happily (as we have often done at Max Gate).

Hodgson was here to-night. I told him my dream, and he said I ought to make a note of it. (But it seems a very tame sort of dream to make a note of.)

Hodgson told a story about how he once went to see two people at Harringay, newly-married after waiting ten years. (A large stout wife and a small husband.) She stood talking, with her arm round his neck all the time, interposing 'We're a pair of loving 'earts!' Five months later they were legally separated. We discussed Blunden. R.H. said 'Little Blunden is like a landscape painter who has painted one masterpiece ("Almswomen") and now goes on exhibiting sketch-book work. At his best he's as good as Goldsmith. "Some bell-like evening when the may's in bloom"—one of the finest lines in English poetry.' R.H. cited places with H. and vowel names in North London. 'Hounslow, Harringay, Haggerston, Hornsey, Hammersmith, Ealing, Acton, Islington'. He said 'There is probably an ethnic reason for this. Saxon sounds?'

An example of Turner's vagueness. This afternoon he was arguing about forms in art, with a painter named Marston (an early friend whom he has 'outgrown'). Turner mentioned

Gosse's objecting to one of his poems because it began in blank verse and then had some rhymed couplets in it. T. (with great conviction and authority) adduced Milton's 'Lycidas' as an example of similar 'looseness'. After Marston had gone I pointed out that 'Lycidas' is elaborately rhymed. (Except for one line.)

Turner's merits are *independence and seriousness*. A combined merit and defect is his habit of improvising confused notions ('exaggerated facts' to prove 'convictions' which he soon afterwards forgets all about). His defects include inaccuracy about details, carelessness in constructing (prose and verse), general rawness and violence of opinion.

January 30

The last ten days have been mostly *night* for me. January 20 was the last day on which I 'lunched' before 4 p.m. Mrs Binks encourages me to carry on my routine as if the Turners weren't here, and brings me up kippers etc. at 5 p.m. (rather to the annoyance, I suspect, of Turner). But I've been making full use of my *D.N.B.* exploration impulse.

It was in October 1920 that I began to file my way out of prison by a systematic effort to form an individual vocabulary. In the last few days (particularly when I read the *New Statesman* proof of 'Primitive Ritual') *I have felt* as if the door is beginning to swing slowly back.

Yesterday morning, after lying awake from 4.15 to 7.15, I got up to get a drink of water in the bathroom. Watching the milkman looming at our gate in foggy twilight, *Chatterton*[1] came into my thoughts, with a sense of exquisite emotion. I skipped him in the *D.N.B.* when I was searching for clowns, criminals, eccentrics, and forgotten poets, and knew little of his work or the details of his life. But the picture in the Tate Gallery has always appealed to me, with its glimpse of summer daybreak through the garret window, and the 'home from the ball' beauty of the dead boy on the bed. So I have since read about him in the *D.N.B.* ('It is wonderful how the whelp has written such things' said Dr Johnson) and cursed Horace Walpole for not sparing him twenty guineas which might have saved a second

[1] Thomas Chatterton, poet (1752–70).

Spenser to the world; and ended by reading 'Sweet his tongue as a throstle's note' in the *Oxford Book of English Verse*. As I went to the club 'I thought of Chatterton, the marvellous boy',[1] and when I got there I searched the library for books about him.

All this excitement has ended in a sonnet and I am feeling pleased. How rarely one gets that sort of excitement about literature. (And how little authentic information there is about Chatterton.)

February 3

Took Turner to dine with the Heads. 'Men's activities are episodic; women's are the contrary' (cumulative?) said Head. He quoted someone saying 'Ideal woman should be the physiological complement of my highest joys.' 'You react with your totality (sex, intellect, everything). No good talking about an emotion being "due to sexual causes". If it *is* an emotion (and not a crude automatic lust) you react with your totality to the phenomenon of causation.' Henry was very skilful and urbane, when *managing* Turner's wild improvisations on the future. Henry mentioned James Stephens's review of George Moore's *Conversations in Ebury Street* (in today's *Observer*). I hadn't read it. Apparently Moore attacks Hardy. But Turner had read it, and quoted Stephens's support of Moore's assertion that T.H., in his novels, 'makes pessimism trivial'. Turner then said that when he'd read the review he 'suddenly realised' that his appreciation of T.H's poetry was only 'secondary' and acquired from me. (T. has read very little of T.H's work, and might, with advantage, study his exactitude of observation.) Worst of all, Turner said, 'When I read that (about T.H. "making pessimism trivial") I thought to myself *"That's one for S.S.!"* ' (Henry, of course, entirely disagreed with Turner.) All this will rankle. Queer, how antagonistic I often feel toward Turner. (I never used to.)

[1] Wordsworth, 'Resolution and Independence'.

1924

SHENSTONE REMEMBERED[1]

One sleepless night, when dusk was growing grey
And sparrows chirped pert compliments to day,
I heard a voice; I glimpsed a life-worn face,
And insubstantial fingers touched me lightly . . .
  'For William Shenstone can you find no place
  Among these elegies that you ponder nightly?
  I also penned some elegies; my breast
  To rural elegance vowed time and care;
  From bowery solitudes I oft confessed
  My limpid raptures that the world might share.
  Those rills are silent now; those arboured nooks
  No more command trim vistas for the gaze:
  My groves are gone. Dust settles on my books;
  And harsh posterity refrains from praise.'

Sad Shenstone! . . . Recollecting what he said,
This, my remembrance of his drooping fame
I carve beneath a myrtle-guarded urn.
Perchance in some cool grotto where the dead
Converse with Pope and Prior and Gray, he'll turn
My mortal pages to perceive his name.

4 February 1924

February 5

Last week I gave Hodgson a pretty little 1836 edition of
Isaac Watts's poems. To-day he sends me a literary curiosity
called *Pirated Poems*. They are by an American whose name has
never transpired. H. writes, 'I have a real tenderness for him—
so n'er-do-well and likeable. I fancy him as finishing up playing
a cornet outside a tavern in the Bowery, New York, and later at
the Gate of Heaven, where Peter, after looking round to see that
nobody's looking, kicks him in.'

February 7

My poem 'Primitive Ritual' appeared in the *New Statesman*
on February 2. Hodgson writes 'I did like it very much indeed.

[1] William Shenstone, poet (1714–63).

Its force and carry, so gay and sombre—savage too : most of all for doing what it set out to do and with simplicity in spite of some words that ain't no friends of mine usually : so pleasant to find myself on good terms with 'em here.' E. M. Forster writes that the poem 'is not the sort of thing that he enjoys; the images don't leap'.

February 8

Last night was a bad one (futile efforts to shake off depression about recent writings, and so on). Went to bed at 5.30 after regaining some serenity by reading Henry Vaughan,[1] but awake till 10 a.m. and then only fitful slumber till 2. Jaded and irritable all the afternoon, E. M. Forster to tea downstairs, but I remained up here, unable to face even him. Dining alone at the club, I heard Arnold Bennett's laugh a little way off; hadn't observed his presence. He soon came across and was genial. (I hadn't seen him since November 19.) Afterwards I sat with him and Massingham and Walter Roch[2] for an hour, and came away feeling quite fresh and cheery. (Although A.B. mentioned 'Primitive Ritual', saying he couldn't read the damned thing.) My Blenheim lines are in the *Nation* this week, and look better than I'd expected.

MEMORANDUM

For *A Compendium of Military Genius*

Entering the strawberry-foliate demesne,
I pause (a tourist in the present tense),
Spectator of an architectural scene
Of Doric and Corinthian opulence.

Set to the musings of an autumn day
Serenely skied with undistracted grey,
Ducal redundancy (all balustrades,
Pilasters, porticoes, and colonnades)
Confronts me. (Vanbrugh made it for the man

[1] Welsh poet (1622–95).
[2] Walter Francis Roch (1880–1965), Liberal Member of Parliament for Pembrokeshire (1908–18).

Who carved rococo conquests for Queen Anne.)
In wars that burst before the South Sea Bubble
Muskets explode, hussars and pike-men plunder,
While Churchill, stimulating martial trouble,
Perturbs Palatinates with smoke and thunder.
Events unfold. The George Quartet contrives
William, Victoria, Edward; and at last
George Windsor's ermined; ruled by whom, arrives
Myself, obscurely pondering on the past—
Sententious thus . . . 'From halted History comes
The gusty bugling of Malbroukian fame;
And what was once imperious in a name
Recedes with desolate drub of death-led drums.
On regimental flags his fights persist;
But I've no zeal to bolster up the story
Of an imperiwigged stingy strategist
Who caracoled upon extortionate glory . . .'

Meanwhile the sun reburnishes the vanes
And orbs of Blenheim Palace; and the clock
Clangs out a modern hour, as if to mock
The mustiness of Marlborough's campaigns.[1]

February 10

Was cheered up yesterday by a nice letter from Robert
Graves, containing a few helpful suggestions for the improvement of 'Primitive Ritual'. He is an admirable critic of the *shape*
of a poem, and understands my methods. At present he is strong
on the theory of conflict (acquired from Rivers) and reads
conflict-interpretation into everything.

A man called yesterday evening, saying that he came from
Osbert Sitwell. Suspecting a hoax, I refused to see him. But he
forced his way in to Turner's room. Turner, who was busy
writing an article, describes him as a man of repulsive aspect
and manners, a sort of crazy poet. He accosted T. with 'I was
talking to Osbert this afternoon'. T: 'Osbert *who*?' *The Man*: '!!'
T: 'What is your business?' *The Man* (mumbling): 'Have no
business—Called to—' T: 'I don't want to see you. *Get out!*'

[1] Published in the *Nation* 9 February 1924, then in *Lingual Exercises*.

Exit *The Man*. (I heard long afterwards that the Man called on O.S. who sent him straight on here.)

February 11

Have been reading a book about 'Perdita' Robinson[1]—light historical journalese—which has made me feel the futility of the 'epigrammatic elegies' I've sweated at since January 21. Of those fifty-one pieces scarcely half-a-dozen now seem tolerable. I suppose the Chatterton sonnet is all right (I sent it to Gosse, who thought it 'very beautiful'). But most of the fifty-one short pieces are mere trivial scribbles—a parlour game. But I suppose I have picked up some smatterings of history from the *D.N.B.*

Heavens! what fortitude one needs, to become a decent writer. One runs madly through green thickets, enamoured of the bird-notes which last but a few moments; one stumbles, picks oneself up, and emerges into a barren waste; one ruminates miserably for a while, dragging desolate feet through the dust of dead dreams. And then, if one is lucky, one plunges into another fool's paradise of 'poetry'. And at the end, perhaps, one will meet death with half-a-dozen 'immortal' lines scribbled on half-a-sheet of note-paper. Lucky is he who does that!

February 12

Went to Hammersmith with the Turners, and saw Congreve's *The Way of the World*[2]—very refreshing.

February 13

In bed all day (as usual). Haddock and baked apple at 5.30 p.m. Soup, omelette, and stewed prunes at the Monico 10.45. Since then, reading Wycherley's *Plain Dealer*, and very dreary stuff it seemed. It is now 4 a.m. and I've just had some tea and bolted three sponge cakes. I now take my pen and wonder inkily what I've got to *show* for my nocturnities of tea and toil since October 1. *Then* I said 'No hunting; no sociability;

---

[1] Mary ('Perdita') Robinson (1758–1800), actress, author, and mistress of King George IV when he was Prince of Wales.
[2] With Edith Evans as Millamant and Robert Loraine as Mirabell.

five months of seclusion—if I can achieve it—and we'll see what happens.' No more was demanded of the lustrum of dark months than that I should add 350 lines of *Recreations* stuff.

As regards the *Recreations* part of the programme (sponge cakes are causing abdominal pains—a three-cornered fight, I suppose) I have added 132 lines to the previous 628, but only 69 lines are *new* (the remainder being the revised poems on Hyde Park[1] and Blenheim). A few of the little elegies may be added, in which case I have a book of sixty pages to publish. But I am already jibbing from the idea of the reviewers and their shoddy patronage, and I dread being left 'cleared out' and empty-desked. I suppose I've added to my awareness of the English language, through looking up thousands of words in Webster, and wearing out the binding of Roget's Thesaurus. And I've read a lot more than in any previous winter of my life. *What?* *Seven Pillars* (350,000 words) for a start. That was worth doing, and needed concentrated effort.

A great deal of promiscuous poetry (no one poet specially—I would like to study Milton and Wordsworth properly some day). As usual, very little history. (Must have a go at Gibbon.) The *D.N.B.* researches count for something, though they merely showed my preference for the eighteenth century. Music has advanced a lot. I can now play Bach fugues without getting completely lost after the first half-page, and have discovered his long organ-works.

My routine habits have differed from previous winters. Thanks to Mrs Binks (who delights in looking after my needs) I have succeeded in persuading the Turners that it is essential for me to have my first meal 'at home'. That meal is neither breakfast, lunch, tea, nor dinner. It occurs any time between 3 and 7—and is always sole, haddock, kippers, or omelette, with coffee and cooked fruit. I have almost abandoned my Reform Club dinners, and have given up wine, when alone. I am clearer-headed and less liable to nerve-tantrums than at any time since 1918 (except when feeling well and in the country). I know that I've lived too much in books and have received no new impressions of scenes and events and people. ('People' have been limited to E. M. Forster, Berners, (the Turners, of course),

---

[1] 'Observations in Hyde Park', published in the *Nation* 29 March 1924, then in *Lingual Exercises*.

Shanks (whom I avoid—he has slept in this house for the past ten days and I've never spoken to him), the Hodgsons, who come here one evening a week, and a few habitués of the Reform Club.) I have been three times to see the Heads; nowhere else more than once, except to Schuster's, which is only five minutes away. (He went to the South of France a month ago, and I am to join him there early in March.)

February 14

Mrs Binks disturbed me to-day at 2 o'clock (I'd been awake till after 10). She has inclinations toward drama and romance, as I've noticed before; and now she spoke in the solemn tones of one who 'breaks bad news'. Someone, she said, had rung up from 'Lord Bernard's' (her rendering of 'Berners', who has rung up several times this winter). 'Lord Bernard is very, *very* ill indeed, and has asked to see you.' Much perturbed, I made a neurotic toilet, talking to myself in the bathroom (as I always do when upset) and visualising the sad state of affairs at Chesham Place (while Delphine playing Mozart downstairs sounded ravishingly mournful). The gifted nobleman sinking rapidly; the specialist's motor outside the house; William, the chauffeur, tiptoeing about the house with stricken looks; clavichords standing poignantly mute; music scattered about on the piano, 'just as he left it', and everything suddenly awakened from inanimate objectiveness to heart-breaking significance. The dying man has 'asked for me'. I see his head moving restlessly on the pillows, and catch the rapid murmur of his delirious patter. Once again the deceitful, the ever-obvious shadow has caught us napping; and now we remember the gay and intimate humanity of the departing guest. Or—to be more exact—we are confusedly conscious (as I was in the bathroom, and while I bolted a pair of poached eggs funereally served up by Mrs Binks, and in the taxi which butted among the buses down Victoria Street and trundled through Belgrave Square)— yes, we are confusedly conscious of such images and sensations ('reacting with our totality', as Henry Head would say) while the first numbness of the shock wears off.

I found myself thinking (and probably muttering) 'This makes me realise that I have very few friends. If Berners dies,

it will make a great difference to me.' Passing the Army &
Navy Stores I rebuked myself severely. 'Silly rot, don't make a
fool of yourself' etc. Passing St Peter's, Eaton Square, I took a
self-controlling squint at its architecture, decided that it was
unpleasant, and lapsed into gloomy forebodings. 'I don't like
it at all' (meaning the telephone message, not St Peter's); 'these
things always catch one unawares, and another one is just about
due'. Mixed up with this, I asked myself 'Are you really so
upset about Berners, or is it only self-pity?' (In the bathroom I
had actually caught myself imagining letters of condolence—'I
know what a great friend of yours Lord B. was' etc.) I even
fabricated a deathbed reconciliation with O. Sitwell—the
expiring peer, with a final flicker of his characteristic humour,
amiably reuniting us in the hour of his own dissolution! His
mother will be there, of course, I thought, imagining her saying
something incongruous which would give 'the poor gentleman'
a misty spasm of amusement on his way to the ultra-Stygian
'Green Room' whither he goes (in a phantasmal Rolls-Royce)
to pay his respects to Bach and Wagner.

Marooned by my taxi in Chesham Place, I stood on the pavement in a pitiless north-east wind at half-past-three on a sunless
afternoon, and couldn't 'for the life of me' remember whether it
was No. 3 or No. 4 (though I'd been there at least a dozen
times). Instinct said No. 4, but I rang at No. 3, rather surprised
that there was 'no straw down' and everything looking as usual.
After a longish pause, the door was opened by Marshall—B's
tall, mincing-voiced, slightly Semitic-looking valet. He too
looked the same as usual. I passed in, quietly, but with a sense
of ominous intrusion. *S.S.* (in a voice which was expressionless
but sepulchral): 'How is Lord Berners?' *Marshall* (more mincing than ever): 'Lord Berners is much better, but he is unable
to get up yet, and was anxious for you to come and see him.'
S.S. (much taken aback): 'But . . . er . . . a message was given
me that he was very ill indeed . . . Well, I *am* glad . . . I was
throwing fits about it.' *Marshall*: 'Oh no, sir. His lordship has
had a touch of influenza—gastric—but is going on quite nicely,
and not infectious.' As I followed him up the stairs I muttered
'Blast Mrs Binks!' There was Berners, in bed, but normally
exuberant; the clavichord on the counterpane, and books (by
George Moore, Jane Austen, and Congreve) on a table at his

elbow—quite incredibly convalescent, in fact. We jabbered for a couple of hours, and my two-year-old collar-stud dissolved into its two constituent halves, probably from the recent excitement. I told B. how I'd been misled about his condition (without divulging my perturbation, merely saying that I 'was in an awful state about it').

On the whole I am grateful to Mrs Binks for her idiotic behaviour, since her craving for sensational effects reminded me that Lord B. can 'ill afford to be spared' or words to that effect.[1]

February 16

Robert Graves, to whom I sent my Chatterton sonnet, writes that 'Chatterton is a hopeless fraud, to my reading'. R.G. also 'has no sympathy with Vaughan and Crashaw'. I am wondering how much of them he has read. But youngish men are apt to be intolerant and unfair about famous writers whom they've investigated without sympathy. Perhaps my awareness of this is a sign of 'Age with stealing steps'.[2]

R.G. is quite kind about the collection of poems I sent him, and praises 'Evensong in Westminster Abbey'. Rather to my surprise he 'likes extremely' the 'Song, be my soul' lines (which I destroyed before Xmas, and then wrote out from memory, in a faint hope that R.G. would 'pass' them, but expecting them to be dismissed as '1902 poetry' or 'only anthology stuff'). I have now decided to publish nothing till Autumn 1925. This evening I went, rather heavily, to Anerley, in raw and rather foggy weather. (Hadn't been there for eleven months.) The usual Sunday crowd there, mostly friends of the girls—five men and two women. De la Mare has been reading *Gulliver* again. 'I enjoyed it more than ever before, but what a pity he didn't leave out the satire!'

---

[1] After November 1926 I 'lost touch' with Lord B. (who was soaring above me socially) and have scarcely spoken to him in the last four and a half years. S.S.

[2] 'For Age, with stealing steps,
Hath clawed me with his clutch' (Thomas, Lord Vaux, 1510–56).
Cf. The clown's song in *Hamlet*, act V, scene 1.

February 18

Dined with Cyril Tomkinson at the Oxford and Cambridge Club (to which he's just been elected). He always makes me garrulous. (He says 'People confide in me. That is why I am rather a success as a clergyman.') Anyhow I found myself discussing Turner and 'wondering whether he is as devoid of altruism as he asserts himself to be'.

This is a problem which has haunted me lately, and I've sometimes doubted whether Turner really has any affection for me, or trust in me. His 'individualism' *seems* to have grown more aggressive lately, probably because I've begun to criticise him (secretly) which I never did until this winter. I no longer accept his 'dicta' as I used to do. But I'm not well tonight and had best stop, before I commit further indiscretions in ink.

(Tomkinson, like the Heads, was urging me to leave Tufton Street and live comfortably by myself. As usual, I pointed out that if I did this, the Turners would have to leave their house, which they might be unable to sell or let.)

February 20

Was up 'very early' (lunched at 1.30). Feeling moderate, so went to have hair cut before the concert for which Berners had sent me a ticket. Got there later than I intended, and missed all but the last movement of Schoenberg's Quartet (Op. 10), which sounded exquisite. (Last time I heard it, in 1914, I thought it excruciatingly ugly.) Dined at Reform. Weather perishingly cold; felt poorly. Gilbert Wakefield[1] (husband of Isabel Jeans whom I saw as Margery Pinchwife in *The Country Wife*[2] at the Phoenix Society on Monday) talked to me—dreary little chap, always grumbling to the waiters about the food. Read a short story 'England, My England' by D. H. Lawrence after—a devastating affair, but well written.[3] Home at 9.30, feeling wretched. Tried to read *Memoirs of a Midget*[4] (I can never get going with it).[5] Became sleepy and headachy, and went to sleep

[1] Actor (1892–1963).
[2] By William Wycherley (1640–1716). First produced in 1675.
[3] In the volume of that name (1924).
[4] By Walter de la Mare (1921).
[5] Read it afterwards with great enjoyment. S.S.

on the couch in this room. Woke after three hours, mostly dreaming. Made some tea and let some air into the room (which is always either stuffy or draughty, being only twelve foot by ten). The sky has cleared and the wind has dropped; the moon is white above the looming houses of Bennett's Yard. I avoided Berners at the concert, probably because he hasn't thanked me for copying out twenty-six of my Elegies, which he'd asked to see. I took a lot of trouble over the manuscripts and now wish I'd got them back. Spoke to him on the telephone yesterday and asked if he'd received them. He merely laughed and said 'O yes. Very nice!' Evidently thinks them a bore.

Reading Blunden's poems last night. Deeply consoling, and strangely mingled with associations of home and childhood.

February 21

Went to bed at 6 a.m. (after reading Blunden again). Dreamt that E.B. and I were playing cricket for Tonbridge; we had both made a century! Woke at 10.30; ate a boiled egg and opened a large envelope from Robert Graves, containing manuscripts of two long poems which I don't feel eager to read. R.G. pleased with £25 I sent him. Fell asleep, and woke to find the day over —5.30! The only excuse for all this laziness is that I don't waste much time when I *am* awake. Better than walking drearily in Hyde Park, or grumbling with Meiklejohn at the Reform (and being told that 'poets ought to be schoolmasters or solicitors' etc.).

The Turners went to Queen's Hall, so (after my sole and baked apple at 6.30) I had the piano (which I play only when they are out of the house) and blundered through Bach organ-works till 10. Went to the Strand to get a meal. Tried Romano's, but found myself (with Lamb's *Specimens of the English Dramatic Poets*, second edition, 1813) in a dreadful room full of ugly people shuffling round to a jazz-band. Watched them for a few minutes and then fled to Gatti's, which was an empty corridor, where I was able to enjoy *The Duchess of Malfi* in peace. Weather slightly less cold: fleecy clouds round the moon. The Horseguards looked majestic as I walked home. Mrs Binks leaves in March, as she wants a place where she can 'live in' as cook-housekeeper. I shall never be so comfortable again, and

am apprehensive about next winter. Whatever happens, I shall
stick to my present mode of life, and if necessary live on potted
meat and biscuits. I must concentrate all my energies on educat-
ing my mind by reading only good literature. In the summer I
will visit my friends in the country, and then shut myself up for
another six months, and see fewer people than ever. It is the
only way to get everything done, even if it makes me feel ill.

February 22

Turner is shouting down the telephone at Mrs Whitworth[1]—
something about producing someone's play. This morning at
6 a.m. I felt so wide-awake that I went for a walk—through St
James's Park and round the Serpentine. A pleasant grey morning
which made me want to be in the country, and made me realise
the intensity of the glare of my electric lamp on the nocturnal
pages of this winter. Watching the grooms exercising in Rotten
Row, I felt a strong craving to be a brainless fox-hunter again.
A hard-bitten neatly-dressed man came cantering along, whistl-
ing cheerily and leaning well forward on a nice-looking brown
mare. I sighed for Warwickshire. And the stuffy little room
where I spend my bookish nights seemed horrible. Coming
home by Wellington Barracks, the troops were on parade. A
bored-looking young officer (looking absurd in his frock coat
and red-stitched trousers) was inspecting them. I realised the
advantages of being outside the railings. Warwickshire hunting-
people share that barrack-square mentality. 'Thank heaven I've
got a *free mind*!' I thought; and ceased to regret my exile from
Reynardism

February 23

Tip-toeing downstairs an hour ago (Hodgson having
jargoned and departed; the Turners upstairs; and Shanks
snoring along the passage) I found a letter inviting me to

---

[1] Phyllis Bell (1884–1964) married in 1910 Geoffrey Whitworth (1883–1951),
who in 1918 founded the British Drama League, which was largely organised by
his wife. In 1924 she founded and directed the Three Hundred Club, which in
seven years produced fourteen plays of great literary interest, including
Smaragda's Lover by W. J. Turner (1925).

attend a farewell dinner to Blunden on March 11, he 'having been appointed Professor of English Literature at Tokyo'. First I'd heard of it, and a shock. Three years minus little B. isn't a pleasant thought. However, it will get him out of the groove of literary journalism. But this news upsets me considerably.

(After writing the above) I read some more short stories by D. H. Lawrence—all very good, especially 'Wintry Peacock'.[1] Went out at 5.15 a.m. Posted letter to Blunden. Walked along the river to Chelsea Bridge. Night dark and frosty. Dark river. Up Sloane Street, sky lightening. Into Hyde Park at 6.15. Exquisitely beautiful and mysterious (view from bridge, looking along the Serpentine).

Back by 7.30. Woke at 1 and heard a row going on downstairs. Mrs Binks having a 'back-chat' set-to with poor Delphine! Lay there fearing the worst. Sure enough, D. has sacked Mrs B. (for some trivial upset about 'a slice of lemon'). I knew that they were antagonistic. Mrs B. was leaving on March 8, and only stays on my account. (They only pay her fifteen shillings a week, out of which she pays sixpence a day in bus-fares from Chelsea.) I never had any comfort here until she came. Previous servants (sluts) did nothing for me. But the position is awkward. Sometimes I've wondered whether the Turners would want me here if they could afford to get on without me. Probably not. As things are, I can't see that I'm a great nuisance to them. I never have more than one meal a day cooked here, and that's only a bit of fish and some coffee. I bring no one here. They couldn't possibly find anyone else who would give so little trouble. But what do I give them in return? Am I merely selfish and self-indulgent? Sometimes I suspect that Turner resents and envies my financial independence. Small blame to him if he does. O dear! All I want is peace and quiet, a fried sole and a hot bath. Not much to ask of life. By trying to make me comfortable Mrs Binks has created a rift in my relations with the Turners. (But before this winter I wasn't here more than half the time.) Must be reticent and cautious. Anyway I'll be away a lot in the summer.

Later. Went down and talked to the Turners. Delphine upset about Mrs Binks. Turner *hates* her. (Not surprising as she does very little for him.) And I'm afraid her inaccurate tongue did no

[1] In *England, my England* (1924).

one much good. (She was inclined to make mischief about them
to me. I fancy she hoped to get me away from here to rooms of
my own.) Anyhow she has banged the door and departed, so
there's an end of it. Poor soul, I'm sorry for her.

March 1

A week's arrears to write up. *Last Sunday* I went to Weirleigh for the day. (Hadn't seen Mother for six months; but not
my fault. I can't go there and she hasn't been to London.)
Enoch-Ardenish feeling.[1] Tiring day, but a relief to get away
from nearly eight weeks of Tufton Street. On *Tuesday* I went to
Cambridge for the Greek play (*The Birds*).[2] Stayed in King's.
Went to Cottenham Races on Wednesday with R. Wood. Dined
at Corpus with J. MacCurdy.[3] On *Thursday* I went to Clare (not
the College) for farewell visit to Blunden. Five o'clock train.
Snowy landscape, with hares sitting forlornly. Perishing cold
wind. Little B. met me with tub-cart and white pony. Mary went
out to some village beano, so I had a nice chat by the fire,
sipping E.B's weak port-wine and looking at early nineteenth-
century books. Slept well. (House very draughty.) In all day
Friday, except for a slushy stroll round the fields before tea.
(Thawing, but hard frost at night and a gale of wind.) Talking
to E.B. all day. Rotten to think that I shan't see him for three
years. Feel almost inclined to go to Japan to see him! Mary
went to a dance at Bury St Edmunds. Awful Clare chemist called
for her (married to a daughter of T. G. Tickler, whose ration-
jam was a disgraceful feature of the Great War). He was half-
drunk, an atrocious bounder. Poor E.B. looked upset, but they
started at 8, so we had another fireside evening. He impresses
me more than ever as my most kindred spirit among contemporary bards. We share the same feeling for English landscape and country life (Birket Foster charm and village cricket).

---

[1] In Tennyson's poem, Enoch Arden, a sailor, is shipwrecked on a desert island and
presumed dead. Years later he is rescued and comes home to find his wife happily
married to his best friend. Rather than destroy their happiness he hides his
identity. S.S. often referred to this story, especially at Weirleigh, where he felt a
revenant in his childhood home.

[2] By Aristophanes.

[3] John Thomson MacCurdy (1886–1947), Lecturer in Psychopathology in Cambridge from 1923, Fellow of Corpus Christi College from 1926. Author of *The
Psychology of Emotion* (1925) and other works.

On Saturday I caught the 9.57 train from Clare. B. came to the station in the pony-cart, driven by a red-cheeked village girl. Felt very sad, but unable to realise that it is three years' separation.[1] B. looks forward to returning with £700 saved out of his £900 a year salary. Mary refuses to join him in Japan, and will stay at Stansfield with the two children. This morning I went to Cook's and ordered a ticket for Monte Carlo for next Friday. Encountered O. Sitwell in the hairdresser's shop— looking very Hanoverian in a bowler hat and long blue overcoat. I felt confused, but he suavely greeted me with 'Good morning, Siegfried', apparently quite at ease. I mumbled 'Good morning', and hurried past him.

March 6

Have just finished packing one suitcase, and the other needs no selection as it is a jumble of shoes and shaving-things. So my laborious winter is ended, and I can forget, for a few weeks, my struggles to become an accomplished writer. Turner came in while I was packing, and conversed quite amiably for an hour.

March 7 (8 p.m. In the train, Gare de Lyon.)

Pleasantly reminiscent, this journey has been, as all journeys are, when one is alone and undistracted. The sun beamed a little on the way to Dover, and I stared out at Staplehurst, Headcorn, and Pluckley, remembering vanished gallops with the Mid-Kent Stag Hounds. Then a reassuring ocean shimmered away from a half-misty coast, and I knew that I dared to lunch on the boat, and straightway deposited myself at a table for roast chicken and Dutch cheese. But what a dreary assortment of voyagers! I am sure I was the most distinguished-looking, though a few had monocles and fur coats. Coming into Calais, I, as usual, remembered vividly my arrival there (in November 1915, in a cheerless dawn) on my way to Béthune, and actually the first time I'd crossed the Channel. And here I am in the *train de luxe*, sharing a compartment with a dour elderly man with drooping moustaches and dowdy daughter next door; how lucky for me, since he sits with her, leaving me to muse over

[1] I didn't see E.B. again until November 1927. S.S.

Gosse's lecture to the College of Physicians (on 'Literature and
Medicine') which has caused his presence to beam urbanely on
me from the pages of the *London Mercury*, between Abbeville
and Paris. At one point—(at this point the train starts and I go
to eat a very bad dinner).

March 9 (Maison au Coin, Beaulieu)

What I was going to say—forty-eight hours ago—was that
while I was reading Gosse's lecture I came to the words 'He
retorted that their objections were frivolous, frolicsome, and
groundless.' I was reading on into the next sentence when, as it
were, I *overheard* myself (in the *visual* sense of the word) with
apparent irrelevance, on horseback with the Southdown Hounds
near Lewes. Yes; there I was, quite distinctly, riding along a
certain field outside a familiar fox-covert. Instead of relapsing
into a traveller's dream of the chase, I checked the vision and
inquired, '*Why* this irrelevant mind-picture of Sussex?' Then I
remembered that the covert was called 'Folly Wood'. 'Frivolous
and frolicsome' had caused it. If only one could *control* these
delicate spontaneities of the mind-mechanism.

Life here is, so far, livelier than I'd anticipated. Schuster met
me at the station (at 3.15 p.m.) and in a minute Anzie was
retrieved from the barber's to whirl me here in the Rolls. This
house overlooks a pleasant little harbour and the bay beyond it,
and the hills toward Monaco, all much as I'd expected. A
charming little flat, with a decent piano. I was told to be dressed
by 7, to go to *Pelléas et Mélisande*[1] at Monte Carlo. The music
sounded exquisite, and I liked the florid flamboyance of the
Opera House. ('Good old Monte', as Arnold Bennett calls it.)

Schuster, of course, met several acquaintances, mostly hard,
smart women. To-day we lunched with the Gautier-Vignals,
whose large house is opposite this one (which belongs to them).
The Count is tall, white-haired, grand-seigneurish, and deferential, with a pointed beard. He married (second wife) for her
money Sidney Schiff's[2] sister—a wizened little woman who talks
literary jargon—Proust, James Joyce, Aldous Huxley, and so
on.

[1] Debussy's opera (1902), based on Maeterlinck's play (1892).
[2] Novelist under pen-name Stephen Hudson (1868–1944).

This afternoon Frankie Schu had a tea-party. Three middle-aged ladies—Mrs Brinton (formerly Mrs Willie James), Lady Alwynne Compton-Vyner, and Lady Eva Wemyss, a jolly, fat cosy old thing, dressed anyhow, with stuffed-sawdust legs, who lives near here with her mother, Lady Cowley, an aged gambler, who is apparently impervious to bereavement. 'When I told her that X was dead' said Lady Eva, 'she never even looked up, but just went on playing patience.'

Mrs Brinton wears pince-nez, is 'dressed very young' in white and grey, very much 'made up'—talks about 'Bendor's[1] yacht', and evidently assumed that I am a 'real Sassoon', for she asked if I'd 'Been to Philip's[2] Charity Ball'. Bemoaning about the Labour Government, she exclaimed, 'I really don't know what is going to become of us!' (but her pearls looked valuable).

Lady Alwynne Compton-Vyner, in an effort to make the conversation sparkle, quoted the Nice newspaper which announced the arrival of Bendor's yacht—'The Duke of Westminster, *brother of the Prince of Wales*'. She said it was one of the funniest things she'd ever read! 'Ha ha; hee hee!' (We all laughed automatically.) Mrs Brinton capped this with an 'excruciatingly funny story' about someone in Monte Carlo who went up to Lady Hawtrey and said 'How are you, Lady Tree'. (Roars of laughter from Schuster.) Lady Eva Wemyss had 'been to see Mrs Pat' (Mrs Patrick Campbell—historian's note) 'in a Bernstein war-play'. 'Bridget Guinness took me. She was entertaining a great German banker. I'd refused to speak to the German, but I felt so sorry for him during the play that I turned to him and said "We have all suffered too much already through the war!" And we all left the theatre.' (Quite a touching little episode, but the great banker probably suffered more during the inflation of the Mark than during the war.)

They talked about *Pelléas et Mélisande*, and how Mrs Pat played Mélisande years ago. Schuster has a photograph of her in that rôle among the celebrities whose signed portraits adorn the room—Emma Eames, Nellie Melba, Cosima Wagner, Blanche Marchesi, Jennie Churchill etc. One of the dames

---

[1] Nickname of the second Duke of Westminster.
[2] Sir Philip Sassoon, third Baronet (1888–1939). S.S's distant cousin, had been Private Secretary to Field Marshal Sir Douglas Haig (1915–18) and was Under-Secretary of State for Air 1924–9 and 1931–7.

remarked that the room is like a scene in a play (which it was).
I did little except hand them cakes. At 5.30 they all climbed
down the iron staircase ('like leaving a lighthouse', one of them
remarked) and I propelled Lady Eva's large white Aberdeen
Bingo, who was timorous and unwilling to descend. Such is
social life here.

March 10

Waking up here is pleasant, with foreign strangeness,
mingled with certain homely sounds, such as Anzie trolling 'On
the road to Mandalay—where the—fer-lying fishes play' in the
bathroom. Henry the footman bustles up and down the tiled
passage; he also is an exuberant warbler. (Schuster and I
refrain from song.) I feel rather yellow of a morning, and the
glaring coast-scenery out in the expensive sunshine doesn't
allure me. I prefer to puff my pipe in bed, wondering whether
I shall read one of the four (rather un-Riviera-ish) volumes I
brought with me. (Bunyan's *Holy War*; Dickens's *Uncommercial
Traveller*; and a couple of anthologies, one poetry, and one
prose.) I have also brought Skeat's *Etymological Dictionary*—
heaven knows why. The *Uncommercial Traveller* was recom-
mended to me by H. W. Massingham when I lunched with him
last week.

March 11

Yesterday we lunched at Ciro's in Monte Carlo. Countess
Gautier-Vignal at the next table with Mrs Bates (a wealthy
American). Mrs Basilisk would have been more appropriate.
Huge pearls; pouched eyes; vermilion lips; snake-like regard.
Very large, and dressed in white and grey. The Countess looking
like a little gnome; wisps of grey hair hanging from under a
round helmet-hat crushed down over her brow. Very square
chin, which she pokes forward. Dressed dark and dingy. Eating
stewed prunes while the Basilisk gorged chocolate éclairs. As
we came along the arcade, Schuster was greeted by one of his
grey-haired dames who 'hadn't seen him for twenty years'. She

introduced her son, a tall, pink-faced, blond-moustached
monocled, grey-suited tailor's dummy, who towered above her
with an imbecile grin. She exclaimed, 'O Mr Schuster, how well
I remember your *dear* mother at Baden-Baden, and how she
used to say "I can't be bothered with names!" ' etc. She clung
to Schuster, peering up at him from under a large lilied straw
hat with black velvet on it—a weary old woman in white. 'Used
to be one of the wittiest women in London,' said Schuster afterwards. Lunch was amusing (watching the people). Admiral
Beatty pranced jauntily in, wearing a grey flannel suit. Count
Festetic (of Vienna) ordered lunch with hauteur and delibera-
tion. He bowed to Schuster. ('One of the few chic Austrians who
has still got a lot of money,' murmured Schuster.) Count F. is
bald-browed, middle-aged, and rather grim-looking. Three
smart, ghastly, and socially intimidated Germans near us, with
an Italian interpreter of despicable aspect. Five Dago Argentines
at another table—sallow, sinister with their quickly decayed
good looks, like some exotic flower which goes rotten after a
day or two of sickly-smelling display. Monte Carlo is full of
'currency profiteers', dreadful people who have moved from
Vienna to Berlin like vultures preying on dead bodies. After
lunch Schuster and I went to a song-recital by Madame Croiza.[1]
(Very good.) Fauré, Debussy, Ravel. Very pleasant and
relaxing.

March 12 (In bed)

Schuster has just been in to announce that there is 'a biting
east wind'. Very bad for the sunshine *brio* of his luncheon-party
'out of doors on the Cap'. He has toddled off to arrange for a
table 'in the only warm corner' of the restaurant terrace. No
doubt he will succeed. He seldom fails to secure 'the only warm
corner' on the terrace of life.

As long as I am not 'being serious' about anything except the
quality of food, music, the weather, and the 'amusingness' of
passers-by, I find Schuster an admirable companion. (He has
learnt not to fuss about small sums of money—dividing up bills
—in my presence.)

[1] Claire Croiza (1882–1946), French mezzo-soprano.

And Anzie is a source of perpetual good-humour. Yesterday morning, while we were leaning on the sun-warmed wall above the harbour outside our door, he imparted the news of his engagement to the charming young lady who was painting his portrait last winter. They are to be married in August. This was a halcyon announcement. I offered reticent congratulations, while Monaco villas glittered in the noonday light. Sea and sky were uncompetitively azure. Rich people in limousines and well-to-do persons in autobuses whizzed past us on their way to and from Nice. Then Schuster shuffled out, locked the door behind him, adjusted his muffler, and buttoned his grey overcoat. We entered the long grey Rolls-Royce and glided away, up the zigzag road among bougainvillaea-purpled villas. Soon I was gaping down at the Mediterranean, and Schuster was introducing me to the Alps. (A skyward glimmer of whitish-gold snow-fields beyond the humped aridity of foothills.) Beyond the Alps lies Milan, whither we go next week to hear Toscanini conduct Verdi and Wagner. Far below, in the bay of Villefranche, lies an Admiralty sloop (waiting for Admiral Beatty to return from his lunch at Ciro's in Monte Carlo?).

At La Turbie we draw up in the *Place Théodore de Banville*, and consume a large lunch out of doors. I drink *vin rosé* and watch tourists come up from Monte Carlo while unwashed children scuffle and squabble and stare, and La Turbie dogs come sniffing for scraps. After lunch we glide up to the golf course, where ultra-British 'civilisation' is chasing its golf-ball against a background of eternal Alps and shimmering sea.

Anzie tinkers with the tyres, while S. and I toddle a little way up the hill, sagely discussing the engagement, which S. finds *most satisfactory*. 'Her mother is a very old friend of mine; and she will have a nice little income of her own, and £1500 a year after her mother's death.' Then down the hill again and home by Monaco.

Anzie rows me on the bay in a dumpy little boat. After that, opera allures us. Anzie goes off to Nice to *Madam Butterfly* with a lady-friend. S. and I take an autobus to Monte Carlo, dine at Quinto's (in Italian style) and then hear *Prince Igor*. During the entr'actes S. chats with nobby-snobby canary-haired Lady Cunard[1] and her friends, while I lean against a marble column

[1] American-born London hostess (1872–1948).

and watch the absurdities promenading. We are given a lift home by the Gautier-Vignals (chattering in French) and the day ends with Anzie swinging his wooden leg up the lighthouse stairway, bawling an air from *Butterfly*. Such was yesterday, and not a bad one either.

March 13

Yesterday's lunch at L'Ermitage, Cap Ferrat. The Americans were nice 'natural' people, with no pretensions to 'culture'; they were complaining about Debussy's *Pelléas et Mélisande*, which had caused them agonies of boredom and mystification; but we all agreed that the lunch—especially the artichokes—was excellent. 'The Americans' consisted of Mrs Thompson (a homely old lady), her daughter (beautifully dressed in dove-grey) newly-married (second time) to Captain Steele (who is to take charge of the new U.S.A. Zeppelin which has been built by the Germans). We sat in our 'warm corner' under a pink-and-white-striped awning. Anzie sustained the proceedings with his amusing ditties and ejaculations, which are nothing when written down, but very apt in the open air. *An example:* the waiter drops a handful of cutlery with a crash. *Anzie:* 'Come in, the water's lovely!' (The Americans were acquaintances of his.)

The evening provided an acute contrast. Schuster and I were among the nobs, snobs, and profiteers at Ciro's. We dined with Lady Cunard. I embarked on this affair with the intention of 'acquiring satirical material'. There I'd sit, enjoying my dinner in Juvenalian-plus-Olympian detachment—a being 'formed to delight at once and lash the age'.[1] Not so. The withered garland of a splitting headache still encircles my cranium, reminding me of my failure to achieve 'detachment' (and of the infernal clamour and heat of the restaurant).

To begin with, Schuster and I waited nearly an hour for the party to assemble. It was well after 9 before Lady Cunard put in an appearance (what an 'appearance'!). Then there was trouble about a table for twelve, and it was 9.30 before she dumped us, higgledy-piggledy and famished, round the festive board. Everyone was irritable, and some semi-royalty (Bourbon) had to be re-arranged for purposes of prestige. 'Do you mind

[1] Pope, epitaph on Swift.

moving, Captain Trevor,' said the hectic hostess. But Captain T. (the underbred second husband of Lady Juliet Duff[1]) displayed caddish manners and refused to move.

The noise of the band (quite near our table) was terrific, and shouting was the only medium by which 'polite conversation' could be carried on.

I can see myself (as I saw myself then, reflected in a mirror at dazzling, dyspeptic Ciro's) crowded uneasily between poor Lady Juliet (large and good-natured and suffering through her husband's bad manners) and Mrs Dudley Ward (the Prince of Wales's smart lady-friend from Nottingham). I can see Mrs D.W. leaning her elbows confidentially on the table and turning to ask me (her opening remark) 'What *do* you think about Foot-and-Mouth Disease?' (Fox-hunting has been much interfered with by it this winter.) I can see Lady Cunard (that bobbed and bedizened blonde with startled but unspeculative blue eyes in a clown-painted face) leaning across to scream at Lady Juliet— 'I've been lunching with Lord Rothermere. He told me that he's lost all respect for England and its statesmen, and would prefer to live in France.' She added, 'The *Daily Mail* is a splendid paper.' 'But nobody takes it seriously, Maud,' protested Lady Juliet calmly; 'it changes its opinions too often.' This must have been late in the proceedings, for I was now sitting next to a young man named Sir Robert Abdy,[2] who had been lecturing me about the pugnacious and acquisitive propensities of the human race (he must have been reading some propagandist book before dinner). Sir Robert supported Lady Cunard. 'Lord Rothermere is the greatest patriot in England. I don't know him personally, but I judge him by his articles.'

Captain Trevor now rose rudely from the round table, and said 'Come on, Juliet. I'm going to the Jockey Club to have a gamble.' Lady Juliet followed him out; and Lady Cunard exclaimed, 'And *that's* the man I lifted out of the gutter. And I paid for the *very watch on his person!*' (Trevor was in the Army Service Corps during the War—a 'fancy-man' who was picked up by Lady C.) Sir Robert now resumed his efforts to convert me to militarism and materialism.

[1] 1881–1965. Daughter of the fourth Earl of Lonsdale and widow of Sir Robert Duff. She was the recipient of many of the love poems of Hilaire Belloc.
[2] Fifth Baronet (1896–1976). One of Lady Cunard's residuary legatees.

As usual under such 'social' conditions, I gave my all-too serious consideration to these provocative utterances, thereby increasing my headache. He wished me to realise that war is the only possible outlet for human energy in a world where spiritual (and intellectual) redemption is unachievable (and non existent). He is too young to have been in the late War, and is married to a tall blonde Russian who was (I am told by Schuster) 'a mannequin'. But Sir R. has rather a nice face, and I really felt that I must try and hold the fort against his philosophy of despair and violence. 'I should *like* to convince you of the existence of the human spirit,' I overheard myself (dizzy with champagne and vociferation) saying with an air of Christlike conviction. What a remark to utter at Ciro's in Monte Carlo!

March 14

Anzie has gone to a 'Gala Dinner' at Nice, and the insatiable Frankie Schu (undaunted by the nightmare at Ciro's) has gone by train to Monte Carlo in response to another invitation from Lady Cunard, and is at this moment enjoying a second dose of her hospitality. I was included in the invitation, but manoeuvred my escape and am being rewarded by an evening of Cowper-like comfort and domesticity. Boiled eggs, cheese, and coffee were brought in by the amiable Henry, who became chattily communicative about his past life when he came in to clear away the fragments. He is quite a nice youth (only eighteen) but has been under a cloud lately through yielding to temptation and taking a thousand-franc-note out of Anzie's wallet when brushing his clothes. (The incident was ended by Anzie's tact; he contrived to give Henry a chance to return the note.) This evening he was telling me how he worked as a 'butty' in a Rhondda Valley coal-mine when he was fourteen, talking about the miner's life in a most interesting and intelligent way. Schuster says he is 'too stupid to make a good servant, though his *diction is good*'.

March 15

This afternoon I sat, on an Empire chair covered with rose-coloured damask, in a handsome white saloon in a large white

villa on a hill above the prosperous city of Nice. The white walls
of the saloon were hung with small coloured reproductions of
eighteenth-century pictures (Lancret[1] etc.) and large engravings
of mid-nineteenth-century paintings of the sort that 'tell a story'.
I sat, feeling shy, among palms in pots and polite strangers,
mostly well-dressed women. A musical afternoon was in progress. Three young men and three young women stood in a
row on a square of pinkish carpet on the polished floor; they
were singing the sextet from *Don Giovanni* in classic style,
admirably accompanied by an apologetic-faced little man at an
enormous grand piano. Beside the piano, leaning his massive
dark blue body on its closed lid was Jean de Reszke.[2] His
withered face looked immeasurably weary, seeming to express
disillusionment after a thousand thunderstorms of applause in
gala-garlanded Opera Houses all over the civilised world. He
has a little crop of straggling bleached hair low down on the
back of his immense head. His full lips (grey under a haggard
grey moustache) moved with the music. His right hand beat
time with a short stick. His whole face and body (in spite of his
exhausted aspect) showed an intense association with the
performance. Sometimes, when the tempo was too slow, he
tapped imperiously with his foot and his brow lowered and his
heavy chin jutted toward the singers. So, though I've never
heard the great Jean de Reszke sing, I can say that I've seen him
directing his pupils.

March 16
There is a sort of futility in cold-minded descriptions of
exciting physical experiences. A hair's-breadth escape has no
interest beyond its unique instant of crisis. The fact remains that,
but for Anzie's genius for driving, we might all three of us, at
the present moment, be swathed in bandages in a hospital (or
worse off than that). Coming home from Cannes in the dark,
after hearing Hahn's[3] charming operetta *Ciboulette* at the
Casino, we were about half-way between Antibes and Nice (a bit
of road famous for motor-accidents) when Anzie chose to pass

[1] Nicolas Lancret (1690–1743), French painter in the style of Watteau.
[2] Polish tenor (1850–1925).
[3] Reynaldo Hahn (1874–1947), French composer.

another car; we hadn't quite passed it, and were 'doing about forty', when a third car emerged from a turning on the left and came straight at us. I was sitting behind; Schuster was beside Anzie. I knew nothing except the glaring white eyes of the car coming at us. There seemed no chance of slipping through the gap, as the big car on our left was almost level with us. Had Anzie faltered or done nothing or tried to pull up, there'd have been an unholy smash. But he leapt the Rolls forward and we seemed to squirm through, almost to leave the ground, and we touched nothing. It was a magnificent display of nerve and skill. Before I'd had time to breathe again, old Frankie had started slanging Anzie (petulant expostulation, not hysterical scolding). Anzie replied 'If anyone else had been driving we'd all have been killed.' F.S. 'Don't talk to me like that. If you're rude, I'll be rude too' etc. (something about it not being necessary to go so fast and pass other cars in the dark). I felt an extraordinary exhilaration. I wanted to laugh and slap Anzie on the back, but only patted his shoulder and said 'Bloody fine bit of driving, old boy!' After which we drove into Nice in silence.

The crowd lunching at the huge Casino Restaurant at Cannes was a strange spectacle of brainless self-indulgence de-luxe. These 'pleasure-seekers' seem scarcely to *exist* at all. They are phantasmal consumers of jaundice-provoking hors-d'oeuvres. Conscious only of their clothes, they file in and out among the crowded tables and harassed waiters, while a string-band plays Massenet's meretricious melodies, and the hard blue sky glares on the sea, and life is a wilderness of indigestion and vapid conversation.

This evening we dined at the Gautier-Vignals'. We were late, and the 'Grand-seigneur' Count was in a bad temper and didn't conceal it. There was an awkward moment at the end of dinner. The Countess was dallying over her dessert, peeling an interminable apple while chattering about Proust or George Moore or someone. The Count rudely asked her if she was going to be all night over that apple (or words to that effect). She looked scared and stopped munching. It was a bad breakdown, and did away with the first impression (old-world courtliness) created by the Count. The Countess told me she is going to read Doughty's *Arabia Deserta* in the summer!

March 18

A nice quiet day. Wrote rather a good poem, 'A Musical Critic Anticipates Eternity'.

> If Someone, Something, somehow (as Man dreams)—
> Some architectonic spirit-strength omniscient,—
> Has wrought the clouded stars and all that seems
> World, Universe, and Life (poor, blind, deficient)—
> If this be thus, and Music thrills the spheres,
> And I go thither when my feet have trod
> Past Death,—what chords might ecstasize my ears!
> What oratorios of Almighty God! . . .
>
> Yet, seeing that all goes not too well on earth
> In this harmonic venture known as Time,
> I'm not too optimistic of the worth
> Of problematic symphonies sublime:
> And, though I listen aureoled and meek
> To compositions by the Holy Trinity,
> Who knows but I may write (in my critique)—
> *'The music was devoid of all divinity!'*[1]

S. and A. went to Monte Carlo, so I lunched alone at a small place in Beaulieu, watching several English spinsters snatching the English papers from one another. Like tigers they eyed one another. 'That woman's had last week's *Tatler* nearly twenty minutes' was the unspoken message which flashed from bosom to bosom in that E. M. Forsterish *pension-restaurant*.

Three of Anzie's young friends called after tea. I was alone and the door was locked. I addressed them from the balcony. One of them said 'If Anzie comes in, just tell him we're *pipping along* for the odd spot' (which *meant*, I gather, going up to the bar for a cocktail). They are the sons of a Welsh millionaire (tin-plate maker) who saves £30,000 a year (income tax) by being 'domiciled in Jersey', and spends some of it on a villa here.

---

[1] Published in the *Nation* 30 August 1924, then in *Lingual Exercises*.

March 19

Schuster took me to see Maryland—Mrs Arthur Wilson's famous villa and garden at Cap Ferrat. Her daughter, Mrs Ward (formerly a celebrated society beauty, Muriel Wilson) showed us round. We spent a few minutes with Mrs Wilson, very old and failing, sitting under a pergola with the *Daily Mail* on her knees. The garden is exquisite; sunshine, colour, bees, and fragrances; but the villa, in spite of 'perfect taste' having been mobilised for its making, suggested bridge and boredom, a paradise of perfect cooking.

Dined with S. at the huge Bristol Hotel (Beaulieu). Lady Weigall was at the next table (daughter of Sir Blundell Maple, who built the Bristol). She bowed to Frankie who 'hadn't seen her for twenty years'. He also met a man who was at Eton with him—Cecil Lister-Kaye,[1] who was with his wife (a sister of the Duke of Newcastle). S. said 'I thought Lister-Kaye was dead'; he certainly looked fairly near it. When in contact with these bridge-playing acquaintances of his, old Frankie shines as a very bright and vivacious character. The dinner was bad, and a cold soufflé caused S. to 'send for the maitre-d'hotel' and give him hell. At lunch I was arguing with Anzie about social reforms (started by seeing battleships in Villefranche harbour). I said 'To me battleships are like having alligators in one's drawing-room.' Anzie takes the conventional view. No use arguing about such matters.

March 20

Schuster rather fussed about packing and departure, and complaining of his indigestion and taking only consommé for lunch. In the evening we went to hear *The Damnation of Faust* (Berlioz) as an opera, at Monte Carlo.

March 21

Left Beaulieu 11.30. Wet day. Lunched at Sospello; over the Tenda pass; got to Turin at 8. Unpleasant drive. The zigzag roads made me feel rather seasick.

[1] Fourth Baronet (1854–1931).

March 22

A lovely spring day. Left Turin at 11.30. Distant Alps superb in sunshine. Lunched at a pleasant country inn. Arrived at Milan by 5. Heard *Lohengrin* at Scala (very fine performance under assistant conductor).

March 23 (Hôtel Cavour)

Rainy weather. Stayed in bed till lunch, and got up feeling fresher than since leaving London. Beaulieu gave me a sore throat all the time. Schuster came in from a walk exclaiming, 'Thank God! *I've seen a worm-cast* in the public gardens!' This was an admirable comment on the stage-scenery of the Riviera.

Same day   1 a.m.

Smoking my pipe in my little white room with the French windows open and rain dripping darkly down on the courtyard below. Feeling very satisfied, after hearing Verdi's *Falstaff* (for the first time). Toscanini conducting. An exquisite master-piece, superlatively performed. If I'd been alone I'd have come away after the first act. I felt that I *must* retain all that exquisite delight, and that more of it would give me aesthetic indigestion.

March 24

To the Brera before lunch at Campari's, in the Arcade. Motored to Certosa di Pavia after.

March 25

Another grey day, cheerlessly drizzling. At 11.15 a.m. two tourists might have been observed emerging from the Hôtel Cavour. Each puts up an English umbrella. They proceed. The junior stalks slowly, in accordance with the Charlie Chaplin shuffle of Schuster (who will be sixty-nine in September).

What *does* Frankie Schuster *look* like, you ask? Well, he is medium-sized. His grey clothes hang loosely on a figure which is neither obese nor shrunken. His face is Semitic. His grey moustache is tidily trimmed above a large loose mouth—the mouth of a man who has faced the serious problems of life by

turning his back on them. His face has an irresolute look; it is
browned by the sunshine which he has purchased while avoiding
inclemencies of climate and evading all occupations more exacting than a cultivated appreciation of the arts—especially music,
for which he has a genuine passion. His face is neither mean nor
generous. It has been used mainly for 'social amenities'. When
being 'social' it is alert (on the surface), responsive with
perfunctory amiability, like a room when the lights are switched
on for a party. But when the social effort is relaxed, the lights
diminished, the room silent, his face seems to *fall*, and the aspect
of *looseness* is accentuated; vivacity gives place, not to acqui-
escent meditation, but to an unspeculating resistance of *ennui*.

There is Conrad's new novel to be perused; letters to be
written; a bank-book to be ruminated upon; there are newspapers; and there is to-morrow. Next month? No; *that* must be
approached with defensive circumspection; it must be, if possible, a month of fine weather; it must not be monotonous; it
must be 'amusing'. It must be a month where good music pre-
dominates, and chattering rivulets of small-talk sparkle among
acres of asparagus and green peas, and spring-chicken is
followed by a vanilla soufflé (light and liquescent). Supposing
I were to 'accuse' him of turning his back on everything which
makes human existence 'creative' and 'spiritually satisfying'?
No resolutely formulated reply would be forthcoming. It is too
late for that. He must keep up an appearance of frivolity, to the
last. I sometimes wonder whether Schuster has ever been
'serious' about anything except music. Perhaps I am too hard
on him, with the intolerant hardness of youth. Old age must
defend itself against strong feelings. Anyhow, the party is almost
over, and the social effort must be maintained till the last cork
has popped from the Pommery, until the final fragment of
persiflage has fluttered from the disillusioned lips. The gardenia
must preserve its freshness and the white waistcoat its spruce-
ness. But his feet grow weary, and the departing guests leave
no sympathetic vibrations in his depopulated heart. To bed; to
bed. The white tie flutters crumpled to the floor; the patent-
leather shoes shine sardonically, vacated by their owner. Snores
end the evening's work. Does that bald head on the pillow
contain dream-workings? Or, wakeful, does it contemplate the
past? I think not. Schuster once told me that he has 'a terribly

bad memory'. I think he has a convenient faculty for forgetfulness as well.[1]

March 26

Yesterday's lunch (at Campari's) amused me. On the previous
day Schuster had made a non-success of his lunch, and had condemned himself to two dishes which made him envy the choice
of Anzie and self. So yesterday he 'laid himself out' to make up
for it, by ordering caviare, lake-trout, and a special fruit-salad
(concocted personally by the director of the restaurant). To-day
we lunched at a new place, cheaper than Campari's, and bad. (I
mention this because Schuster makes such an incessant fuss about
the food.)

Anzie drove me out to the Villa d'Este Hotel for tea. In the
evening we went to *Falstaff* again, but I didn't enjoy it much, as
Schuster was in a bad temper over the hotel dinner (cold soup,
etc.) and argued with Anzie about our 'plans'. Anzie wants to
go out to Como, and S. wants to stay in Milan and hear *Meistersinger* on March 30. (Finally they arranged to motor in for
Meistersinger.) S. rebuked A. for his way of pronouncing Villa
d'Este. 'It's "Veelah d'Estay"—not "Viller Desty". God, how
it annoys me, the way the English treat every language as if it
were their own!' Poor old Frankie's indigestion seems to be
upsetting him a lot lately.

March 27 (Hôtel Villa d'Este.)

Lunched at Campari's. More grumbling about the food by
Schuster. At 3.45 we quitted the Cavour. I am writing this at
midnight on a glass-topped table in a luxurious bedroom
(luxurious except for the loud connubial conversation of a
German couple in the next room). We dined expensively, the
soufflé earning applause from Frankie, though the trout was 'a
failure'. Anzie showed me two rings which he'd bought in Milan

---

[1] Not a very good summing up of Schuster. There was much more in him than met
the eye. Robbie Ross summed him up as 'a *bad* type of man'. He was certainly a
good specimen of his type, whatever it was. He knew what he wanted, and (being
wealthy) was enabled to get it. S.S. [For a fuller and more sympathetic study,
see Appendix to *Diaries 1920–1922*.]

for his fiancée. The hotel smells of new paint, and a syncopated band crashed and hooted while I read *Dombey and Son*.

Before dinner I walked up the hill among myrtle-bushes. Church-bells tolled melodiously; birds piped and warbled, distant and shrill; and the lights of lakeside houses twinkled in friendly confusion. Como was thinly scarfed by level veils of mist from its chimneys. And above it all was the unsympathetic sublimity of the hills, their brown-looming masses dominated by snow-streaked summits against an opaque blue sky with broken drifts of becalmed moon-white cloud. (How futile such descriptions are!) I wished Mother could see it. But she never will. (Tomorrow is her sixty-seventh birthday.)

There is a queer sort of tranquillity about my present condition, which consists of being carted about foreign countries, seeing new places with no sense of travel-responsibility and no need to organise my movements. Unable to speak Italian (and very little French) I am carried hundreds of miles in a magnificent car. I do nothing except look and listen, and fork out a few pounds.

MY MOT D'ESTE (Modesty)

Most modern minds think Villa d'Este
As a hotel-de-luxe looks best.
But I (by cocktail bars made testy)
Prefer the vanished Villa d'Este.

March 28

Awoke early; fine weather, birds chirping, and a waterfall making a silken rustle. Strange dream last night. I was in the studio at home; my dead brother was embracing me passionately (a thing he never did in real life). Mother intervened and I awoke after a prolonged scene in which I reproached her and a crowd of vague figures (mostly relations) who were antagonistic to my brother. The dream culminated in an agonising fit of 'dream weeping', and I woke as from a nightmare, surprised to find that I wasn't actually crying. When I dream about Mother I am usually having a scene with her, and we are always antagonised. Yet I never do have scenes with her, and in this case I'd been thinking of her tenderly, owing to her birthday being to-day.

March 29
Went to Cadenabbia with F.S. yesterday. Looked at Villa Carlotta (formerly belonged to Grand-Duke of Saxe-Meiningen). White eucalyptus, Canova statues, etc. Across to Bellagio, and back by boat. (F.S. telling me how he used to stay there, and how he went to some place along the lake where he got *'glasses of iced cream fresh from the cow'* or churn.) This morning I wake to find our expedition to Lugano obliterated by rain, so I lie in bed, listening indolently to the charming twitter of birds, with a narrow glimpse of vaporous hills, soaked cypresses, and glassy lake-waters. Anzie comes in, half-dressed and swinging his artificial leg (he left a leg at Gallipoli) to borrow my tobacco-pouch and hand me the *Daily Mail*. 'The donkey couldn't swallow the truth. So they gave him the *Daily Mail*!' he remarks. Delightful Anzie!

March 31
Yesterday afternoon I went for a longish walk up the hill behind Cernobbio. Fine weather, and woods full of primrose, periwinkle, violet and hepatica. Now and again I stopped to jot down a few lines in this book (satirical lines about the Grand Hotel).

THE GRAND HOTEL

From *An Introduction to European Affluence*

Superbly situated on a Lake
World-famed beyond the costliest Prima Donna
Who ever gargled a Puccini shake,—
The Grand Hotel (superimposed upon a
Villa evolved in vanished centuries
And denizened long since by real grandees)
While publishing on poster and prospectus
Its quite unique attractions which await us,
Refrains from offering to resurrect us
To an austere degree of social status.

Resolved to satirise Hotels-de-Luxe,
Shyly I sift the noodles from the crooks
Beneath whose bristly craniums a cigar
Juts and transmutes crude affluence to ash.
The Grand Hotel asks nothing but their cash;
The Grand Hotel contains a cocktail bar
Where they can demonstrate by their behaviour
Hotel-de-Luxe aloofness from their Saviour.
   (The English visitors have motored off
   Into the mountains for a game of golf.)

The band concedes them Tosca with their tea.
Bored and expensive babble clogs the air.
Between two smooth white columns I can see
Gold and vermilion tulips . . . Ambushed there
I criticise the ambulant outer-covers
That, costume-conscious, enter and withdraw;
And in them all my satirist-self discovers
Prosperity that lives below the law . . .
   (You ask what law I mean . . . Well, my impression
   Is that these folk are poisoned by possession.)[1]

At five o'clock I saw what appeared to be a very high wire-fence, a couple of hundred yards away beyond the small trees and undergrowth. A man shouted at me, but I went on, until I saw that he was a soldier, actually pointing his rifle at me. I went up to him and was arrested. It was the Swiss frontier. (I had no notion that it was anywhere near Como.) The clumsy Italian youth conducted me to a guard-house, where my diary was inspected, as a very incriminating item. But they knew no English, and all I could do was to point down the hill and say 'Villa d'Este Hotel'. So I was sent down to Cernobbio with a smart and bemedalled youth, who occasionally laughed and pointed toward Villa d'Este, exclaiming ' *Bello!* ' At Cernobbio I was again debated over in a military edifice, and led to the hotel by an officer. After I'd been triumphantly identified as the innocuous possessor of a passport, the 'international affair' culminated in the cocktail bar, where I stood the diminutive, cloaked and spectacled officer a gin-and-vermouth. He was now

[1] Published in the *Nation* 1 August 1925, then in *Lingual Exercises*.

quite overawed by his environment, and we parted with many bows. Schuster was delighted by the incident, which provided a new topic at dinner, a topic which gushed to life like a bubbling rill on an Alpine hill.

April 2 (Grand Hotel, Arenzano)
Left Villa d'Este this morning at 1.15. Yesterday we motored to Milan for *Meistersinger*, taking a hotel acquaintance of Anzie's—a Mrs Hastings, wife of a doctor; she had a Spanish and a Russian grandfather; a Serbian and a Hungarian grandmother. Almost a record ancestry, I imagine. Very pleasant woman. Toscanini conducted. Opera finished at 12.30. Spoilt by an awful supper at Cora's. (Jazz band!) Home at 2.45 a.m.

Came about 160 miles today. Coffee at Tortona at 5. Then via Novi and over a fine little pass, up into the evening and down into the dusk. Purple-brown hills and glens. Dreary empty hotel here. Spent evening fooling about with a gambling-machine with A. Lost twenty-five lire. Then A. discovered a way of cheating the machine, and cleared it out. (A sort of penny-in-the-slot machine.)

April 3 (Hôtel d'Angleterre, Nice)
Left Arenzano 9.45. Rough sea, wind, and sunshine. Lunched at Alassio. Road so twisty that I was on edge all the time. Superb scenery. Dined with F.S. at the Ruhl. 'Gala dinner' on, which annoyed F.S. (and the dinner was bad and cost 160 francs each).

April 5 (Hôtel de la Poste, Saulieu) *1 a.m.*
450 miles since Nice. We left there at noon and lunched at Grasse. Delayed by tyre-trouble at Sisteron. Dined at Gap. Got to Grenoble at 11.45 after a queer drive through strange-looking landscapes. I slept in a bed occupied by Napoleon on 7 March 1815!

Left Grenoble at 10.15. Lunched at Pont d'Ain. Tyre-trouble beyond Bourg and Tournus. Got two new tyres at Chalon-sur-Saône. Very rich dinner here. (The hotel is kept by a former chef of the Kaiser's!)

April 6 (Trianon Palais, Versailles)

My hotel-de-luxe life is drawing to a close. This one is over-heated and almost empty. We arrived at 7 after 170 miles. Schuster irritable, owing to north-east wind and dust; plus last night's dinner? Lunched at Auxerre (which interested me, owing to the carvings which Pater wrote about in 'Denys L'Auxerrois'[1]). Looked at cathedral at Sens. Tea at Fontaine-bleau. Studying the menu here, F.S. decided that there was 'nothing to eat'. 'No quail, no woodcock! Not a bird of any sort except pigeon, which doesn't count.' These long drives are too much for the old boy, but Anzie is a mileage-maniac (and wants to get home to his fiancée).

April 7 (Hôtel Christol-Bristol, Boulogne)

Left Versailles 1.30 after strolling about in front of the Palace for an hour in dry cold sunshine. Bare trees and twittering birds. The grand vista beats anything I ever saw, in its way. Must see it on an autumn afternoon. We stopped for tea at Abbeville, after going along the road that runs through my land of war-memories, passing below the woods on the hill where the village of Montagne stands, out of sight. I hadn't seen that hill since January 1916. This was the nearest I've been to the topography of my war-experience of 1915–18 (since July 1918) though I've passed through Abbeville in the train twice. It was pleasant to be sitting beside Anzie while war-memories revived. (He would have been an ideal brother-officer.) Anzie's jollity has been unfailing during the past four weeks (a contrast to poor old Frankie's occasional tiresomeness). All my holiday needed was a little more solitude for reflection and assimilation of impressions. Schuster's fussiness about food has often irritated me. He exaggerates its importance. But I am completely 'set up' again in health.

April 8 (The Hut, Bray)

Crossed to Dover in calm weather and came here (calling for three minutes at Tufton Street for letters, but found none).

[1] In *Imaginary Portraits* (1887) by Walter Pater (1839–94).

April 11

Went to town yesterday, and found a pile of letters, which I'd overlooked on Tuesday. Back here after dinner. My letters include Heinemann's account for last year's royalties. Total royalties £3 (England and America). So I am almost down to zero, which gives me a queer feeling of safety. (I feel I'd like *this* year to be a blank as regards sales. Then I could begin all over again.) Total sales in 1923 ninety-eight copies. My trip abroad cost me £77.

Counter Attack	34
„ „ (USA)	36
War Poems	2 (out of print)
Old Huntsman (USA)	26

Coming indoors at midnight on May Day after a last stroll round the garden before going to bed. Chilly air and blurred whisperless trees. The lamplit room happy with its little china figures, its bric-à-brac gay with posies of early summer flowers. I stop in the doorway. The dog laps from his bowl on the veranda; he is thirsty; lap-lap-lap. Two clocks in the room tick away the dozing lamp-shine—one brisk and small, the other large and leisurely. A mile or two away the last train leaves the station; puff-puff-puff, deliberate at first, then accelerating to the bustle which carries it into the gloom. A web of stars is on the world's roof. The room is warm; the sky is cold and silent. I shut the door behind me.

No diary kept April 17–May 15. I was at the Hut most of the time. Wrote a good poem April 23–24. 'Afterthoughts on the Opening of the British Empire Exhibition' (Wembley).

I muse by the midnight coals to the tick of a clock:
On pageants I ponder; I ask myself, 'What did it mean—
That ante-noontide ceremonial scene?'

I have sat in the Stadium, one face in a stabilised flock,
While the busbies and bayonets wheeled and took root on
  the green.

At the golden drum-majors I gazed; of the stands I took
  stock,
Till a roar rolled around the arena, from block after block,
Keeping pace with the carriage containing the King and
  the Queen.

Ebullitions of Empire exulted. I listened and stared.
Patriotic paradings with pygmy preciseness went by.
The bands bashed out bandmaster music; the trumpeters
  blared.
The Press was collecting its clichés. The cloud-covered sky
Struck a note of neutrality, extra-terrestrial and shy.

The megaphone-microphone-magnified voice of the King
Spoke hollow and careful from vacant remoteness of air.
I heard. There was no doubt at all that the Sovereign was
  there;
He was there to be grave and august and to say the right
  thing;
To utter the aims of Dominion. He came to declare
An inaugurate Wembley. He did. Then a prelate, with
  prayer
To the God of Commercial Resources and Arts that are
  bland,
Was broadcasted likewise, his crozier of office in hand.
'For Thine is the Kingdom, the Power, and the Glory,' he
  said.

But when Elgar conducts the massed choirs something
  inward aspires;
For the words that they sing are by Blake; they are simple
  and grand,
And their rapture makes everything dim when the music
  has fled
And the guns boom salutes and the flags are unfurled
  overhead . . .
And the NAMES, the anonymous crowds, do they all
  understand?
Do they ask that their minds may be fierce for the lordship
  of light

Till in freedom and faith they have builded Jerusalem
  bright
For Empires and Ages remote from their war-memoried
  land ?[1]

Trying to write prose sketches at this time. Poor stuff, all
self-conscious smartness. (Trying to be light and amusing.)
Also began a story, which fizzled out by the end of June, after
about 10,000 words.

April 26 (The Hut, Bray)

Rough Notes on the Dean of Windsor

The Dean of Windsor (Albert Victor Baillie, b. 1864)[2] to tea.
He is a light-weight dignitary. A court-official clergyman—the
most insidious form of Christianity. A spiritual man of the world.
Smooth pink ducal-butler cast of countenance. Silver hairs,
placing the port at the end of the table, 'This is the '63, your
grace.' Perfect deportment, perfect complacency, perfect everything (except perfect sincerity). Excessively vain.

April 27
  Lionel Holland,[3] here for lunch, enlightened me about the
Dean. 'Albert Baillie, after he left Cambridge, went in for
asceticism, and lived in one room in a slum in Newcastle, as a
curate.' (Emotional religiosity; fits in with his histrionics.)
'How long did *that* last?' I asked. 'O, not very long. He soon
became private chaplain to one of the Archbishops. When he
was thirty-four he began to think about his future life, and married
a lady with £2000 a year, a daughter of the Earl of Boyne. His
zenith was when he was Rector of Rugby. He kept seven curates
(nice looking young men) who organised the parish perfectly;
and all Albert ever did was to walk about the town rubbing his
hands while everybody came to their doors and bowed to him.

---

[1] Published in the *Nation* 3 May 1924, then in *Lingual Exercises*.
[2] Died 1955.
[3] Barrister and politician (1865–1936). Younger son of the first Viscount
  Knutsford.

He also pronounced the benediction at evening service, with thrilling effect. He ought to have been an actor. He only likes the *Old* Testament. Used to go and sit with his old aunt, Lady Winford, and talk about the Old Testament. She left him all her money.' Frankie Schu: 'I remember a photograph of Albert, taken when he was at Cambridge in '84, lying on a bench. He was a remarkably handsome young man.'

Notes of the Dean's talk at tea

They were all sitting round the tea-table when I came in. The Dean very broad and suave and smileful, a real Canon Chasuble.[1] 'This cake is delicious! Just a soupçon of lemon in it,' he said. (Communion cake.)

He held forth to Frankie, while Anzie, Wendela,[2] and self sat silent like children (or 'the young people' as he'd say). He talked about the longevity of his family, and especially his aunts. (Expectations?) 'Aunt Car lived to be eighty-five. Lady Colville eighty-seven; and Mrs Beaumont eighty-nine. It takes a hatchet to kill *our* family!'

Described Lady Winford's death (Aunt Car). Asthma affected her heart. 'I've enjoyed life immensely; but *this* doesn't amuse me.' She paid her house-books on Monday morning; extra wages for the servants, 'as I shan't be alive next Monday, and you'll need something extra to go on with'. On Thursday she said, when I went to say good-night to her, 'I've put all my affairs in order. Good-night.' Then she just turned over and died.

They talked about the music at St George's Chapel. Frankie S. 'The great *chic* of the Chapel used to be the way the choir held on the last note of each verse of the Psalms.' St George's Chapel is being rebuilt 'stone by stone' at a cost of £125,000 (of which the Dean has already raised £45,000). 'Mr Minter' (the contractor who is doing the work) 'is the best type of self-made man. Has already given £13,000 toward the expenses, and is giving all the gargoyles on the roof of the chancel.'

We adjourned to the next room. He lit his pipe, spread out his skirts on his knees, arranged his shapely calves and ankles

[1] In Oscar Wilde's *The Importance of Being Earnest*.
[2] Wendela Boreel, a painter and Anzie's future wife.

(silver-buckled shoes) and became even more expansive. His hands are large, plump, and salmon-pink, with a massive episcopal-looking ring on each. (I ought to mention that F.S. asked him to tea in order to pave the way toward asking him to perform the ceremony at Anzie's chic wedding.) He talked about his ten weeks in 'the States' last summer. 'Never had a single meal in a hotel or slept anywhere except in private houses. Every meal was a party. Mrs Vanderbilt gave a dinner for me which numbered seventy, and Mrs Hofmann had fifty to meet me. At almost every place I went to I received a letter from an old parishioner.'

Eulogy of the Queen. 'Wonderful woman. Amazing power of application. Naturally pleasure-loving but has disciplined herself to duty and keeping herself in the background. The King *likes* to be dull. Only wants to sit and read his paper after dinner. Prince George has ability, but is such a lazy little creature. The Duke of York will make the biggest man of them all, but suffers from his stammer. The Prince of Wales—obstinate as a mule. But I always fall a victim when I am with him. One can't help being charmed by him.'

The Dean, as will be surmised, was showing off for all he was worth. (Probably a habit which has become permanent.) *'What a broad-minded man!'* exclaimed Schuster, after he'd gone. But is it 'broad-minded' to prattle about actors and publicity agents? (The Dean adores the theatre, and is great on publicity. He was honorary chaplain to the Imperial Advertising Congress at Wembley, and opened the proceedings with a prayer!) Probably most people gush about him as being 'so boyishly interested in everything', but he struck me as a superfine clerical coxcomb, a frivolous old gent with an adroitly-developed social instinct. He keeps in touch with the times by getting asked to lunch to meet Labour Ministers, and patronises them because they lack 'the advantages of a university education'. He gets shown round 'Chelsea Bohemia' by his rather disreputable young press-agent friend Bolitho (whose services he enlisted for the Chapel Royal money-raising publicity).[1] Prides himself on being 'rather naughty'. Keeps in touch with the intelligentsia too. Wrote and asked Middleton Murry to dine with him at the club. 'The

[1] Hector Bolitho (1897–1974). Voluminous New Zealand author. Known in Windsor and Eton as Mrs Dean.

Adelphi magazine seems to have such an influence on so many young men, so I thought I ought to talk to him.' He and Schuster revived old memories of Mrs John Wood ('Ma Wood', a celebrated comedienne), Corney Grain,[1] and the Beefsteak Club in the old days when Toole[2] and Irving were always there. Oscar Wilde was mentioned. '*How* I disliked him! He used to come and see me when I was at Cambridge. So *greasy*; and his epigrams not spontaneous, like Whistler's.'

'Leslie Henson[3]—such a delightful feller, a *great* friend of mine. When I was starting for the States and the Press were worrying me to find out why I was going, he said, quite spontaneously, "Tell 'em you're going for *pleasure combined with bismuth*".' And he let out one of his loud laughs—a sort of baritone cackle. (He always laughs at his own jokes.)

Has let the Deanery to Lady Lowther for 500 guineas a year. Can't afford to live there. (He has at least £6000 a year, Lionel Holland said.)

He doesn't find George Robey amusing, but admires Harry Lauder—'he's a friend of mine too!' 'Don't *you* love Lauder?' he asked Wendela, who had been silent for nearly an hour. W. 'No. He doesn't amuse me at all.' 'Well, well,' the Dean carried on with an urbane flourish, placing himself on the hearth-rug with feet well apart and skirts lifted to warm his Windsor behind—'Well, well, of course that's all right; but what *art* he does it all with, though the material, perhaps, *is* a little poor.' And he digressed to the foundations of St Paul's and the instability of ancient religious edifices in general. Whereupon I tackled him (with intent to catch him bending, sound his serious side, and get him out of the Green Room) about the attitude of the Church to Psychology. 'My friend Dr Rivers once told me that he'd been called in by half-a-dozen Bishops at Church House—and I've often wondered what the consultation meant,' I said (adding, with juvenile diffidence) 'but perhaps it's rather an impertinent question—rather ponderous, too.' The Dean pulled himself together, composed his countenance, twiddled his eye-glasses, and evaded the issue altogether with a two-minute talk on 'the fallacies of modern psychology'. 'You can't

[1] Entertainer (1845–95).
[2] John Laurence Toole, comedian (1830–1906).
[3] Comedian (1891–1957).

judge a friend's character by psychology' etc. 'Of course' (rather flurried, for the first time) 'of course I read up child-psychology at one time, hoping it would help my teaching work. But' (and he became vaguer and vaguer). I admitted that 'there is a good deal of pedantry in modern psychology', but reminded him that 'one judges character by intuition or instinct, and those are the things which psychologists are investigating'.

'Have you read William James's *Varieties of Religious Experience*?' I asked mildly. No, he hadn't. And soon we slithered back to Leslie Henson and all the other 'amusing fellers'.

April 28

The Dean writes a long letter to Anzie. Cosy platitudes about marriage—like extracts from a sermon. His metaphor is that 'sex-attraction is like the match put to a fire. First the fire blazes brightly, but gives out no warmth. Then it burns low, and the more you tend it the more warmth it gives.' 'I am only an old man and an old parson, so you must not think me impertinent,' and so on. I suppose he is kind-hearted, but the letter ends so lushly. 'I love to think of that little annexe, and you two living there and learning to love one another.' (The annexe has been built on to the Hut for them recently.)

Anyhow, the Dean is comfortingly true to type.

(*A Footnote on the Dean*)

He came over after dinner; silk stockings and silver buckles; chattering about the rodeo (cowboy) competitions at Wembley, how he was 'taken into the Stockade'. 'Such charming fellers, the cowboys! One of them asked me for a match; he did it so nicely!' The Dean denies that there is any cruelty in the 'steer-roping' competitions. A steer was killed and one had its leg broken on the first day. But, as he pointed out, one of the cowboys broke three ribs.

May 15 (The Hut, Bray)

Yesterday the first real summer day. Motored up before lunch. Haircut. Talking to Brothers the hair-cutter about his pianola. Twenty minutes late for lunch with Mother at Halcyon Club. Hadn't seen her since February. Took her a hundred of Trumper's best Turkish cigarettes. Usual scramble-lunch—everything 'off' except roast lamb and so on. Dreary-looking women with pince-nez. Mother, for all her wrecked looks and countrified rig-out, far the most distinguished person there. Heart-breaking, Mother seems. Flustered at first, all of a dither about ordering the lunch. Polite 'calling voice' when trying to get hold of waitresses. 'Salad? Are you bringing it?' She had been to the Academy before lunch, but came away at once owing to the heat and the crowd. Usual fragments of parochial news. Everything Mother comes in contact with is given her serious attention. And she wastes herself on such jumble-sale domesticities and villageries. Behind it all one feels her grandeur of spirit, intense integrity and courage overlaid with superficial prejudices and crotchets.

The past history of myself and Mother seems rather epical now—a series of tragic mistakes, mostly due to my own slow development and lack of sophistication (*she* is still a child as regards sophistications). Compare Mother and Frankie Schu. One almost too serious; the other too frivolous.

During lunch she divulged her big bit of news: 'Poor Rachel hasn't long to live.'[1]

This means, I suppose, that we shall be inundated with 'poor' Auntie Rachel's money within a year or two. (We have been waiting for it about twenty years!)

Hope it won't interfere with my efforts to live austerely and simply. Must try and forget about it. It will bring me no peace that I can't attain on my present income.

After lunch Mother confessed that she had nothing to do all the afternoon. I had expected her to be off to 2 Melbury Road to see my aunt and cousins. Forlorn, I felt her. I was due at Covent Garden at 5—*Valkyrie* with Schuster. However I took her to the Tate to show her the Crawhalls,[2] which, as I'd expected, made her enthusiastic. Wonderful to see her, at almost seventy, and

---

[1] She lived another three years. S.S. [Rachel (1858–1927) was S.S's father's sister. In 1887 she married Frederick Beer (1860–1903) and at one time owned both the *Sunday Times* and the *Observer*. From 1904 she was in the care of the Commissioners of Lunacy. On her death S.S. inherited £30,000.]

[2] Joseph Crawhall (1861–1913), water-colour painter, mostly of birds and animals.

battered to pieces by life, as excited and voluble over those pictures as she'd have been fifty years ago. What an unquenchable spirit!

We looked at the goldfish ('diminutive cyprinoid') which I dropped in the fountain in July 1921. Not the same one, I am sure; but I pretended to recognise it, and we had that topic in common. (A link with 'Auntie Rachel', too, for I dropped it in as a joke-protest when they were trying to raise £10,000 to buy her Millais, 'Christ in the House of his Parents' which was on loan.[1])

Cup of tea at Tufton Street. (Had rung up Mrs Gosse to arrange tea for Mother, but Mrs G. was engaged, the parlourmaid said.) So Mother went to Melbury Road and I went to Covent Garden.

Delphine came in just before we left, while I was packing some clean clothes in a bag upstairs. Gave her the bill I'd paid (£15.10 for repairs to the house).

Enjoyed the opera—dinner at Tairy. Gota Ljungberg's Sieglinde very fine—superb gestures. Great acting, I think.

Got to White's Club at 11.20, but stayed there having beer and sandwiches until 12. Awful man Frank Daniel joined us— quintessence of conviviality in a club smoking-room. Not sober; chaffing Anzie. Back here by 1, very tired. Passed accident on the way. Someone had skidded into a ditch—line of cars, and people 'helping'—unpleasant sensation. Two bob-haired straddling girls in aquascutums enjoying it—as they did the war—calling one another 'old thing', hands plunged in their pockets.

Frankie and Anzie went up early this morning. I go up by 5 train—shall only hear the last two acts of *Siegfried*.

Weather glorious to-day. Story still working itself out in my head. Can see the end clearly, and think I have done more than half of it already, in rough draft.

Annoyed yesterday by Jaeger's sending my new shirts to Tufton Street and their man demanding the money from the servant. Took parcel away, as I wasn't there. Kept remembering this at the opera, and in bed last night. Inventing cutting repartees to them. Absurd. 'Not in the habit of being treated like that by shops'—Oh!

[1] See *Diaries 1920–22*, p. 84.

M.W.[1]   What have *you* been doing?

S.S.   Weeding the lawn.

M.W.   Reading the Law?

F.S.   'We've got a cuckoo that *barks*. We must all write to *The Times* about it. Cuck, cuck, cuck, cuck, etc. Didn't you hear it early this morning? But it isn't *possible*! You *must* have heard it! Cuck, cuck, cuck, etc.' (All this while the first course of lunch was being handed.) *Small talk!*

At dinner last night. The Dean got off a bit of gas (out of a book) about German music due to G's poverty in seventeenth and eighteenth centuries. Air of solemn wisdom. Instance of parrot talk which is so usual. Quite harmless—a social effort.

I was inclined to be antagonistic to Lady Maud W. as she is anti-German and ultra-British. Made a few provocative remarks, but she is a wise bird and didn't respond. One imagines oneself making all sorts of withering remarks when one is alone and feeling anti-social toward worldly Deans and smart society!

But in reality, they seldom give me an opening. And of course, it is futile to scold at them and be superior. One should try and make them behave naturally, and give themselves away.

Last night I rather expected Lady M. and the Dean and F.S. to make fun of Labour Ministers. But they are getting canny about *that* now. The Dean likes me, but is, I imagine, a bit nervous of my brains.

After dinner they all played a spelling game. The Dean bad at it. Produced literary words like 'mart' and 'mete'. 'Prey' was his best, but he only did that with assistance from Lady M. The Dean is worth studying. He does anything one expects. Last night he was wearing his 'Garter' round his neck (he is chaplain to the K.G's). To-day the ladies went to Windsor, and he showed them the chapel. He was wearing his scarlet cassock and Garter too! And, no doubt, looked very ornamental. He loves dressing up. Histrionic. (Repressed!) Homo too, I suspect —always talking about young men. 'They always tell me I don't like anything over twenty-two!' he said one day.

Mrs Appleby-Quince! (real name—an American acquaintance of F.S's).

[1] Lady Maud Warrender (1870–1946). Daughter of the eighth Earl of Shaftesbury, widow of Vice-Admiral Sir George Warrender, Bart.

May 19

If I hadn't asserted my independence I should at this moment be shoving my way out of Covent Garden after hearing the *Götterdämmerung* in sultry weather. Schuster went (it began at 4.30) but I generously gave my 25/– ticket to Delphine, having decided on Saturday that I hadn't the slightest desire to spend five hours at Covent Garden when I might be here alone, as I am now. Also I hoped to get on with my story. But the social exercises of the week-end have obliterated the story, for the time being, and I have done nothing to-day beyond polishing up some satirical lines (written yesterday evening before dinner). Also thunder-showers and sunshine have made to-day an indolent one. Now all is cool and tranquil, and I am sitting out on the verandah with the lamp as a lodestar for local insect life, and a full moon glistening beyond the apple-tree on the lawn. The ocean murmur of a Londonward train is the boundary of my world, and a remote plover's pee-wit my acoustic companion.

A glass of ginger-beer assuages my pipe-smoking palate, and I have been playing sentimental Schumann songs since sunset.

After tea I mowed the tennis-lawn and perspired profusely. After lunch I read the *Rosenkavalier*[1] libretto, as I am going to hear it on Friday. It reminded me of P.,[2] with whom I heard it for the first and only time, at Munich in August 1922.

I posted a letter to him this afternoon; he is in Rome, and wants me to go there. I have suggested his visiting London and the Hut next month, but the odds are fifty to one against his coming, and I am not sure that I want him to come.

May 31 (Easton Glebe[3])

After missing the 3.26 from Maidenhead, waiting there forty minutes, crawling to Paddington in a train that accumulated milk-cans and Saturday afternoon cinema-enthusiasts, I taxied to Liverpool Street, tore to Bishop's Stortford in an express, waited there fifty minutes, crawled on to Dunmow, hired a large-bodied underpowered car at the local garage, and drove three and a half miles hither, breaking down 150 yards from the house and arriving at 8.15, just in time to hear H.G. telling

---

[1] Opera by Richard Strauss (1864–1949), first produced in 1911.
[2] S.S's friend of 1921–2. See *Diaries 1920–1922*.
[3] The home of H. G. Wells near Dunmow in Essex.

Charles Trevelyan[1] (Education Minister) that Lloyd George
is 'in the pathetic position of a man who has burnt his boats and
is running about on the beach pretending that they are still
there'. H.G. is lunching with L.G. at the House of Commons on
Monday 'to meet an American who wants to plead for the
League of Nations'.

Trevelyan is an earnest-faced man; his eyes are those of an
ascetic clergyman crossed with a serious-minded Yorkshire
terrier.

You observe that I am influenced by my environment; it
would be impossible for me to write in this style at Schuster's.
I have 'caught' H.G's summing up people, peoples, and international problems, in a quotable sentence.

Last night, at the Hut, I was rambling through *Pelléas et
Mélisande* while Schuster knitted a green-and-orange wool
hearth-rug. H.G. differs from the Schuster mentality as much
as Debussy differs from massed brass bands playing the Rakoczi
March,[2] though H.G. would disapprove of the nationalistic
message of the March as much as he'd despise the shadowy
poetism of Pelléas and Co.

But why compare poor old caviare Schuster with Vesuvius
Wells? The lotus has its place in the world and so has the
eruption. But where do *I* come in? Aesthetically *Pelléas et
Mélisande* are more important to me than H.G's Utopias. But
his intellectual energy makes me feel that I ought to be a man
of action; that I ought to know all about the problem of the
English in India and hold strong opinions about the necessity of
splitting the Labour Party and establishing it on a basis of
scientifically educated communism (to the exclusion of the
Anglicans). H.G. talks vigorously, glancing from Trevelyan to
me, I nod and say nothing. How *can* I say anything, when I am
such an ignoramus as regards racial and political history?

After dinner Lady Warwick[3] comes in—a broad voluminous
white-haired woman in black, with ideals in her eyes—the

---

[1] Sir Charles Trevelyan, third Baronet (1870–1958). M.P., first Liberal then
Labour. Son and brother of historians (Sir George Otto and George Macaulay).
[2] A traditional Hungarian tune, adapted by Berlioz and Liszt.
[3] Frances Maynard (1861–1938) married in 1881 Lord Brooke, who succeeded
his father as fifth Earl of Warwick in 1893. Lady Warwick was Mrs Keppel's
predecessor in the affections of the Prince of Wales. In 1898 she joined the
Labour Party and worked hard on its behalf.

deals expressed by drawing-room meetings convened to give
impetus to movements for social reforms. I scarcely spoke to her
at all, but when she was going away, she held my hand and said
'Your poems—I have thought so much about them. It was the
"rebel" in them that appealed to me so greatly.' Her voice was
as soft as the rain that is soaking down in the sultry darkness
outside my window. (Once she was a celebrated Beauty.) I felt
a shy, flattered young man, looking down my nose and murmuring my gratification. Trevelyan said less, but implied a similar
recognition of my 'achievements' of six years ago.

Yet, as I journeyed from Maidenhead to Easton, I was
grumbling to myself about my futility and failure to produce
anything impressive, anticipating the feeling of inferiority
which H.G. always causes me. And I was wondering why I was
coming here at all, when I might be lotus-eating by the Thames
and playing modern French music in the twilight of Schusterism.

These people remind me that, after all, I *am* 'someone' in the
eyes of the cultivated classes. They remind me that my internal
gestures against publicity are a little exaggerated—like T.E.
Lawrence's (though his are more externalised).

And they (H.G. included) remind me of the peculiar detachment of my self-lacerating mentality. How remote they are from
the Narcissus-pool of my introspection.

June 1

The glimmer of my uncurtained window awoke me at 4 a.m.
As I swam up out of sleep I was conscious only of a lark that was
shrilling upward. It climbed, dropping links of chromatic vocalis-
ing which seemed to draw me upward with it. Then a thrush sang
loud and piercing from the lime-tree whose branches almost
touch my window. I leant out. It was a glooming gusty dawn;
belts of trees loomed dark under a clouded sky.

Later

My lark and thrush stuff was interrupted by H.G. and I spent
the rest of the morning playing his famous ball-game in the
barn. He and I beat Mrs Wells (Jane) and R. Temple. One of
his sons arrived after that, a yellow-haired blue-eyed unkempt
creature, rather repellent at first sight. With him three friends.

[129]

(All from Cambridge, none of them interesting.) Mr and M
Scribner (the New York publisher) had arrived from Londe
soon after breakfast, a dreary couple. Twelve of us and a litt
girl aged six at lunch.

The day became rainy. After lunch some bridge was playe
and people loafed around with small talk and looking at book
Mrs Wells has just carted the Scribners off to see Thaxte
Church. They were becoming heavier every minute, and I fe
that they were such a bore that they'd fall through the flo.
unless someone took them out of doors to dilute them, thoug
the atmosphere outside is humid and sultry and headachy.

As regards my last night's pages, I doubt whether I give an
thing like an exact impression of H.G's conversation, which wa
mostly light and amusing.

Most of my pleasure in this delightful house and garde
evaporated with the advent of these four crude and unattractiv
young men. Sitting next to Mrs Scribner at lunch finished i
Since lunch I have been bored, uneasy, and anxious to slip awa
by myself, but the rain prevented that, except for half an hou
before tea. When I came up here at 10.45 a.m. my mind wa
fresh and actively appreciative of the day, but that feeling fle
And this evening, with 'sixteen to supper', doesn't promise wel

After lunch I spent some time skimming *Lifting Mists*,
school story by Austin Harrison.[1] The usual thing, flogging
cricket, sex-suggestions, etc.

Also did a little 'spying'—pulling out presentation volume
to read the inscriptions, many of them inscribed by people H.C
has long since alienated, Edmund Gosse among them, als
Belloc.

Hardy's *Selected Poems* (Golden Treasury Series) has 'T
H. G. Wells, after reading *Mr Britling*, from Thomas Hard
1916'.

How easy it is to entertain oneself. How difficult to be ente
tained. What a happy day I could have had if I'd been alone
this house all day and not seen anyone till dinner. As it is the da
has become a jumble and I can't even record Mrs Scribner
typical U.S.A. banalities. (H.G. worked hard with her at lunc
telling her about Portugal. He was there, with the Galsworthy
in the winter, and she goes there next week.) She also asked hi

[1] Author, journalist and editor (1873–1928).

questions about the Royal Academy Exhibition, which he answered with levity, and about Wembley Exhibition, which he hates and she admires. By teatime he was replying to her queries about climate, camouflage as an art, etc. with difficulty and obvious discomfort. And Mr S. was waiting for a chance to have a confidential talk to him about the Collected Edition of his works, every detail of which has already been discussed ad infinitum. Is there anything more exhausting on earth than a well-organized American?

The rain-drops are still pattering down in the dark, but I am feeling more hopeful and less irritable than I did before dinner, which turned out to be a cheerful affair, quite jolly and alive.

The young men have gone back to Cambridge, after improving on the primal impression they made on me. Mr and Mrs Scribner have toddled decently to bed to prepare for their early departure in the morning. A worthy couple; I can now regard them with equanimity, since I shall probably never see them again.

After the departure of youth, we sat round in the long library, and H.G. discoursed in soberly subdued tones—mostly about contemporary reputations in literature.

About Conrad, whom he ranks well below H. M. Tomlinson,[1] as a prose-writer. Also women; he puts Katherine Mansfield above Virginia Woolf, 'a too-well-educated woman writing her best', and 'Stella Benson's *Poor Man* proves her a more considerable person than the author of *Jacob's Room*.' I disagree, but H.G's taste is not for *delicate* writing. Most of this was drawn out of him by my queries. He spent some time relating the early history of Conrad (meeting Galsworthy etc.) which was done mainly to entertain the Scribners and three others who came in to dinner, a Mr and Mrs Starr, and Mrs G. D. H. Cole, a scraggy, dark, intelligentsia-type of youngish woman who looked as if she had slept in her clothes for a week, very much emancipated and ungraced. Ambrose Bierce, Arthur Morrison, Dorothy Richardson, Ford Madox Hueffer were also mentioned.

After they'd all gone except R. Temple, the Wellses and self, I broached the question of 'one's audience' (Virginia Woolf's 'patron' idea). H.G. was very sympathetic and gentle about it; and evidently was trying to encourage me toward writing when

[1] Author and journalist (1873–1958).

he revealed details of his method of writing a novel, processes which I'd already half-formulated for myself; it was consoling to be taken into his confidence in this unostentatious way.

On the way upstairs he took me into his bedroom and showed me the manuscript of the novel he's working on and said how comforting it was to have it to live with and evolve. It was nice of him to do that, and it sent me to my room resolved to finish, somehow or other, the little story I'm labouring at (since May 7) and have lost faith in.

H.G. this evening was more human than I've ever known him before. I felt rewarded for my championship of *The Dream* against the sneers of young 'intellectuals'.

June 2 (Hardy's 84th birthday)
Left Easton 10.15. A wet morning. H.G. drove me up. We conversed occasionally. He said he thinks that 'the despair and hysteria which followed the war are ended. People begin to realise that the old institutions which seemed, at first, to be re-established, were only dummies and that great changes are actually happening.'

I asked how he liked Huxley's *Antic Hay*. He said he thought it could do no one any harm to read it, as it adopts 'a cheerful attitude toward copulation'. I suppose he is right. But, as H.G. says, the act has no connection with 'passion' in the real sense of the word.

After lunching alone I went to the dentist at 2; he caused me acute pain which left me rather incapable of coping with my tea party with Miss Burton and Meyerfeld[2] at 40 Half Moon Street. Turner is in bed with a gastric attack, so I couldn't bring M here to meet him.

I feel stimulated by my week-end. Am staying here till Saturday, when I return to the Hut. R. Graves sends me his *Mock Beggar Hall* (new poems). He is camping in a tent on Prewett's[3] farm at Abingdon this week, and wants me to go there

Dining alone at Reform—was joined by H.G. who stood m

---

[1] Wells's novel (1924).

[2] Dr Max Meyerfeld (1875–c. 1952), who had translated some of Oscar Wilde writings into German. Robbie Ross dedicated the 1908 *De Profundis* to him.

[3] Frank Prewett (1893–1962), Canadian poet and farmer. S.S. met him at Convalescent Home in 1918.

a glass of G. H. Mumm. So I dined pleasantly after all. I'd been feeling very arid and solitudinous.

H.G. discussing Galsworthy (whom he thinks a gentlemanly ass) and his lunch with Lloyd George, Margot and Mrs Snowden.

June 2–7 (at 54 Tufton Street)

Turner in a state of nerves, so I hardly saw him. He has gone to stay with William Nicholson. Have done nearly 6000 words of re-writing story since Monday, which is as much as I hoped to do. The weather has been wet until to-day. Lunched with Berners on Tuesday and Wednesday (Meyerfeld there on Wednesday, and got on well with B.). B. told me that P. is mixed up with a no longer young but once beautiful Baroness in Rome. She is 'in love with him' and has lent him two rooms to live in. It means that P. won't come to England (though that was unlikely in any case).

My life has been complicated, however, by the gift of an 8 h.p. two-seater car, which R. Temple has pressed upon me, explaining that he's 'made over £5000 this year' and wants me to get more fresh air. So I am taking it down to the Hut tomorrow (with a man to drive it) and shall get Anzie to teach me all about its entrails and manipulation. It may prove a godsend. I'd never have bought one on my own initiative, as I've an antipathy to engines of any sort. It is brand-new and must have cost over £200—tax-paid and everything. R.T. is an extraordinary character. I was quite overcome when he asked me to 'accept it as a favour' (to him).[1] No doubt, as he explained, it means no more to him than if he'd stood me a good dinner. But it shows a very warm heart, and the episode has done me good. At first I felt unwilling and regretted having accepted it. I have a strong feeling against owning things. And (in my relationship with the Turners it is always being tested) I am continually trying to escape from acquisitiveness.

I am hoping that it will be possible to 'share' the car with the Turners. But if I get to enjoy driving it, it will be difficult. My affection for inanimate objects will assert itself (as in the case of the piano).

[1] He got it for nothing for advertising it! S.S.

June 6

To-day I received a note from Secker the publisher[1] informing me that J. C. Squire[2] is including six of my *Recreations* poems in his *Second Selections from Modern Poets*. It was the first I'd heard of it. After prolonged rumination (during which I went to Great Portland Street to be introduced to 'my car'—how absurd it sounded when the automobile-emporium manager phoned from the shop to the garage, 'Bring Mr Sassoon's car round at once') I decided to refuse to be included in Squire's anthology. Is this a self-lacerating gesture? Genuinely I dislike the idea of my poems being hauled into the limelight of this representative volume of contemporary verse (it will probably include a lot of the dull stuff which Squire prefers to the genuine poetry of Edith Sitwell and Charlotte Mew). Nevertheless, I am aware that my absence will, for the time being, increase the accumulation of the poppies of public oblivion which already adorn my reputation of five years ago.

And I am secretly comforted by the thought. My whole attitude—anonymity etc.—about my recent work is a self-conscious fakir-like self-torment. Mixed up with it is an intense resolve to produce something strong and significant, to express the 'big stuff' of which I am capable. And, no doubt, I am afraid of failure. No half-successes will satisfy me. I have got beyond being able to deceive myself with a few laudatory reviews from careless critics.

I want to overwhelm all the people whose judgments I respect. Technical adroitness doesn't satisfy me. I must be 'dynamic' as well. The story I am writing is mainly an exercise in restrained narrative, and restrained vocabulary. It isn't 'dynamic', because it is free from sexual interest. Why write about sex at all? I must try and avoid it, I suppose. But spirit needs flesh as a dress. I can't write about spiritual abstractions.

This evening I went to hear *Pelléas et Mélisande* given (in English) by the British National Opera Company. But came away after the third act. The libretto was murdered by the translator. And the whole production was impossible after the Monte

[1] Martin Secker (1882–1976), publisher of great distinction.
[2] John Collings Squire (1884–1958), poet, parodist and critic. Founder and editor of the *London Mercury*. Knighted 1933. S.S. described him as 'most generous of men'.

arlo one I heard in March. Even the orchestra sounded thin
nd lacking in sonority. Also the opera had been heavily cut.

Back here by 10.15, I wrote to R. Graves about his book,
hich is satisfactory, on the whole. But I flinch from seeing him.
haven't seen him since 6 June 1923.

Yesterday I began E.M.F's *Passage to India*. It promises
nely. But I haven't seen *him* since February, though I like him
 well as anyone I know, and always find him stimulating. I
ave felt lately that I am drifting away from my four years'
ental intimacy with Turner. I no longer feel affectionate
ward him, and suspect that he is half-antagonistic toward me.
nyhow I feel inclined to hold things back from him, which I
ever used to do. (Probably my self-revelations were a strain
 him.) Certain things which he said last winter shook my
ith in his loyalty to me. I have been trying to get rid of this
eling. But it crops up again. Also I no longer accept his judg-
ent about books and music, which used to impress me. I have
alised that he rushes to rash and uneducated conclusions about
ings. But my affection for Delphine remains unshaken.

Reading a short story by Aldous Huxley, 'Hubert and
linnie',[1] at the club yesterday, I suddenly recognised in
lubert' a sketch of R.K.W. (who went to see A.H. when he
as at Florence in January). The description of R.W's appear-
nce is well done.

une 7 (The Hut)

Created a 'sensation' by arriving in 'my car' (driven by a man
om the agents). Feel pleased with it, in a diffident way.
unched pleasantly with Berners at Chesham Place. Mrs
/eguelin[2] and Wendela here. Weather sultry, and pouring rain
nce dinner. River about three feet above normal level.

une 8

Meyerfeld arrived 12.30. F. and I met him at Maidenhead.
olonel and Mrs Carslake to lunch, Miss Schuster[3] and Miss

Published in Huxley's *Little Mexican and Other Stories* (1924).
Mrs Arthur Weguelin (died 1931).
Adela Schuster, Frankie's sister, devoted and generous friend of Oscar Wilde,
who called her The Lady of Wimbledon.

Bridstone to tea and dinner. They took M. in car to Wimbledon
Left 9.30.

M. playing *Ariadne*, *Elektra* before tea and Wolf songs after
Felt sorry for the little man; he hates going back to Berlin.

June 9

Tried to work in orchard-room 10–12, but felt livery and
failed to do anything. Vaguely emotionalised by Meyerfeld
(who was obviously much taken with me); the connection with
Robbie Ross moved me . . .

Madame Crommelin[1] to lunch tea and dinner. F.S., Anzie and
Wendela went to a musical party at some rich vulgarians at
Danesfield, some miles away. Weather fine. I mowed the lawn
before dinner and felt better. Sat up till 1 talking to Anzie.

June 10

Had my first driving lesson 11–12. Found it easier than I'd
expected.

Berners to lunch (on his way to Faringdon). Rainy afternoon
B. played his fugue to F.S. who liked it. B. thinks he'll buy
Monkey Island. Mrs Weguelin has just left (5.45 p.m.).

June 13

F. and A. went to town early this morning, and are attending
the Opera, musical parties at Adèle, Lady Meyer's,[2] Mrs Emil
Mond's and a dance (that is their aggregated amusement list)

A day by myself here is always a godsend; solitude at Tufton
Street is less refreshing owing to the homelessness of the
atmosphere. Tufton Street is a place to hide in, but not a place
to live in. Here I am kept up to a certain level of cheerful sanity
by Anzie, who is a perfect antidote to morbidity. And the background is, of course, as pleasant as anything could be. If F. and
A. were away oftener I could do plenty of writing. As it is I've
done nothing since I came here a week ago. The first three day.

---

[1] Wendela's mother.
[2] Née Adèle Levis, she married in 1883 Carl Meyer, who was made a baronet in
1910. She died in 1930.

were infested by visitors; and the everyday distractions plus 'my car' plus bad weather plus worrying about Dick have spoiled the last three. I have read *A Passage to India* with interest and admiration, though the characters are all more or less repellent (except Fielding who is mostly Forster himself).

But my brain has been either sluggish or exhausted by social efforts. And yesterday was muggily draped and muffled in thunderstorms. To-day has been coldish, windy and grey until after tea.

Tomorrow I go to Tufton Street for three days. I couldn't stay here even if I wanted to; the Italian Ambassador and his wife, and Wendela Boreel and her mother, and two men arrive tomorrow. On Sunday there is to be a vast musical party; dowager-countesses and music-loving frumps will come from London in shoals. Lady Cunard [*page torn out*].

But how empty and arid my life seems, for the moment. I shall ask myself what I shall do in London till Tuesday. I can talk to Turner, but I feel definitely antagonistic to him now. (As an example, found myself resenting the idea of taking Forster's novel back for him to read. 'He will only disparage the book' I think. 'Let him get a copy of his own if he wants to read it.') London seems a desert sparsely populated by a few middle-aged or elderly people whom I have neglected going to see for several months.

This morning I received a long letter from Squire (eight pages) urging me to reconsider my refusal to appear in his anthology. The letter flatters me:

> The book is propaganda for the best modern stuff. I was aware when I made my list that you might decline. But I put them in on the off chance. I had to, since I thought them very good and perhaps the finest things you have done. I haven't asked for the whole book; only for indisputably, manifestly fine poems; and I want you to consider whether the time has not now arrived when you can at least acknowledge these. The book, robbed—by age—of de la Mare, Davies, etc. will be crippled without you—not commercially but as a representation of the best recent work in poetry. The question is whether the time hasn't now come when you can (and I'm sure you must have

found your friends unanimous about them) confess to these poems.

I may add, as one who looks forward to every line you write, that I believe the habit of keeping your work dark must be cramping if too long persisted in. I don't think anybody accuses me of being over-prone to enthusiasm for experiments, but these things captivated me from the start, both because of their Art and because of the spirit of Truth that is in them. If you assent I shall be very glad and relieved. If you refuse I shall understand while deploring.

Impossible to stand out against such an assault of amiability! So I altered his list from

Early Chronology		Early Chronology
First Night		Solar Eclipse
Storm on Fifth Avenue	to	Wittlesbach Fantasia
Villa d'Este Gardens		Storm on Fifth Avenue
Case for the Miners		Concert Interpretation
Fragment of Autobiography		Falling Asleep

and let it go at that. Shall demand three guineas apiece for the poems from the publisher. And shall probably be interested to see what the reviewers say. It makes it easier to postpone publishing a book, too. Seven years ago I was hanging my tongue out for a favourable review by Squire. And had to wait till *Counter-Attack* was published before I got it.

June 14 (Tufton Street)
Arrived here an hour ago after a lonely dinner at the club during which I perused and deplored a silly 'attack' on Alfred Noyes[1] by O. Sitwell in the *Spectator*. How drearily O.S. wastes his time and talent with sterile spitefulness directed at authors who don't admire him and his family. After lunch (a man named Julian Sampson had arrived—a Saki character who frankly 'lives on' rich people and is well over forty and rather pathetic) we motored to Turville Court (beyond Henley) to attend a musical party at the Conways (formerly Conway Wertheimer).

[1] Poet (1880–1958).

Harold Samuel[1] and Helen Henschel.[2] In a renovated barn, 'all the old beams preserved' etc. A collection of prosperous elderly persons listened to the music. We left before the end. Tea at the Hut. Bright sun and north-east wind. Wendela and her mother arrived. I picked a posy for Burton and a bunch of roses for Delphine, and took the 6.10 train. Mark Gertler is here talking to Turner, so I must join them, though I have a headache from the sun. Gave a rose to the deputy hall-porter at the Reform. Nice old man. Felt virtuous in consequence.

June 15

I spent an hour at the hairdresser's. And had tea with Burton. Took strawberries and cream with me. Stayed there till 6.30 and came away with Meyerfeld's manuscript of Synge's *Well of the Saints*,[3] which I have promised to sell for him. It is typewritten, with numerous manuscript corrections by Synge. Worth about £50, I think.

Am feeling disinclined to return to the lotus-eating luxury of the Hut. Feel I can no longer work there. But life here is arid, and hourless. I have difficulty in filling up the day. And the Reform Club is a wilderness.

June 17

Awoke at 6. Felt inclined to get up and go out, but didn't, and remained in bed till after 10!

Then rang up Mrs Gosse and arranged to go to tea there this afternoon. A fine warm day. Sallied forth with Meyerfeld's Synge manuscript. Called at the Treasury and saw Meiklejohn, whom I've neglected lately. Arranged to lunch with him. Had a cup of coffee at Stewart's and then was going to Sotheran's when I observed O. Sitwell emerging from Hatchard's in a blue suit and a small round bowler hat. Followed him along Piccadilly (it always amuses me to *watch* people when they are unaware of my presence). But he must have seen me, and suspected that I was in the wake of his large blue body with its too narrow shoulders

[1] Pianist and composer (1879–1937).
[2] Singer and pianist (born 1882), daughter of Sir George Henschel, singer, composer and conductor (1850–1934).
[3] A play (1905) by the Irish dramatist John Millington Synge (1871–1909).

and wide hips; at Piccadilly Circus he looked back with a hunted air. I quickened and overtook him; an impulse to speak to him overcame me. (Perhaps it was the spirit of Robbie Ross which impelled me, since R. was fond of O. and also of Meyerfeld, whose manuscript was in my hand.) So I overtook O. in the middle of the traffic and touched him lightly with the slim parcel. He turned and greeted me with apparent unconcern. I shook him by the hand, looking gravely into his eyes. Then I felt confused, and blurted out 'I saw you and couldn't help feeling amiable'. 'I am always amiable', he replied urbanely. (I wish he were, in his writings!) The manuscript provided a topic, since Meyerfeld saw O. several times and liked him. We walked slowly down Waterloo Place and back to the Circus, discussing the chances of selling the manuscript. Just before we separated I remarked, 'I like reading people's books. But I find that knowing literary people personally leads to disaster. I like to be aloof—to watch people as I watched you when I was following you along Piccadilly.' I glanced at him; his face was flushed. Evidently his unconcern was disturbed.

Afterwards I felt a sense of relief. Quarrelling with the Sitwells has been an effort which has caused me a great deal of discomfort. I suppose I did the right thing in speaking to him to-day.

After leaving the manuscript at Sotheran's (to be bound in green morocco) I lunched with Meiklejohn at the Reform, and talked in the usual style (slightly dreary, and as if talking to the family solicitor) until 3.15. H. G. Wells joined us for a while.

Walking back to the Treasury I told Roderick I'd seen Osbert and spoken amiably to him. Rested here till 4.30. Then to the Gosses', buying ten shillings' worth of sweet peas in Bond Street on the way. Found Mr and Mrs G. entertaining a pawky white-haired Scotchman from Selkirk (Fowler by name, a Stevenson enthusiast[1]). Fowler stayed till 6. He was modest and much impressed by E.G. After that E.G. and I sat on his balcony and chatted, as usual, about Hardy and contemporary letters. And I was persuaded to stay to dinner. And E.G. read me some of his intimate notes, about Doughty, Morley, etc. I felt more able to be candid with him than usual. I begin to realise lately

---

[1] William Fowler (1862–1933), clerk to the Parish Council of Selkirk from 1900; one of the founders of the Stevenson Club in Edinburgh.

how one can affect people by being gentle and tolerant and quite genuine. It is a difficult art, because one is in danger of being merely 'easy-going'. Anyhow I came away at 10.30 feeling that I had given E.G. pleasure by my conversation without having said anything insincere. When he was seeing me out he complained of the unpleasantness of growing old. 'One gets tired, and all one's faculties flag' he said. What can one say to a man twice one's age who is indisputably seventy-five and on the wane—especially after such a delightful evening? I said nothing, but held his hand for a few extra moments, feeling a real affection for him. And so out into the balmy twilight.

How difficult life is! How difficult to assimilate a number of friends who don't all get on with one another. E.G. cuts Turner at the Savile. He can't bear H. G. Wells. He has been rude to the Heads but likes the Sitwells and Squire. The Sitwells loathe Turner and Squire. H.G.W. dislikes Turner, E.G., the Sitwells, and Squire.[1] Yet I like all these people and want them to like one another. The list of people to whom I've given copies of *Recreations* is a catalogue of little groups of incompatibilities.

So I conclude the day by inscribing and putting into an envelope a copy of *Recreations*—the seventy-third I've given away. The envelope is addressed to O. Sitwell. Peace is signed.

Next day I decided *not* to send the book after all. It was only an impulse. Ramshackle reconciliations are a snag.

June 19 (The Hut)

Yesterday, after lunching with Tomkinson at the Oxford and Cambridge Club, I came here to find F.S. and A. away for the day. So I spent the evening writing a long letter to Bob Nichols who has sent me eight weak lines of verse from Los Angeles. Partly because I have been thinking about his brother, and partly because I'd not written to him since last October, I found it easy enough to concoct something which would amuse him. But was feeling very tired and rather bilious, and still feel indolent to-day. J. Philbin has just arrived after nearly five years' absence. F.S. seems much excited and moved. A few

[1] In 1926 H.G.W. was on good terms with the Sitwells and with Gosse. And in 1930 Squire was asked to tea by Edith Sitwell. E. M. Forster also dislikes Gosse, who was violently unfair about *Howards End*. S.S.

lines from E. M. Forster (in the Isle of Wight) unwilling to come here. Turner has read *A Passage to India* (I lent him my copy) and admires it as much as I do.

Review of O.S's volume of stories[1] in the *Literary Supplement* today. 'Dislike, contempt, or ridicule is Mr Sitwell's cardinal feeling for his characters.' (Evidently they are imitations of Aldous Huxley.) I have left my own story in London and feel a strong aversion to it. The idea of finishing it appals me. Even my satirical verses seem more worth while.

June 22

To-day has been as indolent as a bowl of roses. Perfect food in perfect weather. Digging weeds out of the lawn before and after lunch. Playing the piano after tea and dinner.

No one here except Philbin (and a Guardsman brought a lady to tea but I avoided them).

Yesterday we drove to the Crystal Palace after lunch—and heard Verdi's Requiem.

Friday was quiet. Anzie away all day with Philbin. They returned for a late dinner. I tried to begin some writing but failed to function.

Philbin's presence causes a change in the atmosphere, and is on the whole a relief. He came over (working his passage) on a 7000-ton sailing ship from South America (Mexico).[2] S. greeted him affectionately, but has since found that he is 'on the rocks' and in a neurasthenic condition. And is terribly afraid that he will 'exhaust his (Schuster's) vitality'. He shows no *pity* for poor Philbin. Only uneasiness lest P. may cause him inconvenience. Was it for this that he embraced him when he arrived? Of Philbin more must be written. He is an interesting case. I am too tired to-night.[3]

June 23–24

Mrs Brougham arrived. Crazy croquet. Fine weather both days. Tuesday quiet. Weeding croquet-lawn. Mrs B. tiresome.

---

[1] *Triple Fugue* (1924).

[2] This has since become problematical. It is suspected that he came on a liner. S.S.

[3] Philbin turned out to be rather a fraud! 11.3.27. S.S.

Asked me if I wrote books or 'only bits'! Drive to Royal Oak in 'my car' with A. and P. Jollity. Arrow game. Beer.

Talking to J.P. in Orchard Room on Monday night. (Anzie in town all day.)

June 25

To town before lunch. Hot day. Left sweet-peas at 40 Half Moon Street. Lunch with Mother and Mrs Gosse at Halcyon Club. Bought Mother gloves. To Zoo. Aquarium after. Tea at Gosses'. E.G. there. Dinner at Heads'. Took J. Philbin. Very pleasant. Left him at White's. But I left Bob Nichols's letter to H.H. in a bus on way home. Letter from Buhlig[1] (in England).

Enoch Arden idea cropped up again in conversation with Heads. After death! If only I could get Enoch glimpses of my friends. Same idea as Romains' *Mort de Quelqu'un*,[2] only from the *Quelqu'un's* view.

June 26

Called at Chatto & Windus before lunch to find out (for Meyerfeld) about securing the German rights of Strachey's *Queen Victoria*. Coming down St Martin's Lane again (with an hour to fill up before lunch) I thought 'I may as well call and see my own publishers', though I had no reason for calling except that I hadn't been there for ten months. In three minutes I was entering Heinemann's, and at once bumped into my distant cousin H. V. Marrot (himself a publisher—Elkin Matthews is his firm). He was slinking out with a hangdog look on his semitic countenance, and looked even more despicable than usual. (In reality there is nothing wrong with him except that he is a bore, writes bad verse, and licks Galsworthy's boots.[3])

Inquired for Mr Evans[4] and waited a few minutes, scanning the shelves of recent publications, and remembering my embarrassed interviews with William Heinemann in 1918–19.

---

[1] Richard Buhlig (1880–1952), American pianist.
[2] Novel by Jules Romains (1885–1972), published in 1911. English translation (*Death of a Nobody*) by Desmond MacCarthy and Sydney Waterlow, 1914.
[3] Marrot was Galsworthy's biographer and bibliographer.
[4] C. S. Evans, managing director of William Heinemann Ltd.

Was shown up to Evans, who emerged, with Maurice Baring in a light grey suit giggling nervously as usual and giving instructions about review copies of some new book of his. (He produces one every three months.) Talked to Evans about Secker's anthology (Secker is paying me £15 for my six poems in it). Told Evans that I wanted to have control of the format of my poems when they are published by Heinemann's, and inferred that I would be willing to publish next year. E. was very amenable, promised to allow me a free hand in the matter, and protested much about his anxiety that my book should bear their imprint. He gave me a copy of Herbert Palmer's[1] *Unknown Warrior*, which seems poor stuff, on the whole—very shoddy technique, and a lot of over-emphasised emotion and rant.

Philip Nichols[2] lunched with me. I like him quite as much as his brother Bob. Roderick joined us after. Walked back to Tufton Street (hot weather) reading Palmer's poems in St James's Park.

Then went to Melbury Road to see Mother. Found her having tea in the garden by Uncle Hamo's studio, with Uncle H., Aunt F. and Mary Donaldson. Mother looking rather absurd in a funny little round straw hat, extremely unbecoming. Sat there, conversing heavily about Architecture, Liverpool Cathedral, Nature, and the children of relations, until nearly 7. T. Donaldson (Aunt F's eldest son) joined us later on; I hadn't seen him for at least eight years; he is an engineer; a round red-faced clumsily-built man, of the lowland Scotch type of his father. A gentle, simple, conscientious man, with no initiative and all the conventional virtues. A thoroughly good man with whom I have nothing in common except blood-relationship. I don't suppose he has ever done or thought anything dishonest in his life (he is nearly twenty years older than I am). All the Donaldsons are good and conscientious and loyal to their friends and their family.

I hadn't been to Melbury Road for over a year (they have never asked me) and I am always feeling that I *ought* to go and see them. But I suppose neglecting one's relatives is a human platitude.

From Melbury Road I went to the Reform to entertain

[1] Poet and critic (1880–1961).
[2] Diplomat and future Ambassador (1894–1962).

Festing-Jones to dinner. Enrico is much more of an uncle than
any of my real uncles. We went on to 40 Half Moon Street with
Roderick and sat in his room till nearly 12. I glanced at O.
Sitwell's book of 'stories', and lit on a description of the Haw-
thornden Prize Meeting, with a malicious burlesque account of
E. Gosse. It all seemed such trivial stuff. I am sure that even
my diaries—scribbled as I am doing now—are more interesting
and less futile. I can't understand O. thinking such stuff worth
printing.

June 27 (at The Hut)

A letter from my lawyer informs me that he has paid a quite
unexpected £219 into my account at the bank (some payment
which was overlooked owing to the mix-up of dividends in the
combined estate of my brother, self and Mother). This sets my
mind at rest as regards my finances for 1924, which were
beginning to assume their usual midsummer aspect of 'not
enough to last me till December'. On an impulse I offered
Turner £50 for his summer holiday; he said he'd rather wait
till he needed it more urgently. Met Mother at Paddington and
arrived at the Hut at 1 o'clock. Mother returned to London
(alone) by the 6.10 train. She'd never been here before, and it
was queer to see her in the Schuster surroundings. She thoroughly
enjoyed it all—the garden etc. But the only person who really
made me feel that he appreciated her *humanly* was, of course,
dear Anzie. Mother chattered away in her unsophisticated way,
taking F.S. into her confidence and showing her utter lack of all
the shams and insincerities of social intercourse with which he
surrounds himself in his acquaintances. S. behaved quite nicely
(Mrs Brougham, of course, was odious and patronising) but I
felt that he was slightly embarrassed, and would have preferred
Mother to be smart and sophisticated and 'amusing'. Mother,
of course, is like a child in her impulsive, *literal* homely way of
behaving. She never tries to impress people. And she is devoid
of levity.

But I didn't feel any confidence that F.S. wouldn't, as soon as
Mother was out of earshot, turn to Mrs B. and cast his eyes up
with a gesture of ridicule, because Mother hadn't said the sort
of things that smart conventional people say. Whereas with

Anzie I felt that he instinctively sympathised with Mother and realised her greatness. Ten years ago, under such circumstances, I should have felt snobbishly ashamed of Mother's homeliness and lack of 'smart' sophistication. To-day I felt, more and more, how her integrity withered and demolished all the 'chic' associations of the Schusteristic atmosphere, which I have inhaled so often. And Mother's courage, and her pleasure in being with me, always give me a heartache now. Life has played havoc with her face. She has suffered and been unselfish; and still she can spontaneously enjoy herself, and trust strangers and go on her way without bitterness, apparently oblivious of the sneers and snobbery and petty meanness of people like Mrs Brougham.

Miss Schuster and the Miss Springs came to tea and stayed to dinner, and didn't clash with Mother, in my sensing of the subtleties of the scene. Anyhow Mother has had a happy day, and thinks Mr Schuster 'an old dear—and very sympathetic'.

I shall be glad to remember this afternoon; Mother sitting with her feet up, in the Orchard Room, looking out at the green tangles of the riverside trees, while I played Bach and Gluck's *Orpheus* (which she is fond of). I sat there alone, after she'd gone back to London. And, if I'd become willing to allow myself that luxury, I could have cried quite a lot; the thought of Mother's pleasure seemed so pathetic, and the thought of all our conflicts and misunderstandings so poignant.

It was a deep emotion which she brought me in this familiar paradise of shallow emotions and self-indulgent recreations. Mother made Schusterism seem a despicable affair.

At dinner F.S. remarked to me from his end of the table, 'I can't understand your saying that your mother gets overtired. She seemed so strong—as if nothing could tire her.'

I answered in a challenging way, so that they should all hear me, 'She has suffered a martyrdom for twenty years with her eczema—brought on by worrying and doing things for other people. And I have never heard her complain.' They were silent for a few moments. I had a sensation of defying them all as if they were my enemies. In reality the only person present who was my enemy was Mrs B. And she is not worth troubling about. Mother's heart is big enough to contain a hundred Schusters.[1]

[1] Rather unfair to Frankie. He wasn't *all that* shallow and snobbish. S.S.

June 28

Last night I dreamt that I was holding a severed head—caressing it with an emotion of regret. I can remember how deathly the face looked; also the hair, which was dark and thick, was streaked with a few silver hairs where it lay in a wave across the front of the head. The face only vaguely resembled my own, but I associated it entirely with myself. Evidently it was a symbol for some fragment of my life. I can only think of one possible suggester of the symbolic head. I read (on Thursday night) in the appendix of O. Sitwell's book a quotation from some description of the brass head of him by Frank Dobson which I have seen in the Tate Gallery. I can't see that the dream could have any connection with my emotions about Mother yesterday evening.

E. M. Forster writes (from Isle of Wight) 'Have just had four very enjoyable days with T.E.L. He is a rare remote creature, uncanny yet attractive. I suspect him of "practices"—i.e. some equivalent of yoga—otherwise I can't understand his attitude towards the body, his own and other people's. He thinks the body dirty, and so disapproves of all voluntary physical contact with the bodies of others. I should like to know whether he held that view *before* he was tortured at Deraa. He had one of your Palestine notebooks[1] and spoke of it with enthusiasm.'

June 30

A day of much-needed solitude. Weather breezy with more clouds than sunshine. Mrs Brougham departed at 11; Anzie left at 9 (taking the 'big car' to Cricklewood for repairs preliminary to his honeymoon tour abroad). Frankie and Philbin also motored to town early in the day, in the 'small car'. I saw none of them. My activities were entirely confined to demolition of weeds on tennis and croquet lawns. While weeding I ruminate in an otiose way—usually about quite trivial affairs (such as O. Sitwell's book of stories, which, I am glad to say, was well slanged in the *Sunday Times* yesterday).

Since tea I have been reading *Sinister Street* (Vol. 1),[2] and was rather enjoying it, when Philbin returned, restless and complaining of his tooth and headaches. His nerves are bad,

[1] i.e. S.S's 1918 diary.
[2] By Compton Mackenzie (1913), Vol. II 1914.

poor thing, and he probably suffers under the social exactions
of visitors here (as yesterday when Mrs McLeod and Madame
Crommelin were here).

Last night, when all had departed and Mrs B. had gone up to
finish her packing, I spent a couple of hours reading Princess
Blücher's Berlin diary (1914–19) and became greatly interested
in it.

I seem incapable of exercising my mind on abstractions. My
interests all derive from concrete experiences. My life is only a
series of pictures, punctuated with groans and guffaws. Incapable of formulating theories or constructive ideas, I blunder
past panoramas of sensuous impressions which rush toward me
and occasionally take shape at the point of my pen. My 'ideas'
are merely emotional or introspective ejaculations. My memory
a museum of departed passions!

Reading the Berlin diary made me sentimental about P. In
fact I dreamt about him (in an idealised shape). But I knew that
I could get no satisfaction from seeing him again. I should soon
find him heavy, and he has probably deteriorated since I last saw
him. Of course I am suffering from the need of a new sexual
adventure (probably it will turn up when I least expect it).

In the meantime I have been wondering to-day (mindful that
it is the last day of the month) whether I have got any benefit
from my Schusterised summer, for I have been here nine-tenths
of the days since April 20.

Certainly I am in good health, through my absence from
London life. And, apart from Tufton Street, I had nowhere else
to go (and no one to go with). But I have grown mentally slack
and sluggish during the last three weeks—have dropped my
French reading, and entirely lost touch with my unfinished
story, which now seems quite trivial and insignificant.

I am pledged to stay on here, more or less, until July 26. After
that a few visits (Garsington?, see T. Hardy, the Loders). Then
August 28–September 10 Glastonbury and Hereford Festival
with Schuster, and stay a few days with the Heads near Malvern.
And after that there will be the problem of how to get through
the winter profitably. Tufton Street doesn't feel possible. Paris?
Anyhow I shall have enough money to last me till December
thanks to the unexpected £219 which arrived from my solicitor
last week.

How futile my existence sounds! It can only be judged by results (literary product).

July 3

After lunch alone (all the others gone to London); a drenching shower going on; and the 'rare American lime' and two horse-chestnuts in dark-green gusty perturbation against whitey-grey flatness of sky-scenery.

Feeling rather pleased after driving Philbin to the 11.35 train in 'my car' ('wonderful little bus', Anzie calls it) and for the first time found myself in unchaperoned control of the vehicle. The main street of Maidenhead was a procession of Henley-Regatta-ward motors meeting me, but I got to the garage (the petrol-tank was nearly empty); my activities included reversing into a very deep gutter; but I arrived home uninjured, after quite a pleasant little tour round by Holyport and Bray Wick. I have now owned this 8-horse Gwynne since June 6, but have only driven it six times, and still regard its interior mechanism with an awed and uneasy ignorance which I have made no effort to dissipate. Up till to-day I was inclined to treat the thing as an embarrassment and a nuisance, but driving it along the road by myself has given me a sense of property and independence. And I begin rather to like the vehicle. It is not so uncontrollable and explosive as I had imagined. It is in fact positively amenable to my wishes, and I can face the prospect of fetching Philbin from the station at 4 o'clock without apprehension. My feeling for Philbin, by the way, is solidifying into quite a tough friendliness. The fact of his straitened circumstances helps. I like to feel that I can help him.

His position is a quarterly £21 pension from the Army (for his disabled arm). No relations. And no friends except Schuster and Anzie and Lionel Holland, plus potential aid from Lady Astor (a War connection) plus some people at Basingstoke who are rich and have an only daughter who is interested in him. He is a Ph.D. at the University of California, and also a qualified mining engineer. Has a charming tenor voice, adequately trained, and sings 'Where'er you walk' (Handel) and 'Now sleeps the crimson petal' (Quilter) of an evening, with F.S. at the piano. He sang these two last night to the Dean of Windsor who came over after dinner with one of his sons, a very pretty blond pink-and-white teeth-smiling twenty-year-old, *too* pretty to be interesting, and saturated with the Dean's traditions as to gentlemanly behaviour. He looked like the hero of a mid-Victorian public-school story, and talked in rather a mincing voice.

The Dean was in all his usual glory—silk stockings and silver-buckled shoes. Philbin took a dislike to him (and his son). But the Dean is to marry Anzie and Wendela on July 16, so he is an asset in the Schusteristic cosmos (until July 16).

On Wednesday (a cloudless day) John Barclay came to lunch and tea, with a friend Richard Hale, a young American baritone whose sister married Heywood Broun (a well-known New York journalist). Barclay is English (beer); six foot four high; handsome: thirty; and has made a success this summer as a 'lyric baritone'. Like most 'performers' he is self-conscious, vain, and shallow.

Hale sang Iago's *Credo* (Verdi) and Wotan's *Abschied* in the Orchard Room before dinner. But gave me no pleasure at all, though his voice is quite good. I wanted my dinner; had been mowing the croquet-lawn and felt sticky; and grand-opera-excerpts always seem ridiculous except in an Opera House. Frankie S. has spent most of his life going into raptures over such 'performers'. It is his hobby. His face was suffused with an expression of weak ecstasy while Hale ('hacking out' his own accompaniment) was singing Wotan. I didn't object to the ecstasy, but it seemed a diluted perfunctory rapture, scarcely skin-deep. The dinner-gong dispelled it. Half-an-hour later we were all 'going into fits of laughter' at Hale's negro stories and facetious operatic anecdotes.

The trouble about 'performers' is that they are forced to be *arrivistes*. Admiration is their oxygen. Press-notices are their pabulum. Engagements are the essence of their existence. All other artists (of their own particular line of business) are their natural enemies.

Moved into small room upstairs—which I prefer.

July 4
Lionel Holland came yesterday (by same train as Philbin). L.H. is about fifty-five; a handsome disillusioned-looking man

with a large nose, heavy grey moustache, and very scanty hair. He has a deep line from below each eye-socket to below the corners of mouth. His cheeks are hollow and his eyes weary. Brother to Lord Knutsford, he failed in politics and is now a director of companies 'in the City'. A pleasant man (addicted to young men). Conceals his disappointment in levity.

Cyril Tomkinson came this afternoon from Beaconsfield (a high-church 'retreat' presided over by one of the Trevelyans).

I met him at the station and drove him back to Beaconsfield before dinner. Very pleasant, with Philbin perched on the door of the 'little bus', shouting directions to me 'Give her some gas', 'both feet', 'Put in the clutch', etc. Philbin seemed very happy to-day, which made the hilly landscape look beautiful in the cloud-strewn evening light. Tomkinson also happy, at being with me. Elgar arrived before tea. He looked rather puffy and old, and regaled us with his usual boring anecdotes about America etc. He greeted me affably, however, and said he'd like to go for a motor-tour with me, asked what I am writing etc. Holland leaves to-morrow and is replaced by Walter Sickert.

After dinner this evening Holland, Philbin, Anzie and I played 'crazy croquet' with much jollity.

After Elgar went to bed we listened with suppressed giggles for the sound of the 'musical jerry' which had been placed in his room. Soon the tinkling little tune struck up, to the intense delight of Anzie who never tires of this urinatory witticism.

Driving home I collided with a dog-cart going full-speed, but only touched the horse's shoulder and did no damage. Increasing confidence makes me genuinely enjoy the car. It makes me feel more human and less pathological. It is a substitute for my hunter, I suppose.

July 5

Weather still windy. West winds have been strong for three days. Went to station with Anzie 10.30 and drove back, assisted by John's ejaculations. Knocked a bicyclist on to the pavement in Maidenhead but didn't damage him at all. On return, Elgar led me to the music-room and played the piano for nearly an hour. It was delightful. He played snatches (from/of) my piano-music, Mozart A major Concerto, Bach Organ Fugues,

Chaconne, etc. Afterwards I got him going on his own choral stuff, and he played through 'Death on the Hills', 'Te Deum', and 'Light of Life', making it sound superb. Quite sketchy unpianistic playing, but the rhythmic sense of course wonderful.

He also played some of Schubert's Rondo Brillante (for piano and violin)—lovely melodies: 'the best *natural* music ever written' he said (of Schubert as a whole) and 'I could listen to it for ever'.

It was splendid to see him glowing with delight in the music, and made me forget (and makes me regret now) the 'other Elgar' who is just a type of 'club bore'. At lunch, regaling us with long-winded anecdotes (about himself), he was a different man. The real Elgar was left in the music-room.

E. smokes innumerable pipes of fragrantly strong tobacco. His eyes blink a lot, and look small and weak. (They are rather close together.) He seems to like me, and when we are alone always talks to me as to a fellow-craftsman, which gives me a satisfied feeling.

EYES

My Youth has looked at Life; has looked and seen
In a strange mirror only his own stare,—
His own unanswering gaze of circled green
That holds two pigmy pictures of the scene
Where Youth sits mute, only of himself aware.
My Age will bid the looking-glass good-bye
And read his microscopic tales of being
In every face but that which answers 'I'.
In every face he stares at, Age will throne
The microscopic picture of his own,
Exchanging glory by that act of seeing.

5 July 1924[1]

July 6

Sickert–Elgar meeting yesterday. S. arrived about 6. I was in my room reading Herrick. Butler came up to borrow my

[1] First published in the *Decachord* (Exeter) November 1924 and, much revised, in S.S's *Rhymed Ruminations* (1940).

black evening tie and hair-brush for him. Then I went downstairs and saw his sunburnt straw hat on the table in the passage.
Weeding the croquet-lawn; they appeared pacing amicably on
the grass between the 'blue border'. I advanced to greet S. who
reminded me of our previous meeting (at Gosse's dinner-table
twelve months ago). S., shaven, bare-headed and pale, looks
like a distinguished French actor. (Wearing short black coat
and dark trousers.) Rather high-pitched voice, fine diction, eyes
tired and rather screwed-up. Trick of rounding off a story or
pointed remark by throwing up his head and laughing with his
mouth a wry hole in his face, rather as if he were going to
whistle. Eyes rounded also. Heavy eyebrows, but fine arch of
brow. Upper part of face beautiful. Mouth and chin not so good
—a little meagre and peevish.

At dinner.

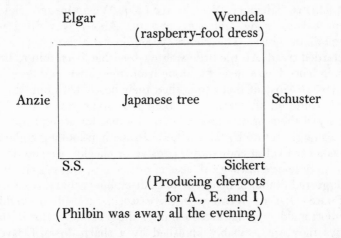

Elgar wears sleeve-links given him by Edward VII. Sickert
couldn't possibly be imagined doing so.

Sickert 'knows nothing about music', which makes Elgar want
to tell him about it. If S. were knowledgeable about music Elgar
wouldn't want to discuss it. Both like telling stories. E's are
long-winded and trivial. S's terse and witty. Several times
during the evening S. told stories in French: at these moments
E. and I laughed tentatively—neither of us really getting the
drift of the idiomatic French.

After dinner Wendela and Anzie in garden. F.S. to bed early. W.S. talking about W.K. Haselden[1] and black-and-white men.

Went to Beaconsfield (with Philbin) in car, to lunch at White Hart with Tomkinson. Japanese Ambassador lunching there.

Drove to Amersham and Princes Risborough (for tea) and back to Beaconsfield by 6, to drop Tomkinson. Home by Slough and Windsor. Went sixty-two miles during day, and felt quite confident in my driving. Very jolly day.

July 7 (Tufton Street)

Elgar, Sickert and Wendela all gone before lunch. Came up by 3.26 with Schuster.

This evening (6–7.45) I went (with Schuster) to a Festival Service of Cathedral and Collegiate Choirs at the Abbey. Eighteen choirs were represented (in addition to Westminster). Seven Deans attended, Windsor, Chichester, Ely, Rochester, St Albans, Salisbury, Winchester (plus Westminster). Solemn words were sung and said, and the Abbey was filled with melodious noise. The choirs paced in with bored face and retarded tread. All the little singing-boys had been told to brush their hair. I was near the door from the cloisters where they entered. Most of them smoothed their heads with one hand as they came in, after removing their mortar-boards. Little faces, many of them pretty, followed one another for several minutes, charmingly set off by their frilled Elizabethan-looking collars. It was a carnival of choir-boys, pensive or cheeky, shepherded by the middle-aged liturgical faces of precentors, whose grim looks suggested (though, no doubt, such disciplinary measures are out of date) that a percentage of the cassocked cherubim would be unbottomed and smacked soon after the ceremony. But in these days they are probably punished by a sharp dose of psycho-analysis instead.

After the choirs had made their picturesque entry, the seven Deans appeared, through a different door, headed by the Dean of Windsor, that worldly man whose article on rodeo and cow-boys at Wembley appears in *Country Life* (current issue). The procession ended with the 'Members of the Collegiate Church of St Peter at Westminster'.

The service was impressive, though clogged by an intermin-

[1] Cartoonist and caricaturist (1872–1953).

able anthem by Samuel Sebastian Wesley,[1] 'Ascribe unto the Lord worship and power'.

Weelkes's[2] 'Hosanna to the Son of David' and Byrd's[3] 'Sing joyfully unto God our strength' were superb.

After 'the Old Hundredth' (and a collection for King Edward's Hospital Fund) Psalm 68 was sung—'Verses in faux-bourdon; interludes founded on the Antiphon'. The choirs sang the odd verses, while the Westminster choir sang the even verses, walking round the Abbey as they did so. The effect, as they went further and further away, was beautiful. 'It is well seen, O God, how thou goest; how thou, my God and King, goest in the sanctuary. The singers go before; the minstrels follow after' etc. The climax came when they went up to the altar singing Parry's[4] 'I was glad when they said unto me, We will go into the house of the Lord'. The singing and the organ rose to a tumult of exultant praise, while the evening light seemed to transfigure the solemn architectural interior and the many-coloured congregation.

The figures of the Cross Bearers, as they passed with flushed intent faces, moved me. There were two in particular (they carried the Cross and the blue-and-gold banner of Westminster). Young men in girdled white cassocks, like beautiful young saints in a picture; tall and straight and strong, gazing steadfastly before them; their athletic heads rising nobly from red-and-gold collars; the Banner-bearer was blond and joyous, flushed with mortal pride; the Cross-bearer had the set and suffering aspect of martyrdom; he might have been St Lawrence going to his torment. Three times they passed within a few feet of me; my eyes were suddenly full of tears when I looked at St Lawrence as he went up the nave toward the altar—accompanied by Parry's triumphant music. 'Peace be within thy walls, and plenteousness within thy palaces'.

The service ended with Bach's E flat Prelude and Fugue (St Anne).

It will be apparent from what I have written that the ceremony was (for me) quite a pagan affair. The service had no significance

[1] Organist and composer (1810–76).
[2] Thomas Weelkes (1575–1623), organist and madrigal composer.
[3] William Byrd (1543–1623), composer.
[4] Hubert Parry (1848–1918), composer. Knighted 1898.

for me. 'O God, wonderful art thou in thy holy places' said the Psalm. But God has given me a body, and it was my body, and not my spirit, which delighted in the sounds and the scene of his pomp and circumstance. God is not easy to get in touch with.

On my way to dinner at the Reform, going up Waterloo Steps, I overtook the Earl of Lonsdale in his frock-coat and top-hat; he turned to whistle to his three dogs. He was smoking a cigar, as usual, and his face was the face of a genial dog. If God has a pack of fox-hounds, Lord Lonsdale will be their master. Yet he looks distinguished, and I inwardly wished him well (from a discreet distance) as he sauntered along Carlton House Terrace in the fine evening light. At the club I talked to Hugh Sturges (County Court Judge and Recorder of Windsor)[1] who thinks the Dean of Windsor 'a conceited chap'. One of them asked me 'what sort of a writer' I was. Only a scribbler, I muttered, and left them to their port wine.

July 8

A pleasant sort of day. Fine weather.

Met Tomkinson at the Reform 12.30. Went to Gunter's, in Berkeley Square, for lunch. (Was accosted by the Dean of Windsor on the steps of the Travellers Club. He looked immense, pink, and complacent, and wanted to know what I thought of the music yesterday.) Went to Oxford v. Cambridge at Lord's. C.E.T. had never been to Lord's before. All was as usual and Cambridge doing well. Stayed till 5.45. Saw Alec Waugh[2] as I went out, and spoke to him for a few minutes. Lord's is his spiritual home.

Called at 120 Maida Vale but Enrico was away. Called at the Foreign Office to look for Philip Nichols and met him on the steps. He came to dinner to meet Tomkinson and brought H. Straus[3] who lives with him in the Temple. Quite a jolly party, as they both seemed to like Tomkinson.

July 9

Sat up till 4.30 a.m. last night trying to write a piece of verse about the Varsity match, but felt no pleasure in the effort. Turner

---

[1] 1863–1953.
[2] Novelist (1898–1981), elder brother of Evelyn.
[3] H. Straus married P.N's sister Anne in March 1927. S.S.

lunched with me to-day at Reform. The first real talk I've had
with him for several months. It was quite a revival of our old
relationship. After buying a copy of Herrick for Wendela's
wedding present (£4.15.0 at Sotheran's—a charming two-
volume edition in blue morocco with Sir E. J. Poynter's[1] book
plate) went to Trumper's. Was having my hair cut when I
heard O. Sitwell's voice come in. He came and sat down on the
leather sofa, behind my chair, and rather diffidently greeted me
(as if he weren't sure whether I'd be civil to him). I felt pleased
at seeing him and conversed amiably, telling him a few amusing
things. He told me that he talked to Philip Sassoon at a large
dinner at Mrs Greville's lately. 'P.S. has become as brown as a
walnut.' O.S. is evidently extremely anxious to regain my
esteem, and carefully spoke politely of Turner. 'I hear his play
has had a success in America' etc.

July 10
Last night worked at varsity match poem 7–8.30.

THE BLUES AT LORD'S

From *A Guide to British Ball Games*

Near-neighboured by a blandly boisterous Dean
Who 'hasn't missed the Match since '92,'
Proposing to perpetuate the scene
I concentrate my eyesight on the cricket.
The game proceeds, as it is bound to do
Till tea-time or the fall of the next wicket.

Agreeable sunshine fosters greensward greener
Than College lawns in June. Tradition-true,
The stalwart teams, capped with contrasted blue,
Exert their skill; adorning the arena
With modest, manly, muscular demeanour,—
Reviving memories in ex-athletes who
Are superannuated from agility,—
And (while the five-ounce fetish they pursue)
Admired by gloved and virginal gentility.

---

[1] Painter (1836–1919). Elected President of the Royal Academy and knighted
1896.

My intellectual feet approach this function
With tolerance and Public-School compunction;
Aware that, whichsoever side bats best,
Their partisans are equally well-dressed.
For, though the Government has gone vermilion
And, as a whole, is weak in Greek and Latin,
The fogies harboured by the august Pavilion
Sit strangely similar to those who sat in
That edifice when first the Dean went pious,
For possible preferment sacrificed
His hedonistic and patrician bias,
And offered his complacency to Christ.

Meanwhile some Cantab slogs a fast half-volley
Against the ropes. *'Good-shot, sir! O good shot!'*
Ejaculates the Dean in accents jolly . . .
Will Oxford win? Perhaps. Perhaps they'll not.
Can Cambridge lose? Who knows? One fact seems sure;
That, while the Church approves, Lord's will endure.[1]

Dined alone and skimmed O. Sitwell's book, which is a con-
glomeration of spiteful gossip and 'pretty' writing (the Aldous
Huxley method). Back here 10.30. R. Hodgson here, looking
thin (after his operation for piles) but full of his usual ardours.
I asked him whether he shared Sickert's admiration for W. K.
Haselden's cartoons. He said W.K.H. is far the best black-and-
white man of to-day. A social historian as important as Rowlandson[2] or Leech.[3] Not a first-class technique but a genius (as
good as Caldecott,[4] he said). I showed him my cricket-match
lines, which he approved.
The Hodgsons leave for Japan next week.[5] Over-excited, I
slept badly; as I have done every night since I left the Hut. So
here I am, with only my Haselden cartoons and Gabriel's[6] letter
to prove that I have been alive on 10 July 1924. The night is still
and warm and the metropolis is whispering in its sleep. I am

[1] Published in the *Nation* 27 December 1924, then in *Lingual Exercises*.
[2] Thomas Rowlandson (1756–1827).
[3] John Leech artist and *Punch* cartoonist (1817–64).
[4] Randolph Caldecott (1846–86), chiefly known as illustrator of children's books
[5] Hodgson was Lecturer in English at Sendai University in Japan 1924–38.
[6] Gabriel Atkin, artist. See *Diaries 1920–1922*.

alone after all the 'jollity' which circumstances have imposed on my temperamental moodiness, a man suffering from sexual starvation, but otherwise in good health and the prime of life.

To-morrow, well, I am dining at 120 Maida Vale with good old Festing-Jones. And there is Eton v. Harrow, if I feel like slinking in there to make observations of social phenomena.

July 11

Another hot day. Sat up till 4 a.m. working on cricket-match poem which is getting better and has reached forty-eight lines.

Berners rang up this morning and asked me to lunch ('to meet Mrs Carew'). Both the lunch and Mrs C. were pleasant. B. has finished orchestrating his new Fugue. Mrs C. likes the Sitwells, and they were discussed, as usual. They have 'gone to Dieppe to escape from Baba Brougham'[1] (a lady who lives opposite Berners and is said to possess a rather mischievous tongue). The Sitwells enjoy fabricating these persecution legends. Berners was sending off a telegram, to hoax them. 'Osbert Sitwell. Royal Hotel. Dieppe. Arriving this afternoon. Must see you. Most important. Baba.'

Mrs Carew was a great friend of Robbie Ross.[2] Her father was Wylie, a wealthy American newspaper magnate who built a large villa at Antibes. She is a kind lady, with a rather bird-like mind.

After lunch I toddled off to Hyde Park, listened to the band and compared the scene with my last year's poem.[3] Last year I sat there on a similar day (in a heat-wave). It was the first day of Eton v. Harrow, as it was to-day.

On my way home I ate a raspberry-water-ice at Gunter's little shop by Lowndes Square. A scarlet and busbied soldier was on guard at the door of 2 Albert Gate (my great aunt's house). Also a red carpet down. I 'asked a policeman', who told me that the home is at present occupied by the Prince of Abyssinia!

Spent three quite characteristic hours at 120 Maida Vale.

---

[1] The Hon. Eleanor Brougham (1883–1966), daughter of the third Lord Brougham and Vaux. She published several anthologies of prose and verse.

[2] She contributed £2000 to the cost of the Epstein statue on Oscar Wilde's grave in Père Lachaise.

[3] 'Observations in Hyde Park' (see p. 87).

Those tête-à-tête dinners with Enrico are very much alike and always leave me soothed and consoled. He always begins, at the dinner-table, with a sort of monologue (which I have learnt not to interrupt). I think it is his way of settling down and avoiding the strain of listening to my rather inaudible remarks (he is getting a little deaf) before he has revived his energy with food.

This evening the monologue consisted of an outline of his journey to Genoa etc., 'meet Giovannini at Genoa, then go on to Venice or Ancona or Rimini or somewhere with Valery Larbaud,[1] then probably stay with "Elizabeth" (Countess Russell)[2] at her Montana chalet, followed by a detailed account of how one spends one's day at Elizabeth's, breakfast at 8; then the post arrives; at 10 Elizabeth comes down on her way to her morning's work in her garden chalet' etc. Meanwhile I imbibe soup (which Enrico doesn't take) and sip some yellow, rather sharp-flavoured wine out of a little silver (shiny anyhow) goblet. Sole and shrimp-sauce follow and he tells me about Richard ('Moritz' he calls him) Buhlig's visit last week to lunch, tea and dinner, and yesterday to lunch. There is quite a lot to be said about Buhlig (a not-first-rate pianist whom I met in America and now wish to avoid). Soon the tranquil rhythm of our sympathetic exchanges has fixed its tempo and we go rambling on until [*several pages torn out*].

July 13

A few weeks ago I reminded J. C. Squire (in a letter) of the approach of October and the eightieth birthday of Robert Bridges. The matter had been in my mind for some time, but I vaguely and indolently hoped that I should hear of some projected recognition which would not cause me any exertion beyond forwarding a guinea to some industrious devotee of the Laureate's lyrics. But no reply has come from Squire, and I have gradually become confident that no one will do anything at all—nothing adequate anyhow. As I was pacing past the Albert Memorial yesterday afternoon I came to a decision. 'I will order

[1] French novelist and Anglophile man of letters (1881–1957).
[2] Mary Beauchamp (1866–1941), author of *Elizabeth and her German Garden* and other novels, married first Graf Henning von Arnim, secondly the second Earl Russell, who had previously been imprisoned for bigamy.

 one of Dolmetsch's[1] clavichords, and I will collect the money myself.' So it was settled. I went to tea at Chilswell last January, when I was staying with Berners at Faringdon House. At my instigation Berners came with me and brought his clavichord, as I knew that it would please the Poet Laureate.[2]

July 16

A crowded day, which began cloudy and cooler, but became gloriously fine in afternoon.

Put on my best clothes and started off to Holy Trinity, Sloane Street, just before noon. ('Mahon Murder Trial. Sensational Developments' on *Evening News* posters.[3]) Anzie's wedding half-over when I got there and tiptoed in to sit at the back of the church. Sorry for this, but I went late to avoid being ushered to a front pew and the embarrassment of sitting among Schuster's acquaintances and relations.

The backs of Anzie and Wendela (far away under a large and not gaudy modern stained-glass arch) looked dignified and reverent. Their 'solidarity on parade' was impressive. A single fidgety motion would have spoilt the effect.

The Dean of Windsor hovered above them, broad, scarlet-shouldered and benevolent. By the chancel-rails Lord Lambourne,[4] uncle of the bride, cocked his chin at a formalised angle; an elderly coachman, he looked. He is President of the Society for the Prevention of Cruelty to Animals and an enthusiastic game-shooter. Gave the bride a donkey for wedding present and has £15,000 a year. An old-fashioned obsolete Tory.

Best man a tailor's-dummy type, good-natured and middle-class virtuous, son of a Nottingham mercantile magnate. 'Ideal best man', has done it four times before, and endowed by nature with the appropriate demeanour. 'Seeing Anzie safely through the ceremony' etc.

The congregation included the Dutch Ambassador, the

---

[1] Arnold Dolmetsch (1858–1940), expert on early instruments and a virtuoso on the recorder.
[2] The clavichord was duly given to Bridges on his birthday, 23 October.
[3] Patrick Herbert Mahon murdered and dismembered his pregnant mistress in a bungalow at the Crumbles, near Eastbourne. He was hanged in September 1924.
[4] A. R. M. Lockwood, first and last Lord Lambourne (1847–1928). Former Conservative M.P.

Italian Ambassadress, and George Moore (silver-blonde in
back row and showing the meagre aspect of his physi⟨
exterior).

'God is a spirit' well-sung by a quartet of Schuster's friends-
Lady Maud Warrender, Marcia Van Dresser,[1] O'Conn
(budding tenor discovered penurious in Nottingham) and
Hubbard, a nice chap who sings in the Abbey Choir. I w
among a sprinkling of uninvited and inquisitive femal⟨
'Doesn't the bride look sweet?'

I felt lachrymose from the start, as I did at Bob Nichol⟨
nuptials two years ago. But repressed successfully. (I feel t⟩
same sometimes at cinemas!)

The Dean's address was rather inaudible, and I recollect on
one phrase. 'Marriage is the supreme opportunity in life f
happiness.' I trickled into the vestry behind J. Philbin (w⟩
brought his San Francisco hat to the ceremony and looked ve⟩
distinguished). In the vestry were the main human ingredien⟩
of my summer at the Hut.

Took Philbin to lunch at the Reform. Saw H.G.W. the⟩
and was invited to Easton Glebe for a week-end in August. H.⟨
looked me up and down, in my unusually respectable attire ⟨
wedding-guest minus top-hat and tails to coat).

Philbin and I went back to Tite Street to see them off. The⟩
2.45–4.30. Only Schuster, Wendela's mother and marri⟩
sister, McRath, the Dean, and Anzie there (plus bridesmaid⟩

Wendela looking charming in her long veil and beflower⟨
cap fastened with a diamond brooch. Her silky-yellow Germ⟨
dog looking wistful and out of it. The Dean, blond, cross-legge⟩
and talking about foreign food. 'I know it's vulgar, but
secretly adore German food.'

McRath and I sat in the big studio upstairs while Anz⟩
changed into a grey flannel suit and clicked shut his beautif⟩
brand-new dressing-case (gift of the best man). At last th⟨
went. Schuster going through the motions of being a benevole⟩
uncle, Madame Crommelin exhausted, genuinely sad—with h⟩
grey hair, perfectly chic dress, and remnants of beauty. One f⟨
that she would put up her feet, close her eyes, and become, qui⟩
candidly, an old woman, as soon as they'd gone.

Schuster took an over-exuberant farewell of the bride. H

[1] American dramatic and concert soprano (1880–1937).

good wishes were spectacular and too over-stressed for genuine feeling. And away toward Folkestone they spurted, in the superb grey luggage-laden Rolls-Royce. The indispensable family butler sighed and retired to his pantry to finish the champagne. We speedily dispersed, I to 40 Half Moon Street to have tea and gossip with fat Nellie Burton (after buying at Fortnum & Mason's a pound of raspberries, which we gobbled, and a cold chicken for dinner at Tufton Street with the Hodgsons).

The dinner had been planned as a farewell feast. The Hodgsons leave for Japan on Friday. But Mrs H. arrived minus Ralph who has been unwell lately, but would 'come in about 9'.

Mrs H. spoke anxiously about him. His operation (for acute piles) early in the summer seems to have been unsuccessful. Since last Friday he has eaten nothing except bacon and eggs for breakfast every day. Refuses to eat anything else all day. And yesterday was using fomentations from 9 till 3 (in the day). Refuses to allow her to consult the doctor. H., she said, is taking several hundred books to Japan, packed in army ammunition-boxes which he managed to pick up somewhere.

She seems pleased at the prospect of the adventure and relieved to escape from their wretched little flat in Ebury Street Mews. During dinner she spoke of the 'wonderful letters' Ralph has written to little Michael McKenna. (He creates great enthusiasm in children.) Also the wonderful letters he wrote to her—five a week—before they married.

Soon after 9 Ralph arrived, looking drawn and pale. He asked for a pen and while we went on talking (about health and diet—rather a tactless topic!) wrote a letter with exhausted sighs (I never heard him sigh before) and took it out to the post. On his return he settled himself on the sofa with his legs up, lit his long-stemmed briar (he has abandoned his stumpy clays apparently) and started off with his usual conversational virtuosity.

Hodgson has been here regularly once a week (except when he or the Turners were away from London) since early in 1920. He recently described his visits to Tufton Street as 'something in his life which nothing could have replaced'. At a reasonable estimate he must have been 150 times and have smoked at least 1000 pipes on our premises. (Sometimes I have come in, seen his old bowler-hat hanging at the foot of the stairs, and gone

up to my room to remain aloof.) How much of his conversatio
can ever be recovered? I have a few pages of scrappy note
Gertler has probably incorporated a few significant scraps o
anecdote in his racy repertoire of reminiscence. But Turner, th
main partaker and stimulator of R.H's talk, has no gift fo
retaining or recording such experiences. He is a talker, not a
observer. Delphine, the discreet and taciturn sharer of the
symposia, how much will she remember when she is an old lad
being questioned, perhaps forty years hence, when we are a
dead?

And now R.H. has gone up the steps into Tufton Street fo
the last time in the four-year sequence, after shaking our hand
with reticent finality. No 'See you next Friday, old boy' can
from his invisible head as he passed the gate, the upper part o
his body hidden by the roof of the porch. We *shall* see him o
Friday, though; at Euston Station, 10 a.m.

Characteristic enough was his talk this evening betwee
9.30 and midnight. It had all its usual flavour, most of i
familiar themes, and the fire of faith in his eyes was unabate
though the eyes were sunk and narrowed by illness and pai
The 'black-and-white men' of the last century cropped up–
what a book he might write about them! Caldecott and 'Bil
Baxter',[1] and 'Phiz'[2] and Keene[3] and Phil May,[4] and Leech, an
all the rest of their graphic journalists.[5]

'Billy Baxter', the wild drunkard and genius who expresse
himself through *Ally Sloper's 'Alf 'Oliday* for three year
Caldecott, with his quality of poetry which none of the othe
possessed. Old Keene, 'who used to wink at you when he co
fessed that he admired Leighton'.[6] Phiz: 'the only gloomy thin
in his work was that he died so young.'

And Dickens emerged from a conversational patch whic
began with H's observations about 'village life' in London—th
local interest of humble folk, communities of parochial feelin

---

[1] W. G. Baxter (1855–88), cartoonist on *Ally Sloper's Half-Holiday* 1884–6.
[2] Pseudonym of Hablot Knight Browne (1815–82). Illustrator of *Pickwick Pape*
and other works by Dickens.
[3] Charles Keene (1823–91).
[4] 1864–1903. Contributor to *Punch* etc.
[5] Hodgson himself had worked as a black-and-white artist for magazines in th
1890s.
[6] Lord Leighton, P.R.A. (1830–96).

confined within an acre of not-yet-demolished dwellings. 'Any-where you'd find material out of which Dickens would have made one of his finest stories, merely by taking the people as they are and adding himself.' One got glimpses of R.H. explor-ing some district by St Pancras with a couple of old maps in his pocket, searching for Dickens topography. 'Dickens!—what a genius—creative—creator of a whole population to-day of people for whom his characters are living people—the inns and streets they haunted, living actualities.' (Levelling the long stem of his pipe like a pistol.) 'I simply can't understand how intellectuals in the Nineties *managed to kid themselves* into believing that Dickens was no good.'

Black-and-white men and the homeliness of Dickens were the intimate Hodgson, the Hodgson who used to ferret about in St James's Park in the spring looking for seventeenth-century clay-pipes among the excavations, the Hodgson who hobnobs with some old back-street bootmaker-craftsman who used to make all Baron Rothschild's boots and took a pride in his technique.[1]

Then there is the humanitarian Hodgson, who is 'haunted for weeks by a dog's suffering face or a dying cat curled up in the snow'. Yet that Hodgson, with his passionate pity for animals, can be tolerant and unembittered toward Lord Lambourne and Lord Banbury[2], in spite of their (ineffective) political and social infamies—can extract from his hatred of them as types of the class he abhors the one good quality—love of animals—though it is mixed up with their callousness as sportsmen. 'Their faults,' he says, 'are only habits. We should make use of their one good quality. And when we have used them thus, reject them for ever.'

'There is only one thing,' he said, 'which seems to me worth doing. And that is' (with emphasis) 'for one man *to give birth to an idea* which two, or ten, or forty other men can develop. It may

---

[1] I remember R.H. once telling me (when talking on this favourite topic of 'old-fashioned craftsmanship') how he went into 'Whippy's' (the classic saddle-makers in South Audley Street) to buy a leather dog-lead for his famous brown bull-terrier Mooster (who has died lately, to Hodgson's great grief). The dog-lead only cost a few shillings, but the man who sold it reminded him to 'remember *just a drop of sweet-oil for the swivel* now and then'. How R.H. appreciated that little touch, and how zestfully he spoke of 'the old saddlers at Newmarket'; such homely prestige is, to him, part of his feeling for the preservation of 'the honourable craft of poets'. S.S.

[2] Frederick George Banbury (1850–1936). Diehard Conservative M.P. 1892–1924.

be an idea whose effect will have become dim and diluted in a
few generations. But life seems to work that way, an idea being
taken up by one decade after another until it has served its
purpose and expressed what the world was waiting for. Such
movements seem almost to have been *pre-arranged*. I feel that,
when a man has such an idea in him, he is safeguarded; he's just
incapable of dying of smallpox or typhoid, or of breaking his
neck. Coleridge did it when he wrote "The Ancient Mariner",
putting it in the form most suited to the age he lived in. All the
"humane societies" of the last century were based on those
words "He prayeth best who loveth best all things both great
and small".

'It was the crystallisation of the religion of pity. It was an
idea which had become a necessity but had not yet been formulated in such a way as to make people aware of it.' (After a pause
he went on) 'In the Forties and Fifties Evolution was in the air.
The world was full of it. But it had to wait for Darwin in 1859.
And then there were cultured men, all over England, locked up
in their libraries and refusing to speak to their wives, because
of what Darwin had put in their heads! And it seems we are
approaching something similar now. Why is it that all sorts of
people—fools and scientists, charlatans, and poets, and theo-
logians—are all groping after the idea of *the psychical*? Aren't
they waiting for the man who will find the solution?'

This leads to the big-visioned Hodgson, the archaeological,
anthropological Hodgson, with his intensely imaginative interest
in history and geography and biology, his belief in the ultimate
victory of good. 'Progress. The word had become vaguely
sentimentalised. So, in accordance with English character, they
now call it *Change.*'

'I'd like to see a man—and I *can* see him doing it in the next
five years—starting a school, with immense success, where
Shakespeare would be eliminated from the teaching, and Shaw
and Ibsen substituted.'

He had used up all the pungent-smelling tobacco in his little
round metal case, so I gave him some of mine. I also gave him
my little Clarendon Press Milton. (I underlined a line on page
63 : 'I see clear honour shining in your eyes,' having chanced on
it first time, in a *sortes Virgilianae*[1] quest for an inscription to

[1] Divination by chance opening of the works of Virgil.

McKenna, and the Turners were also there, an unknown man with a young boy and girl, and two shy spectacled Japs.

R.H. was in a fluster; there'd been some mistake about their carriage; finally he rushed back to the booking-office to get a rebate on his fare, as he'd paid for first-class and been put in a third. We grouped ourselves at the carriage-door; Mrs H. leant out, holding a small bunch of red rambler-roses. Whistles blew; doors slammed; fifty seconds before the start R.H. appeared at a shambling trot. I had gone down the platform to look for him, and as he appeared I felt protective and pitying; he looked so middle-aged and ill and rattled. 'Don't hurry, don't hurry,' I exclaimed, putting my hands on his shoulders, and steering him toward his carriage-door.

Then he was up and inside and leaning out, and everyone was shaking his hand and ejaculating good wishes. The last thing he did was to stoop and kiss the little girl (about fourteen). I think she and the boy are the children of some people at Pinner, with whom he used to lodge before he married for the second time. The train drew slowly out and we waved him away to Japan with our hats. Turner and I and de la Mare walked sedately down the platform. 'How funny old Hoddy going off like that,' remarked de la Mare. We stood about talking for a few minutes, and then emerged from the station to board a bus. On the top of the bus was a young medical student with a human skull. I pointed out this to de la Mare, who at once entered into conversation with the youth. (He told him that Leigh Hunt tried on the hats of Lamb, Shelley, and Byron, and all the hats were too small for him.)

July 20

After lunch, while coffee was being imbibed in the sunshine of the river, everyone became amiable and 'jolly' over a blue Kerry sheepdog-puppy which Constance Collier[1] gave Anzie for a wedding-present. At 3 I went off to Windsor (to see my estimable relations at the Vicarage) and remained there till 7, playing tennis with young Hamilton, and being shown his architectural drawings, which are dull and thoroughly efficient.

---

[1] Actress (1880–1955). Tree's leading lady at His Majesty's. Once briefly engaged to Max Beerbohm.

The homeliness and sincerity, though rather tedious, were a contrast to the chic and sophisticated social atmosphere of Schusterism. The Rev. Hamilton, pink and beefy and conscientious, and his consumptive little grey-haired wife, and the earnest young architect, and Mrs H's brother (Eric Donaldson, a stout and ponderous young doctor) were all so pleased at seeing me that I felt inwardly caddish at my awareness of their essential conflict with my distaste for smugness and acceptance of conventions. I object to their 'disapproving' attitude toward so many things which interest me. But I suppose my own 'disapprovals' are just as regrettable. Anyhow I drove home in 'my little bus' with a sensation of having done my duty. And the mild game of tennis had made me feel well.

At dinner I sat beside Constance Collier, who had been to tea with a Mr Bookbinder at Marlow, and had fallen and hurt her arm. She flattered me by showing a deep respect for my opinions about the theatre (which I know nothing about). But her own opinions emerged as very shoddy and superficial. And she is much concerned about 'spiritism' [*page torn out*].

July 21 (E. M. Forster at home)

Luckily we found the famous fiction-fabricator entirely accessible in his unassuming semi-detached red-brick residence on Monument Green. I made Philbin ring the bell and go in (while I hid behind the shrubs at the gate).

In went J.P. in his loose brown woollen jacket and cowboy hat, and was shown into the drawing-room and Forster's mother (the same high-waisted, bunchy, dowdy, white-haired, delightful old gossip as ever). J.P. caused a most entertaining little flutterment in her afternoon (most of her afternoons are humdrum enough, no doubt). 'A strange young man, giving his name as "Mr Sassoon"! And looking so sunburnt and wildwesterly! Who *could* it be? And such a nice young man too!' Then, of course, explanations, and Forster hurrying downstairs, and myself at the front gate, and lots of laughter and jocularity all round.

And only yesterday Mrs F. had won the cake-guessing competition at the hospital fête, had guessed its weight to be 2½ pounds, but the cake, when weighed in her kitchen, only weighed

½ pounds! What was to be done? Evidently there had been a gross error in the award. *Should* the cake be returned? etc. etc.

E.M.F. gentle, unassuming, whimsical, pleased but unexultant at his novel having sold ten thousand in five weeks, thoroughly enjoyed being chaffed by me and John (who did it very nicely and appropriately in spite of it being his first meeting with F.).

After tea we brought him back to stay the night here. And we had dinner by the boat-house in quiet rather sultry weather. And played crazy croquet afterwards on dew-soaked grass.

This morning I received an immense epistle from Bob Nichols (in California) lamenting his enslavement to the brainless barbaric cinema people.

July 22

At Garsington were the Turners, young Bob Gathorne-Hardy[1] (a plump pink undergrad with a monocle), a young Levy, Mark Gertler, Julian Morrell[2], fresh from her 'short, first season' of dancing in London (under the wing of Lady Howard de Walden), Ottoline, rather yellow, but very jolly and friendly. Philip Morrell arrived after lunch from London; and Schuster and Philbin (who had lunched in Oxford) came to tea.

It was Garsington at its best, and I felt very contented at being there, with the 'freshness' of 'my car' to stimulate small-talk.

Pleasant, too, to see the Turners enjoying their change of air, and to take Delphine out for 'a spin'. What one might call a *human* sort of day. The sort one recalls afterwards, with a pang of regret at the memory of people light-hearted in summer weather.

July 26 (Tufton Street)

Feeling better to-day. After being alone here a couple of days I note a slight regurgitation of possessiveness; this takes the form of antagonism to the Turners. I begin to arrange my bound

1902–73. Son of the third Earl of Cranbrook. Author and printer. Edited the Memoirs of Lady Ottoline Morrell.
Lady Ottoline's daughter.

volumes of music (there are about twenty of them) and at once
I am exasperated by the thought of Turner 'using them'; using
them on *my* piano, too! And not even using them well! (His
playing is much more fumblesome than mine, which is none too
good.) Last winter, when the Turners were abroad for two
months, this sort of feeling got very strong. The fact is I
secretly crave a house of my own. Also I am intermittently
poisoned by having 'given' money to Turner; they are undoubtedly under an obligation to me financially, and this is not
easy to escape from. It probably makes Turner *hate* me at times,
though we seldom mention money. There is no doubt that one
can't *share* one's intimate possessions with anyone.

Music is my main recreation, and I have to more than share it
with Turner (by this I mean that when we are both here I cannot
use the piano when I feel the need of a little music; and often
when I am craving for it, I must overhear, from above, *his* playing, which is too clumsy to give me any pleasure at all. He plays
slowly and laboriously and appears to seek no satisfaction in
tone).

I suppose I shall some day find that I have got much benefit
from this conflict with my acquisitive instincts. I have felt the
same thing with my car. I don't really *like* John Philbin driving
it (though I have learned a lot about motoring from him). But,
since I have *been given* a car worth £220, I suppose I have no
cause for complaint! Also I have enjoyed Schuster's hospitality
for about ten weeks (though that is a '50/50' affair).

(Dined alone, and tried to work here after, but did no good.)

July 27
The rain is dripping quietly down after a day of Enoch
Ardenisms. Westminster clock was booming eleven when Philbin drove me across the Thames in my car. River and street were
glistening-dark with gold reflections.

We left here at 10.45 this morning in fine half-clouded
weather. I drove. After passing Sevenoaks I felt a new little
emotion at driving a car for the first time into the country of my
youth where my previous perambulations have been made on
bicycles and horses, in dog-carts and pony-carts. The familiar
district has the deep significance of early associations.

Being with Philbin (who belongs only to my 1924 life, but now seems an old and trusty companion) gave the day's excursion an additional queerness.

Always when I visit that home country I feel the same Enoch Arden detachment from my early (pre-1914) life.

Always my sensations are acute and vivid. I see the well-known landscapes, roads and villages (once so stale, once the background of my provincialism) with the new eyes of my liberated maturity. I pass through Tonbridge with feelings of affectionate tolerance, remembering my futile efforts to make runs on the County Ground, and how serious my cricketing career seemed in 1911. Threading the narrow by-lanes between Tudeley and Matfield, lanes where I have walked and ridden until they were almost invisible with familiarity, I became quite a sentimental traveller.

And how little the countryside has changed in these ten years of cataclysm and recovery.

Weirleigh was the same haunted background, invaded by the new crudity of my brother and his wife.

Mother, as usual when at home, fidgety and fussy, her mind incessantly occupied with lamentable antagonisms toward her daughter-in-law, who can do nothing right, poor thing, according to Mother. The presence of Philbin however made things rather easier than when I go there alone, as he got on well with all three of them.

Mother was in a flurry about a garden-party she is giving tomorrow. Seventy-five local gentry expected. 'What are you going to do to amuse them?' I asked. Michael intended some very inadequate clock-golf, which could only occupy the energies of four people at a time. Four more could play tennis. But most of the guests will be too old for tennis. I became quite seriously concerned, visualising a fiasco of unemployed guests hanging about the lawn from 4 till 7. So I set to work cutting golf-holes and by tea-time had 'laid-out' a tolerable nine-hole course round the garden. In pre-war days my putting-tournaments at Weirleigh garden-parties were quite celebrated. So the guests of tomorrow will be reminded of me, though they will not see me; and only a very few of them *have* set eyes on me since 1914. I have become more or less mythical at Matfield since achieving reputation in the outer world. In old days I was famed only as the winner of a few local point-to-points, and as an inferior club-cricketer.

'What's become of the fly-squirt, Michael?' asked Mother at tea. 'We've got a fly-squirt. Such a splendid thing!' she explained to me. Most of Mother's conversation at Weirleigh is confined to things like fly-squirts. She seems obsessed by domestic trivialities. While she was watching me at my putting-course work, Michael and John were busy investigating the electric inefficiency of my car. (Mother, of course, had to be deceived about my ownership of the car; she would worry herself to death if she knew that I am driving it; 'the roads are so dangerous. People drive so recklessly!' etc.) Michael's verdict was that 'the dynamo's got no guts in it at all'. His two elder boys are still at school; the little boy (aged four) ran about the garden, fair-haired and blue-eyed, a charming child, but he finds no favour with Mother, because he is 'so like his mother'.

All Mother's affections are centred in the black-and-white cat I gave her a year ago. She keeps him *shut up* in her bedroom all the time, never lets him out in the garden at all. 'So many cats have been poisoned. People put down rat-poison' etc. The pussy however, seemed cheerful and active, sitting at the window (covered with wire-netting) and looking out across the lawn with feline complacency.

As usual I brought back a few books. (There are still five or six hundred of my books at Weirleigh.) This time I carried off six volumes of the Cambridge Shakespeare, and a couple of old manuscript books of my juvenile poetry-scribblings in Swinburne–Tennyson–Rossetti style. Automatic poetising—not an idea in it—only a delight in the noise of polysyllables. I always seem to carry away a scrap of my early life from Weirleigh to London. I go there seldom. I was there, alone with Mother, for ten days last August. Since then I've only been twice, to-day and in February (for a Sunday). To-day I soaked up a little more of my past and brought it back here. The place is saturated with intimate associations, but they grow weaker, and I more detached from them, every time I go there. And I take with me, when I go there, very little of my post-war self.

I go there disguised as a sort of ramshackle imitation of my long defunct *Weirleigh* self. I did try, in 1919, to make Weirleigh more or less my home again. (That was before Tufton

Street became my home.) But Turner was a failure there. So was Osbert Sitwell. Then I went to America, and my brother came from Vancouver to live there again, in the autumn of 1920. And since then I have gone there as a stranger, revisiting the glimpses of an existence gradually becoming more and more memorial.

Remembering that, after all, October is less than four years ago, I realise how much I have developed, how intensely I have lived, in those four years. And how utterly obsolete my old self has become.

We left Weirleigh at 8.30. John drove, at full speed, singing operatic snatches in his charming tenor, his San Francisco stetson hat jaunty on his head, evidently he had enjoyed his day! We averaged nearly thirty miles an hour to Sevenoaks. So (partly to interrupt his high-speed mood) I made him turn off as we entered Sevenoaks, to make a detour of three or four miles so as to pass the New Beacon, which is the preparatory school I was at in 1900–1.

I hadn't seen the place for fourteen years, and it was a splendid Enoch Ardenism. Very quiet and deserted, at 9 o'clock on a Sunday evening, the last Sunday of the summer term. Mellowed and much enlarged since I was there. New chapel (as war-memorial), new gymnasium, new swimming-bath, new assistant masters' house, new and imposing 'new wing'.

The only person visible was the school carpenter, in his shirt-sleeves, leading a fox-terrier on a string. He too was new. I chatted with him for a few minutes in the twilight. 'Won't you go in and see Mr Norman?'[1] he asked. No, I hadn't time. (How crude the idea seemed, smashing up my emotions with an inter-view with my old headmaster, now seventy-one.) 'Would I leave my name?' No; I wouldn't. 'They' (the Normans—father and two sons) 'might feel hurt if they knew I'd been without going in to see them.' Yet I suppose I am the only author of reputation the school has produced in its forty-five years of increasing prosperity. (There are ninety boys now; in 1901 there were barely fifty.)

When I arrived there—a big, home-tutored, backward boy of nearly fourteen—kept at home by Mother's distrust of schools (she kept her children at home as she keeps her cat shut up in

[1] J. S. Norman, headmaster of New Beacon School. See *The Old Century*.

her home now)—I was four years behind in the school-knowledge of a boy of fourteen. Now I am probably mentioned as one of the glories of the New Beacon, though I was super-annuated from Marlborough at eighteen, because I was still in the Lower Fifth. Rather guiltily I gazed at the War Memorial Chapel.

July 30

Yesterday began with the return of the Turners (from Garsington). I only saw them for a few minutes, and they departed for France early this morning (at 6.15, motoring to Dover with the Whitworths).

Turner had to write 800 words for *Truth* (on Music) so I undertook to do this for him. I rather enjoy an occasional jet of journalism, and I sat from midnight till 3 a.m. scratching 850 words about the death of Busoni and the impending Promenade Concerts.[1]

Yesterday afternoon (in a thunderstorm) I went at 4.30 to Bloomsbury Square to confer with the Royal Society of Literature, about the Bridges Tribute. The Society was thinly represented (in numbers).

Professor Wagstaff, the Secretary; Sir Henry Newbolt;[2] a pink and genial amateur called Sir H. Imbert-Terry, Bart[3] (Chairman of the Conservative Association or something Carlton-Clubish), and Professor Watson.[4] Terry and Watson might just as well have been elsewhere. Watson (a white-bearded Lecturer on Rhetoric at Gresham College) only made one remark. He suggested that 'it might be seemly to ask the King and Queen to subscribe'. Receiving meagre response, he became a mute appurtenance to the conference. Newbolt sat at the head of the table, a pleasant, institutional, 'broad-minded' sort of man, one of the enlightened Headmasters of Literature. His behaviour to me was impeccable; sympathetic and almost deferential, without a suggestion of pomposity. Our conversation made the Bridges Tribute an academic certainty. Already I

[1] They appeared, unsigned, as 'Pianists and Busoni' in *Truth* on 6 August 1924.
[2] Poet (1862–1938). Knighted 1915.
[3] Author (1854–1938).
[4] Foster Watson (1860–1929).

can visualise the presentation; a distinguished assembly; 'a delightful literary event,' beams Mr Gosse. The Sitwells, dignified, but on the look-out for something to be malicious about afterwards. A sort of super-Hawthornden in fact. How funny to think that the whole affair began in the brain of the secretary (myself).

After the meeting Newbolt walked with me as far as Westminster Abbey, talking all the time, and being as nice as he knew how, telling me what Lord Grey[1] told him at the Athenaeum about August 1914 etc. Newbolt is a continuation of Victorianism, the Liberalism of Lord Morley, etc. His kindness was a little oppressive. But gratifying—most gratifying! It will be fun to watch the development of this Bridges clavichord affair. And I am now absolved from any further efforts, except to make a list of the names of younger writers.

To-day I felt rather marooned. My car is unfit to take the road until to-morrow; the weather is sultry but fine.

I lunched with Roderick and discussed his new house in Connaught Square. Afterwards (at a loss for occupational interest) I called at the Nonesuch Press and demanded a free copy of *The Week-End Book* (they hadn't sent me one, though I contributed four poems without fees).

Saw Vera Mendel[2] and took a strong dislike to her. Before that I called at Chatto & Windus and despatched an inscribed copy of Owen's poems to Newbolt. Then I took a bus to Ludgate Hill, and called at the *Mercury* office to ask why they've kept my Westminster Abbey poem since February without printing it. No one there but a clerk, who took my message respectfully. (I went because I sent them my only fair copy.) To-morrow, perhaps, I shall set out for South Wales with J. Philbin.

July 31
John Philbin rang up this morning to say that the car isn't ready till after lunch, so our departure was put off till to-morrow.

---

[1] Sir Edward Grey (1862–1933). Foreign Secretary 1905–16. Created Viscount Grey of Falloden 1916.
[2] The beautiful second wife of Francis Meynell. They founded and ran the Nonesuch Press together.

J.P. lunched with me at the Reform. He seems well and has been
trotting around to Wembley (the Empire Pageant) and theatres
with Schuster all the week. After lunch I went (alone) to Lord's
to watch the Rugby v. Marlborough match. Curiously enough it
was the first time I'd ever seen this match. (I left Marlborough
exactly twenty years ago.)

The afternoon was fine (with clouds) and the match exciting
When I arrived Marlborough had lost five wickets for 80 in
their second innings (after leading Rugby by 26 on the first
innings). They were all out for 109 and at 4.25 Rugby went in
to make 136 on a 'wicket which was giving the bowlers assistance'. Their best bat was out in the second over, yorked by
Coleridge, the Marlborough captain, a very erratic fast bowler
who didn't get anyone else out. The next was out for two. The
next made ten (three wickets were down for 25). Then the
Rugby Captain came in and made 34 very well. Marlborough
fielded superbly, but E.F. Longrigg (the left-hander who went
in first) was missed at mid-off before he'd made 10. Except for
this he played perfectly, and had made 31 when the fourth wicket
fell at 83 (a hard drive back at the bowler which he caught)
The next three Rugbeians all failed to score, and were caught
from half-hearted strokes, the bowler Knight taking all four
wickets in three overs. Longrigg then began to hit very hard
and the next man managed to stay in until the end. Longrigg
made 46 of the last 54 runs (four of which were byes). His 77
not out was one of the best match-winning innings I have ever
seen. After playing with restraint at first, he took all possible
risks after the seventh wicket fell, and Rugby must have lost had
he shown less enterprise.

It was an ideal school-match. He was carried into the pavilion
by his excited schoolfellows. It was quite in the *Tom Brown*
tradition. He looked such a nice sturdy boy. I came away feeling
refreshed. The game was a fine contrast to the accomplished
dreariness of ordinary 'first-class' cricket.

The people who perambulated the greensward between the
innings, however, looked excessively commonplace. A good
many of the boys were wearing their khaki uniforms, as they are
in camp this week.

Poor Longrigg! He has probably had the most triumphant

moment of his life.[1] And how few will remember it by the time
he is thirty. The only face I recognised at Lord's was that of
E. W. Dillon, a former Rugby hero, and Captain of the Kent
eleven for several years before the War. I remember seeing him
play his first match for Kent and make a century at Tonbridge
in 1899. He had just left Rugby and was wearing his blue shirt.
The match was against Hampshire, and old Walter Humphreys,
the famous Sussex lob-bowler was playing for Hampshire (he
must have been over fifty, and was making a belated reappear-
ance after having retired several years before).

Dillon, now a bored-looking man of forty-five, came out of the
members' stand, a little girl hanging on to his hand—his
daughter, no doubt. How sad is the fate of the ex-athlete!
Dillon's day is done. Twenty years ago I would have given a lot
to be as successful a batsman as Dillon. There are consolations
in being an artist—even though a disgruntled one.

After dining alone at the Reform (which closes for a month
to-morrow) I saw Arnold Bennett. He is getting very stout, but
looked well. I went up to him, rather diffidently, as I'd not seen
him since February. 'Hullo, you devil!' he exclaimed, removing
a large cigar from under his grey moustache. He was sprawling,
rather ungainly, on a sofa and chatting to A. G. Gardiner[2] about
Guernsey and other places he's been touching at in his yacht.
'Well; how's the work?' he asked. 'What work? Mine?' I
replied, adding : 'It's no bloody good asking me about *my* work
—it's always in the same condition.' A.B. looked pained.
'Aren't you well?' he asked. 'Moderate,' I mumbled. Somehow
I always feel defiant and rather petulant when A.B. (with such
genuine kindliness and interest) asks after 'the work'. A.B.
writing successful novels (and dud plays) and journalism at
1s.6d. a word makes me feel sensitive. Probably I envy him his
prolific powers, and his belief that the words are worth writing.
For him literature is a glorious game. For me it is a struggle
against disillusionment and disgust.

I asked had he read Forster's novel. No; he hadn't. 'It's
interesting, isn't it?' he said. (I remembered that I lent Forster
Riceyman Steps and he returned it, after six months, without
having been able to begin it.)

---

[1] He was later a well-known Somerset player. S.S.
[2] Author and journalist (1865–1946). Editor of the Liberal *Daily News* 1902–19.

So end another eleven weeks of my diarised existence.
Another 20,000 words or more (for which I shall never receive
any remuneration). At 1/– a word it would be £1000!

August 2 (Garsington)
Left Westminster 2.30 yesterday, in grey weather (and my
car). J. Philbin drove all the way. We arrived here about 5
(fifty-four miles). Gertler and Walter Taylor staying here.
(Miss Mary Smith arrived on Saturday evening.) Julian
Morrell away (staying at Welbeck).
Expedition to Brill after lunch. I drove Ottoline. Weather
rainy. Fine after tea. Pleasant sauntering drive home through
lanes between Beckley and Brill. The Spa at Brill. Arrow game
in p.m. Playing card-game after dinner (Sevens).

August 3
Very wet after lunch. Croquet 'tournament' before lunch.
Kitchin,[1] Montgomery, and young Swede to tea. Self playing
Bach Chaconne before dinner.

GRANDEUR OF GHOSTS

When I have heard small talk about great men,
I climb to bed; light my two candles; then
Consider what was said; and put aside
What Such-a-one remarked and Someone-else replied.

They have spoken lightly of my deathless friends,
(Lamps for my gloom, hands guiding where I stumble,)
Quoting, for shallow conversational ends,
What Shelley shrilled, what Blake once wildly muttered . . .

How can they use such names and be not humble?
I have sat silent; angry at what they uttered.
The dead bequeathed them life; the dead have said
What these can only memorise and mumble.

3 August 1924

[1] C. H. B. Kitchin (1895–1967), novelist. Author of *Death of My Aunt*.
[2] Published in *Lingual Exercises*.

August 4 (Bank Holiday)

Weather better, but grey. We left the Manor House at noon. News of Conrad's death in paper. Lunched at Wantage (the Bear). (I drove to W.) (By Sunday I'd decided to change plans; give up South Wales and go down to Dorchester instead—to see T.H.—and T.E.L.). An hour's drive from Wantage (J.P. driving) brought us to Marlborough. My second visit there since I left in July 1904. The last visit was with Nevill Forbes (we drove down from Oxford) in May 1911. Hospital fête going on in College Court. Lane's Fusiliers Band playing, which rather interfered with reminiscences. Walked up to Cricket Pavilion. Talked to groundsman, who told me that P. O'Regan dropped down dead a year ago, in the College Court. Stayed there an hour. Arrived Amesbury 5.30. J.P. drove too fast, and got on my nerves slightly. 25 m.p.h. is my pace, and he prefers 40. Tea at Avon Hotel. Coaching relics etc.

Stopped half an hour at Stonehenge. Arrived Sutton Veny[1] 7.30 in a slight drizzle. (I drove from Amesbury.) We did about ninety miles in the day.

Expected to find Robert Graves and family here, but only found Mrs William Nicholson and Kit.[2] Admiral Sir Morgan Singer,[3] wife, daughter, and naval-cadet son to dinner. Very pleasant people. Dancing to gramophone after, in ancient hall. J.P. got on well. He is admirable, and seems to be a success with everyone. His quiet dignity and unconventional Colonialism are splendid. (The Graveses left last week, and William N. is in Scotland painting a portrait.) T.E.L. was here last week.

So far the 'tour' has worked well. Garsington was a success, and it seems as well that the uncertain weather stopped us going to Wales.

STONEHENGE

What is Stonehenge? It is the roofless past;
Man's ruinous myth; his uninterred adoring
Of the unknown in sunrise cold and red;
His quest of stars that arch his doomed exploring.

---

[1] Where William Nicholson lived. Near Warminster and very near S.S's future home at Heytesbury.

[2] Nicholson's youngest son.

[3] 1864–1938. Knighted 1923.

And what is Time but shadows that were cast
By these storm-sculptured stones while centuries fled?
The stones remain; their stillness can outlast
The skies of history hastening overhead.

4 August 1924[1]

August 6 (The Antelope Hotel, Dorchester)
Left Sutton Veny this morning at 11. Pleasant, cool day with occasional sunshine. I drove all day. (Did about sixty miles.) Went by Maiden Bradley, Mere, Shaftesbury; lunched at Sherborne. Went up church tower. Left Sherborne 3.15; stopped at Cerne Abbas for half an hour.

Got to Max Gate 4.45. A motor-bike leaning against some shrubs suggested T.E.L. Sure enough, there he was, grinning genially at me through the window of the sitting-room; back-view of T.H. also visible. Loud bark from Wessie (tied up on the lawn out of sight). Mrs Hardy very smart, all in white silk, greets us in the hall, and T.H. is close behind her, looking exactly the same, and brisk as ever.

We stayed there till 7.15. After tea Mr Graham Anderson (Editor of *Country Life*) turned up (with wife and two strapping daughters). Anderson has been to Cerne Abbas to inspect the Giant, who needs a little attention as his outlines are getting slightly blurred, and Charles Whibley[2] has raised a small renovation fund. Anderson said the Giant is evidently Phoenician. The Phoenicians had small necks and a habit of lifting the right shoulder when wielding a club. The Phoenicians probably came up to Cerne to try and discover tin-mines. This led to a discussion of the Phoenicians, and T.E.L. spent the next half-hour earnestly demolishing all Anderson's archaeological ideas about Egyptian and other ancient civilisations. ('Dilettante Knowledge' he called it after A. had departed.)

THE CERNE GIANT

Hardy (the famous Dorchester magician)
Suspects this giant to have been Phoenician;
But local folk quite ignorant of his origin
Merely conjecture that he went out foragin'

[1] Published in *Lingual Exercises*, with 'hurrying' for 'hastening'.
[2] Essayist and critic (1859–1930).

(Prompted by antique erotic urgin's)
Ravished the prehistoric Dorset virgins;
Cerne Abbas maidens of the moment thrill
To see their gallant standing on the hill;
While many an archaeological society
Climbing the slope to make their safe inspection
Newly investigates the impropriety
Of this most immemorial erection.

A. is a big red-faced, clean-shaven, white-haired man.

T.E.L. has sold his gold dagger for £120 to pay for doing up his cottage on Cloud's Hill. We are going there on Friday afternoon.

T.E.L. has a motor-bike which will not go less than forty-five miles an hour in top-gear. It can do ninety-three if necessary!

After tea (before the Andersons came) we all trooped out into the garden to inspect the new half-acre of ground Mrs H. has purchased from the Prince of Wales. On it vegetables are grown and chickens kept. We stood looking at the chickens for some time, while Wessie barked at them. It was all (as E. M. Forster would say) 'rather tame', but as long as T.H. is well and bright one doesn't mind the tameness.

Yesterday was quiet. We went up to Scratchbury Hill after lunch. And I walked down to the river Wylie after tea, and sat on the charming little weir watching a very Wiltshire landscape with a square church-tower tucked away among dark-green trees under the hills.

To-day has been rather spoilt for me by a bad headache, but I enjoyed the drive. And J.P. is an admirable companion, and seems to be enjoying himself, though he too has headaches, worse ones than mine, I expect.

The last event at Max Gate was listening in. They have a loud speaker' in the dining-room. A voice announced the death of two airmen, the cricket-scores, the foreign-market etc. T.H. listened with apparent interest, but refused to 'come for a spin' in my car.

August 7

The first really fine day since we left London. I left J.P. to explore Dorchester, and was up at Max Gate by 11, to take Mrs

Hardy for a drive. Drove her round the lanes toward Wimborne and Blandford for a couple of hours, talking all the time. She says she would like to have a small car, but T.H. is very firm against it. His young brother (aged seventy-two and stone-deaf) has lately scandalised his parish by purchasing an expensive Sunbeam which he drives furiously. 'My husband was so annoyed that he refuses to look at the car,' said Mrs H. He is quite wonderful for his age, but I suppose it is too much to expect him to begin to be buzzed around in a two-seater by his second wife at the age of eighty-four.

Mrs H. told me this morning that he has been writing a lot of poems and has thirty or forty—nearly enough for a new book. 'Mr Cockerell is afraid of his writing too much, like Wordsworth, and has warned him about it.' What a subject for Max! S.C.C. gazing sternly down at T.H. sitting at his desk. 'Now, Hardy, I really must forbid you to write any more poems until you are ninety.' Poor T.H. looking rather rueful, murmuring 'I suppose Cockerell is right. But I thought that last one was rather good, I must confess.'

After a very pleasant lunch, when we had 'adjourned' to the drawing-room, T.H. read to me two scenarios he's drafted for the Hardy Players. One is *The Romantic Adventures of a Milkmaid*. The other *The Mayor of Casterbridge*. I suggested that *The Mayor* was rather too big an undertaking for the local Thespians.[1]

At 3.30 I came back and fetched J.P. and we went up to Max Gate again for tea. Mr and Mrs Edmund Selous[2] were there. The Selouses were elderly and amusing. Mrs S. (daughter of M. E. Braddon, once famous fiction-writer), square-faced and jolly, with features not very near together. Mr S., white-haired, bearded and rubicund, with a big blobby nose and a round bald brow; he ought to have worn an antique ring round his tie, but didn't. He has the high-pitched, wood-wind voice of a connoisseur. Seemed shy. (Mrs S. was talkative and quite at her ease.)

---

[1] Drinkwater dramatised *The Mayor*. S.S.

[2] Edmund Selous (1858–1934), barrister and ornithologist, wrote many books of natural history for children and adults. He regarded all animals, even poisonous snakes, as friends, and the thought of killing any one of them filled him with deep distress. His brother Frederic was a famous big-game hunter who shot anything that moved.

At tea we discussed cathedrals. Mr S. and T.H. bemoaned the destruction of old Temple Bar and other antiquarian objects. Said T.H. 'There were six large Abbeys in Dorset. If they'd been preserved Dorset would be quite a *show county.*'

Mr S. had never met T.H. before. When T.H. was seeing him off, in the hall, I heard Mr S. murmuring something about it always being 'a cherished memory'.

The S's disappeared down the narrow shrub-infested drive in their large cumbersome car. (They live at Wyke Castle, near Weymouth.)

J.P. and I went into Weymouth and dined at the Gloucester Hotel.

August 8
Splendid weather. My face is burning with sun and wind, and my brain buzzing with the incidents of the day. After J.P. had purchased some films for his Kodak and a pair of garters for his socks, we set off at 11 to Abbotsbury. H. M. Tomlinson is staying near there. I learned this from Mrs Hardy, so rang up the post-office at Abbotsbury, which said that T. is staying at the old (sounded like 'Coach something'). Arriving at Abbotsbury, I inquired from the post-master in the flesh; Old Coast Guard Station is the place. Off we buzzed toward Bridport, and reached the old C.G.S. after a mile of bumpy and almost obliterated road opposite the Chesil Beach.

A tall young man was on the beach, drying himself after a bathe in the halcyonic ocean. 'Is Mr Tomlinson here?' I asked. 'Yes. He's just round the corner, doing some writing.' And there, sure enough, sitting in a sun-baked niche among the sand-hummocks, was the little man, with his pipe in his mouth, and a writing-pad on his knee. Exuberantly I bounded down on him. 'Hullo, you old coastguard.' I felt excited and delighted; not having seen H.M.T. for eighteen months at least (the idea of seeing him at the *Nation* office never seems to attract me, though I always think of him with affectionate enthusiasm). He scrambled to his feet, and peered up at me with his queer gargoyle face. Recognition dawned. 'Sassoon!' Jabbering away at his deaf ear, I introduced him to J.P. (who read *The Sea and the Jungle* at Bray lately, and was very keen to meet H.M.T.).

I duly delivered the invitation to tea at Max Gate tomorrow. 'May I bring the Missus?' asked T. 'Of course.' So that was arranged, and I am to fetch them in my car.

H.M.T. led me up the path to the Old C.G.S. 'The Missus' was believed to be engaged in domestic affairs. I'd never seen her before. She came in, a homely garrulous body, and we sat round talking, in a small parlour, rather short of furniture. (The T's only arrived last week.) T. informed me, rather apologetically, that the place belongs to J. M. Murry, who is on the spot with his new wife. Soon T. was talking to J.P. about ships—the *Cutty Sark* and old Woodgate, her skipper. 'Saw a five-masted barque in the West India Dock the other day' etc. T. hollowing his deaf left ear in his hand, and not catching much of J.P's conversation. (Afterwards J. said 'The greater men are, the simpler they seem to be.')

The tall young man came in; he is T's son. Then we emerged into the sunshine, J. M. Murry appeared, and I was aggressively hearty with him. I haven't seen him for about four years. (He made it difficult by his unfriendly article on *Counter-Attack* in the *Nation* six years ago.) However, we discussed T.H. and George Moore's attack on him;[1] and he showed me his Trojan car (solid tyres) and I showed him my Gwynne Eight. And we all four looked at the ocean and observed the black antics of a ten-foot porpoise.

And then J. and I bumped away to Abbotsbury for lunch. Inspected the ancient Abbey barn and the Swannery, and lunched off liver and bacon and plum tart to the strains of a 'loudspeaker' broadcasting a concert in Paris.

What a queer mixture the last week has been! Garsington with its elaborate table-talk; Gertler painting in the garden; Philip Morrell spouting about Cooperative Farming at the Liberal Summer School in Oxford; Ottoline reading a letter from Robert Bridges at breakfast (R.B. thanking her for sending him Charlotte Mew's poems, and being facetious about her name); then the comparative simplicity of Sutton Veny, the Alsatian lady-dog catching tennis-balls off the roof, and young Kit Nicholson dancing with Miss Singer to the gramophone after

---

[1] Tomlinson said George Moore's head was like a dumpling with onion sauce over it. S.S.

dinner; and four-year-old Penny Nicholson riding her toy-
tricycle; and then Max Gate and Weymouth beach swarming
with holiday-makers.

The old Coast Guard Station was followed by a brisk drive to
Wool, and up the hill to Bovington Camp, where the Tank
Corps contains Private Shaw (otherwise known as T. E. Lawrence). We overtook the little man just beyond the camp, on his
way up to his cottage, Cloud's Hill, with a towel rolled up under
his arm. He turned and smiled ruddily, and hopped up on the
car. In a few hundred yards we were at the cottage, a tiny four-
roomed house surrounded by rhododendrons and neighboured
by a fine old ilex. It had been described to me by E.M.F. who
stayed there four days in June, and broke a tile by shying a stone
at a nightjar—an exploit which I should not have expected him
to indulge in. The outer walls of the cottage are yellow, though
T.H., who went there to tea, suggested 'duck-egg green' as
the correct colour. There is a kitchen on the ground-floor; and
up some stairs a small roof-convex chamber containing four
shelves of books (North's Plutarch in six vols. and Tudor
Translations among them), a fine gramophone and a lot of
records. An old leather sofa, a table, and a dark half-lustre tea-
service made by a local potter.

Before entering the house, we climbed the bank by the house
and looked at the wooded view toward Dorchester. The hideous
camp being invisible, the surrounding scenery is superb.

T.E.L. said, 'You'll find a fragment of the Tank Corps in the
cottage. He has a strong country accent, but doesn't say much.
His name is Russell.'

I had heard of 'little Russell' from E.M.F. and felt inquisitive
about him. He appears to be the Patroclus[1] of the piece. We
found him upstairs getting tea ready. He is a sturdy, not
ungraceful, fair-haired youth, with pleasant face, not quite good-
looking, but charming when he smiles. He was very silent and
discreet, and behaved almost as if he were an orderly. He has
been attached to T.E.L. for at least a year, probably longer. He
stood up or leant against the wall all the time, distributed the
tea, and helped T.E.L. with the gramophone (always addressing
him as Shaw).

T.E.L. showed me a copy of *St Joan* inscribed 'To Private

[1] The favourite friend of Achilles in Homer's *Iliad*.

Shaw from Public Shaw'. He also showed me some experimental proofs of his book, and the amusing illustrations by Kennington. J.P. said little, but was at ease, and T.E.L. seemed to accept him quite naturally and confidently. Josef Hofmann's[1] Scarlatti record was put on; and the whole of the Bach concerto for two violins; and two movements of a Mozart quartet.

I asked L's permission to attach his name to the Bridges Tribute. He fully agreed that the tribute is a necessary affair, and admires Bridges. All the time I felt inclined to try and draw Russell into the conversation, but he was shy and remote, without seeming awkward. His relationship with T.E.L. interested me more than anything else, but my speculations as to its sexuality are probably mistaken.

I asked L. how many people have ordered copies of the book (a hundred copies at £30) and he said 'About fifty'. He has refused to let Barrie have one 'because he is an insincere artist'.[2] Has refused a musician named Sorabgi 'because he is too poor—'it is only a plundering affair' (I suppose he means to reprint it again at a lower price) and 'another author—a low creature, whose name also begins with B.' (I guess it to be Beith—Ian Hay.)[3]

L. is coming to tea at Max Gate to-morrow, to meet H.M.T. who, he thinks, is 'a great prose-writer who hasn't yet written a great prose-work'.

That tea-party in the little house among the rhododendrons on Egdon Heath will remain 'a cherished memory' (as Mr Selous would say). But why, for the nth time, should T.E.L. be a private in the Tank Corps?

He has sold his seven first editions of Herman Melville for £120. He wears large heavy army-boots. He looks brown and healthy. And he is, obviously, getting very fond of his cottage. On the high ground overlooking the cottage stands a pole with wires attached. It is Russell's wireless apparatus.

At 9.30 every night L. has to be back in his hut, standing to attention by his bed—a fellow of All Souls, who has refused all the decorations the King of England could offer him. Well, well, he is an enigma.

---

[1] Polish-born pianist and composer (1876–1957).
[2] This he afterwards thought better of. S.S.
[3] Major General John Hay Beith (1876–1952). As Ian Hay, author of *The First Hundred Thousand* and many other books.

August 11 (Royal Hotel, Winchester)

My tour with Philbin is finished. I have left him at Bourne-mouth with Schuster and Lionel Holland, and am on my way back to London. The last three days have been brilliantly fine. Saturday (August 9) was a *busy* day. Before lunch I buzzed Mrs Hardy round the lanes for two hours—Puddletown, Piddle-hinton, Piddletrenthide, etc. At 3 o'clock I went off to Abbots-bury to fetch Mr and Mrs Tomlinson to Max Gate. Went by an excessively rural route; I had to get out and open (and shut) sixteen field-gates, and arrived at the Old Coast Guard Station half an hour late. Got them to Max Gate by 4.45 however. A large tea-party; in addition to Private Shaw there was a Mr Jeune and a Lady Brackenbury, who had toddled over from Stinsford House (Mr J. is father of Mrs Hanbury who lives there). Mr J. is an elderly, large, monocled, walrus-moustached, Roman-nosed remote relative of Charles Doughty. He seemed to be the last survivor from Whyte Melville's novels (or du Maurier's drawing-rooms). 'The last of the masters' in fact. What a contrast to shabby little H.M.T. with his almost cockneyfied accent. Yet H.M.T. is a far more dignified man than Mr Jeune, for all his aristocratic airs and gallantries. H.M.T. would probably describe him as a 'silly old geyser' (which would be strictly accurate).

Yes, du Maurier was depicting Mr Jeune in the 80's—the pages of *Punch* are populous with him. He was to be seen con-versing with the Duchess of Towers[1] in Hyde Park every Sunday during the Season.

Lady B. is also a fashionable figure, though more up-to-date. She seemed shallow-minded enough, sitting between Philbin and self at the tea-table and discussing, with an affectation of horror, the two recent murder-trials, and gazing at T.H. with fulsome admiration. H.M.T. sat on my left, next to T.H. (who was being bored by Mr Jeune, who was also boring Private Shaw). H.M.T. was observing T.H. all the time, with steady, discreet deference. Mrs Tomlinson, homely, pink-faced and nervous, sat on the sofa beside Mrs H. She looked rather over-powered by the occasion ('the great Colonel Lawrence', as she called him afterwards, was, I think, more startling to her than T.H.). The simplicity and genuineness of the T's is sublime.

[1] A character in *Peter Ibbetson* (1891) by George du Maurier (1834–96).

They made Mr J. and Lady B. seem sham people.

At 6.15 I carried the T's off in my car, dropped them at Upwey Station to catch a train to Abbotsbury (stopping in Dorchester where H.M.T. bought two pounds of butter) and then rushed back to Max Gate. T.H. was in the dining-room hovering round the wireless apparatus. He was listening eagerly to hear Big Ben strike seven. Minutes passed. Nothing struck. The machine merely went plop-plop. Then Mrs H. came in and put it right. (T.H. had put the wire in the wrong socket, and he looked slightly ashamed of himself.) At once a voice began to retail the evening news; hurricane in South America; twenty people perished; Brighton Races, result of 5 o'clock race; cricket-scores, close of play. Alas, Big Ben had already struck. And J. and I set off for Bournemouth, which we 'made' by 8.30, and found Schuster, Holland and two young men, eating a rich dinner in the Royal Bath Hotel (where everyone dresses for dinner and the rooms are upholstered in Pullman Car style). The smart, pretentious hotel seemed loathsome, and J. and I were very untidy. So we wandered out and ate a steak in a dingy commercial hotel just off the Square.

Returned to the Royal Bath. Holland had engaged a room for J. The hotel was full, so I shared J's room. The evening paper announced the death of Sir Claude Phillips,[1] which caused Schuster to look rather sad. (C.P. was one of his oldest friends and they went to hundreds of concerts, parties, and Wagner operas together.) C.P. always struck me as an obscene old gentleman, but no doubt he had his good qualities.

On Sunday the two young men left. Schuster, Holland, John and I lunched at Branksome Tower Hotel and bathed (Schuster a spectator of our aquatics). After dinner we went to a Wagner concert at the Winter Gardens [*pages torn out*].

[From a separate itinerary we can trace S.S's movements for the rest of August. He left Tufton Street on the 15th and then stayed as follows : 16th the Red Lion at Henley-on-Thames; 17th the Plough at Cheltenham; 18th Speech House, Forest of Dean; 19th–20th the Castle at Brecon; 21–28 at Manorbier; 29th the Metropole at Swansea; 30th the Green Dragon at

[1] 1846–1924. Art critic and Keeper of the Wallace Collection. See *Diaries 1920-1922.*

Hereford; 31st the Shakespeare at Stratford-on-Avon; 1st
September back to Tufton Street. At Manorbier he wrote the
following poems.]

A RUINED CASTLE

The Castle, built by thirteenth-century hands,
And weathered by six hundred years of Wales,
Wild, austere, and ocean-chanted, stands
Survivor of Time's galleon-splintering gales.
Postcard-attractive interest attaches
To veteran walls; and tourists flock like sparrows,
Unloaded in their motor-bus-load batches,
Immune from boiling lead and bows and arrows.

But I, who seek the picturesque by night,
Come wrapped in blustering wind and cloud-roofed gloom,
To sense the blind invasions of the dead,
Emerging from their architectural tomb
To move with me by waters phosphorus-white
And grope through feuds and sorrows in my head.

23 August 1924

AT THE GRAVE OF HENRY VAUGHAN

Above the voiceful windings of a river
An old green slab of simply graven stone
Shuns notice, overshadowed by a yew.
Here Vaughan lies dead, whose name flows on for ever
Through pastures of the spirit washed with dew
And starlit with eternities unknown.

Here sleeps the Silurist; the loved physician;
The face that left no portraiture behind;
The skull that housed white angels, and had vision
Of daybreak through the gateways of the mind.
Here lie faith, mercy, wisdom and humility,

[191]

Whose influence shall prevail, for evermore;
Here, from this lowly grave, shines Heaven's tranquillity;
And here stand I, a suppliant at the door.

27 August 1924[1]

WITH DE LA MARE AT CAREY CASTLE

From Carey Castle's tussocked tower
Two poets, twentieth-century hatted,
Craned necks, and sniffed a saffron flower,
Culled Carey's ivied charm, and chatted.

Said one of them, 'I'd like to know
Whose arms upon these walls are graven.'
The other one agreed. Below,
A minor creek of Milford Haven
Shone silver among pastures green
Where bygone cows and knights had been.

Thought one man's musing mind, 'How queer
That we have seen no single face
Of all who dwelt and jargoned here.'
And historied visions of the place
Within his mindsight moved and melted.
He was half conscious of the strange
Voice-haunted corridors of change;
Heard bygone horses stamp and snort,
And bowmen shout across the court;
Glimpsed ladies weaving threads on looms
Along Plantagenet-period rooms;
And hailed a mire-stained galloping ghost
With news of Henry Tudor's landing
Somewhere along the Pembroke coast.

On Carey Castle they were standing;
Two poets at the edge of Time
Who thought it worth their while to climb
A hundred feet above the ground.

[1] Published in the *London Mercury* February 1925, then, slightly revised, in *The Heart's Journey*.

Lulled by an ash-tree's streaming leaves
They listened to the breezy sound;
And one of them this memory weaves,
Faintly remembering what he found
On Carey Castle's tussocked tower,
Stooping to sniff a saffron flower.

27 August 1924

September 5

Lunched with Roderick and went to look at his house in Connaught Square, which is still in the hands of the decorators. To Queen's Hall alone; Beethoven Fourth Symphony, Bach D minor concerto for two violins, Handel Grosso Concerto No 12 (the last glorious; the Bach ditto). Cleghorn-Thompson sat with me. (A young man I met at the de la Mares' once. Private Secretary to a Liberal M.P.) Weather very hazy and overcast—like November.

September 6 (Staying with the Heads at Strathmore, The Wyche, Malvern)

Very pleasant feeling of a jaded townsman going off to the country this morning. Motoring seems to have solved my problems, for the present. Left Tufton Street at 11.30. A fine slightly hazy day. Pale-gold sunshine and fluffy clouds, with a cool breeze. Buzzed along to Beaconsfield. Exactly eighteen miles from Tufton Street to the little bridge beyond Uxbridge (where the country begins and London is really escaped from). Lunched at the White Hart at Beaconsfield.

Left B. at 2 and made the best speed I could for exactly three hours. Through Oxford by 3.15. Through Cheltenham by 4.45. In Tewkesbury by 5 (eighty-two miles from B.). Looked at the Abbey. Steady rain came on at 6. Arrived here before 7 (125 miles).

The Heads bubbling with delight at my arrival. H.H. trotted off to show me the way to the garage, several hundred yards up the road. (He is getting rather stiff and seems unable to lift his feet.)

After dinner Mrs H. read the latest letter from Norah

Nichols, and I read my latest from Bob. And H.H. read the German translation of my Stravinsky poem[1] with chuckles, pronouncing it 'brilliantly literal'.

September 7

Kathleen (the Irish maid) who brought me a cup of tea at 8 a.m. informed me that there was 'a fog as thick as your arm'. True enough; a dense white mist obliterated the superb view across Herefordshire.

So the morning was spent indoors. H.H. upstairs working on his big book. Self beginning by trying to read Patmore in bedroom and ending by rummaging among the music in the drawing-room where Mrs H. was doing needlework. The only possible music (mostly dance-music) was Handel's *Judas Maccabaeus*, Beethoven's *Solemn Mass*, and Bach's *Magnificat*. This I thrummed away at on a hollow-toned piano—a complacent instrument, mediocre like all the furniture and decoration in this house (hired from a tasteless middle-class family).

After lunch the rain stopped but the sun refused to appear. I drove H.H. to British Camp and we climbed to the top. He told me a lot about its postulated antecedents.

Then we drove down the hill to Old Colwall Manor and had tea with Mr and Mrs Rayner-Wood. Mrs R-W. owns the place; is forty-nine; was a Miss Holland; two years ago she married R-W. an Eton master; pink; fifty; smooth, and suffocatingly conventional. The adjoining small estate formerly belonged to Mrs Browning's father. Magnificent Tudor yew-hedge in the garden at Old Colwall; house contains some good pictures and furniture. English water-colours; Copley Fielding;[2] David Cox;[3] Callow;[4] R-W. is descended from Sir Joshua Reynolds's niece.

R-W. showed me round. Mrs R-W. seemed lively and pleasant, but I scarcely spoke to her. A homely cosy sort of evening, H.H. showing me a book on wood-carvings in churches;

[1] 'Concert Impression (*Le Sacre du Printemps*)', first published in the *Nation* on 21 January 1922, then in *Recreations* and *Satirical Poems* (1926).
[2] 1787–1855.
[3] 1783–1859.
[4] John Callow (1822–78).

discussing Anatole France etc. The damp autumnal weather makes me feel rather sluggish (plus the usual over-eating one goes in for when staying with friends).

While with the Heads the newspapers are full of the Joshua murder. (A. M. Joshua, father of the girl Nell who stayed at the Hut in May and was rather attractive, has been shot by his mistress—a squalid intrigue with a smart servant-girl.)[1]

The Heads also know the J's: Mrs J. is sister of Lady Lewis the solicitor's wife).

September 8 (My thirty-eighth birthday).

(Fine but cloudy and unsettled.) Received a scarlet handker-chief from C. E. Tomkinson.

Took Mrs Head for a drive 11.30–1.30. (To Bromyard and back by Ledbury.) To Malvern with H.H. after lunch. He showed me round the Priory Church, explaining the stained glass and wood-carvings etc. Very interesting. Walked up to Worcestershire Beacon 6–7.30 (with the H's). Talking about the supernatural with H.H. after dinner. He of course scientific-ally rational about it all. Very wholesome. (De la Mare made me feel that I ought to swallow all ghost-stories whole.)

September 9

Pouring wet morning, but we started at 11.30 in a hired car of the sedate taxicab variety for Ludlow (forty miles). Weather cleared about noon. After lunch looked at Church and Castle. Home in sunshine. Very jolly day. Talking about journals and methods of using one's experience—after dinner. (At dinner H.H. reminiscing about Germany.)

September 10

Weather cold but fine. Drove alone into Hereford for morning and afternoon concerts. (Rather a rush.) Heard Bach B minor

A. M. Joshua, a retired financier, had been the girl's lover for two years and had gone through a form of marriage with her. When she discovered that he had been married all the time she shot him and herself. The bodies were found on 5 September.

Mass, Brahms's Fourth Symphony and Elgar's 'Go song o
mine'. Back by 5. Went up to Worcester Beacon with H.H
before dinner. View splendid. After dinner busy making list o
names for Bridges affair. Letter from Harold Owen[1] who is now
at Henley so I needn't go to Shrewsbury where I thought he'c
be. Schuster and Adrian Boult[2] were at the concerts.

September 11 (Royal Hotel, Ross-on-Wye)

Left the Wyche 10.30. The Heads are dear people and
enjoyed being with them. Heard Elgar's *The Kingdom* befor
lunch. Schuster, Boult, and Philbin there. Fine performance
Holst, *Hymn of Jesus*. Elgar, Cello Concerto, and *Parsifal*
Finale of Act 1 after. Brahms's Requiem, Rossini *Stabat Mate.*
and Parry 'Blest Pair of Syrens' in evening. Drove back to Ros
after, got here 11.15. Fine moonlight drive. (Did the fourteer
miles in twenty-nine minutes!).

September 12 (The Hotel, Church Stretton)

Schuster and Philbin left for London at 10.30. (Adrian Boul
had gone early.) So I was left alone, rather undecided where to
go. The day was cloudy and mild. At 11.30 I set off for
Hereford. Got there by 12. Listened outside the Cathedral for
ten minutes, and heard some Handel *Messiah*. On to Ludlow
Got there 1.30. Lunched at the Feathers (same table as Tues
day). A letter lying in the hall addressed to Lady O. Morrell (in
Julian M's writing). But O.M. wasn't visible. Only 'expected'
(I expect.) Left L. at 3 and went across Wenlock Edge by
Roman Bank to Church Stretton. After tea I started off for a
walk up the hills. Heavy rain at first; fine after. Came bacl
feeling better but rather soaked. Drank half a bottle of Bern
castler Doktor with a lukewarm dinner. Drinking hock plus the
hill-walk plus the solitude reminded me of Berchtesgaden two
years ago.

Once before I came to this hotel. In September 1915 I cam
here in a hired motor from Liverpool with three other officers
One of them was David Thomas, I think (or it may been

[1] Painter and writer (1897–1971). Brother of Wilfred Owen, the poet.
[2] Conductor (1889–1983). Knighted 1937.

R. H. Hanmer).[1] We had tea here. It is a very vague memory.

Strange to think that on that day I knew so few of my present circle of friends. But the *difference* between 'then and now' [*half-page torn out*].

To-morrow!—cloudy no doubt. Where shall I go? I only know that I don't want to be at Tufton Street.

I have promised to write a 3500-word article on Modern Poetry for a German magazine by October 15. I feel averse to doing it. Otherwise my future is blank.

September 13 (George Hotel, Lichfield)

The up-to-date hydropathic comfort of Church Stretton Hotel is replaced by the less modernised and more country-townish cheerfulness of this one. It has been a wet day. I left C.S. at 12.30. Lunched at the Raven, Shrewsbury (run by the same company as the Gloucester, Weymouth). Took a stroll round the town and along the riverside, but gave the Abbey a miss; ditto Wilfred Owen's mother, who lives a mile or two away. Had the weather been fine and my mood more gregarious I'd have paid her a visit. But I felt unsociable and shirked it. Left S. at 4; rain soon came on. Had tea at a pub just beyond the Earl of Bradford's park. Twenty years ago I stayed with his agent there to play in a couple of boys' cricket-matches, in one of which I failed ignominiously.

Arrived here at 6.45, having completed two hundred miles on four gallons of petrol. So confident was I that scarcely a drop of petrol remained in the tank that I lit a match to look, causing a short conflagration which singed my right eyebrow. (382 miles since Sept 6.)

The Midlands feel friendly after the Welsh hills.

I drank half a bottle of sparkling red Burgundy at dinner (a weakness of mine is for sparkling red wine) and read de Goncourt's journal. Afterwards I watched billiards—first three farmers playing pool, then a couple of Yorkshire motorists. The marker, young and not ill-favoured, looked pleasant through the Burgundy. His jaunty, self-conscious attitudes were well worth watching. Poor over-worked youth! What a dreary face it will be in twenty years (*page torn out*).

[1] Thomas and Hanmer had been brother-officers of S.S. in the Royal Welch Fusiliers. See *Diaries 1915–1918*.

September 14 (Globe Hotel, King's Lynn)

When I left Lichfield I wasn't sure of my objective. The sun was shining; I wanted to revisit Atherstone-land.[1] Vaguely I visualised the East Coast. Through Tamworth, passing within a mile of Amington Hall (where Phyllis Loder's father lives)—on to Grendon—past H. A. Brown's house, where he trains his steeplechasers—and then a few miles further (missing the Atherstone Kennels at Witherley by a mile) past the house of Dick Hanmer, whose daughter I was dimly engaged to for a year (1915–16). (Afterwards she eloped with a married middle-aged M.F.H. and had a baby by him.) After passing Sheepy Lodge, I skirted Market Bosworth, sauntering along the narrow, winding lanes, and then went more rapidly on through Leicester. From there to Uppingham, where I lunched (at 2.15) at the Falcon—a pleasant, guestless hostelry, its dining-room adorned with calligraphic pen-drawings of Queen Victoria's august uncles. Left there at 3.15 and did another forty-five miles to Wisbech—very pleasantly. At 4 o'clock I passed Long-thorpe—and slowed up to stare at the oak-encompassed house where I stayed with the Loders five years ago, and wrote one of my best poems ('Falling Asleep').

After several forty-miles-an-hour spurts along the straight stretches of the Fenland road, I entered Wisbech at 5. The place, as I came in, might have been Holland. (Eighteenth-century red-brick houses by a canal—in mellow sunshine.) At the Rose and Crown I had a good tea and talked with the landlord, who is an eminent wine-merchant. (The wine-list of the hotel is a museum of vintages such as I've seldom seen—*never* in a small country town). His name is Tidnam, and he claims, on his Wine Catalogue, to have been 'established 1475'. The town of Wisbech has a pleasant old-fashioned flavour, suggestive of a German town. Almshouses 'rebuilt by the Burgesses of Wisbech' in 1829. A fair was imminent and the canal-side was crowded with bright-coloured caravan-waggons—'amusements on tour'. After a stroll round, I set off through the orchard-fringes, and arrived here at 7. This place was equally attractive. The hotel, though less distinguished than the Rose and Crown, is by no means bad, standing in a derelict-looking square (of the French *place* type) and backed by the river (almost a harbour).

[1] i.e. the country of the Atherstone hunt.

Sunday evening—a red sunset, church-bells tolling, citizens strolling—how pleasant to arrive. (And to read, unexpected, my twelve lines in the *Observer*.) (In me, past, present, future meet.)

And cold pigeon-pie for dinner. Inspired by Tidnam's wine-list, I ordered half a bottle of vintage port (8/6) and drank it all. Hence my garrulity. (497 miles since September 6.)

APOCALYPTICAL INDISCRETIONS

In me, past, present, future meet
To hold long chiding conference.
My lusts usurp the present tense
And strangle Reason in his seat.
My loves leap through the future's fence
To dance with dream-enfranchised feet.

In me the cave-man clasps the seer,
And garlanded Apollo goes
Chanting to Abraham's deaf ear.
In me the tiger sniffs the rose.
    Look in my heart, kind friends, and tremble,
    Since there your elements assemble.[1]

September 15 (Black Boys Hotel, Aylsham)
Aylsham (population 2471) is only forty miles from King's Lynn, but I motored eighty-five Norfolk miles to get here and I am now twenty-five miles further away from the Metropolis, which adds to my sense of serenity. And I have done exactly two hundred miles since I left Lichfield (582 since September 6) and there is still some petrol in the tank (50 miles to the gallon)—enough, anyhow, to carry me the mile and a half to Blickling Hall tomorrow morning. I am looking forward to Blickling (by a lucky chance tomorrow is the day for public admittance).

This morning I awoke at 4 a.m. and peered out of my window. The cobbled market-place wore a glimmeringly forlorn aspect and its eight trees shivered under a cloudy sky. Six hours later I

[1] Published in the *Observer* 14 September 1924, as 'Apocalypse' in *Lingual Exercises*, and thereafter untitled.

emerged from the hotel, feeling slightly invigorated by m
overnight port—a tribute to its authentic quality. I inspected
couple of antique shops; bought a duster for fourpence
halfpenny (to wipe the car with); looked at St Margaret'
Church; purchased a guide to Norfolk (at W. H. Smith's)
entered the Guildhall and was shown over it by a withere
white-haired woman; Fanny Burney's portrait (a copy) wa
there (her father was organist at St Margaret's, and she wa
born at Lynn). A portrait of Sir Benjamin Keene was said (b
the caretaker) to be by Hogarth, but was less interesting than
curious eighteenth-century painting of the Market Place
anonymous, and presented by a Miss Cruso.

A little before noon, in cloudy but pleasant weather, I slippe
out of the town, taking the Hunstanton Road.

I ought to have stopped at Castle Rising, but felt averse t
looking at it. Then, for a few miles, the landscape wore a
atmosphere of Royalty; pine-woods and smug red-brick cottages
and Sandringham somewhere out of sight. And, on the left, th
hazy marsh-fringed sea. A mile from Hunstanton I was stoppe
by a young woman with a small silky dog; she asked for a lif
in a pert seaside manner. When I dropped her in Hunstanton
after a brief and taciturn trip, she said 'Bye-bye' and went ou
of my life—never to return, I trust.

Faintly desirous of viewing Holkham Hall[1], I pushed on t
Wells, and ate a bad lunch at a Trust House hotel at Holkham
A genteel family there, father, mother and daughter wer
talking about Compton Mackenzie (the father had seen him ac
Hamlet at Fowey[2]). Holkham was not viewable (the aged Ea
being in residence), so I never even glimpsed its glories, and b
4 o'clock was threading the streets of Cromer (having halte
for half-an-hour to look at Cley Church, which contains som
amusing faintly-coloured carved figures, one of them indecent)
Cromer streets contained the commonplace modern figures c
seaside visitors, and I hurried on; previously I had passed th
Sheringham golf club, which was populous with inane littl
processions from tee to green, reviving memories of my ow
golfing antecedents.

At Mundesley I stopped for tea; half-inclined to stay th

[1] Home of the Earls of Leicester.
[2] In 1909, directed by Arthur Quiller-Couch.

night there and get a breath of East Coast air; but, though the air was bracing, the Manor House Hotel was repellent with the smugness of villadom. The people staying in it looked too respectable. And I turned inland with a craving for farmhouses and honest unadultered duck-ponds. And now I was to enjoy the little Enoch Arden episode which had been in my mind all day. Twenty-seven years ago my mother rented Edingthorpe Rectory for eight weeks of late summer and early autumn. Thither she conveyed her three sons. The Rectory is a few miles from Mundesley. On the way I looked into Knapton Church, to admire the carved angels of the Irish-oak roof. In the visitors' book was the name of Giles Gilbert Scott,[1] dated a few weeks ago. (His father 'restored' the church.) I would have entered my own august name, but the nib of the pen was broken. (I rarely write my name in visitors' books, warned by the Drinkwaterish habit of my advertising contemporaries, but on this occasion I felt a wish to record my arrival after such a prolonged absence. But had to be content with an anonymous florin dropped in to the restoration-fund box.)

Little more than a mile away, across the fields, was Eding-thorpe church, which is about five hundred years old. Thither I came by circuitous lanes. My memories of the place were extremely vague. I could remember that the Rectory stood among some trees; and that the church was about a quarter of a mile away from it, on some rising ground. I remembered a nut-orchard in the Rectory garden, and the parson's blue sermon-paper in a cupboard, which I used for my childish scrawlings. (I wrote a poem about Norwich Cathedral which still survives in an old manuscript book at Weirleigh.) But the landscape was strangely unrecoverable in the light of memory; sad and remote, it looked now, in the grey end of an autumn afternoon, but the place had a rustic charm, like a poem by John Clare or a woodcut by Birket Foster.

Leaving the car in a farm-lane, I walked across a stubble-field, past some stacks with men working on one of them; skirted a root-field; and rediscovered the little church. It has a thatched roof. I hadn't remembered that. Probably I never noticed it in 1897. The church was locked, but it looked as though it hadn't changed since 1824, except for a new lych-gate, erected to the

[1] Architect (1880–1960). Knighted 1924.

memory of a young Lance-corporal Muriel (son of the late parson) who was drowned in a torpedoed transport-ship in the Mediterranean after taking part in various battles in France. Somehow that little church, standing in its unkempt graveyard among the stubble and root-fields, had a curious dignity and pathos, which will, I know, haunt me. And its name, with the 'thorpe' in it, seemed so appropriate.

I remember a service there, when the austere young locum-tenens parson stopped in the middle of his sermon and came down the church to rebuke some giggling village-boys among the scanty congregation. I remember that Mother thought he had 'a fine face'.

I made my way back through the Rectory's back-premises; the 'nut-orchard' was still there, though tenanted by chickens and disfigured by wire-netting. And the present incumbent has a car (negligently at its ease in an old shed).

Mistily I memorised an elongated old shandrydan of a vehicle with an elderly horse, in which we used to drive to North Walsham. Also I remembered the donkeys we used to ride; I rode mine in a donkey-race at a local flower-show and came in last in a 'field' mainly composed of fat farmers. (That was my first race!)

Edingthorpe is a straggling hamlet, with a glutinous strip of pond. As I drove away from the Rectory my progress was much impeded by ducks and geese. Rural and derelict to the last degree was Edingthorpe. I heard a shotgun, and a young man came out of a field-gate with a rabbit.

Through North Walsham and on here (by the wrong road) I buzzed under a lowering rainful sky. And in the twilight entered the friendly little square of Aylsham, and was allotted a small room in this rather musty inn. Excellent cold duck for dinner, in an empty room hung with Alken prints.[1] While eating I cut the leaves of my recently-acquired edition of Dorothy Wordsworth's journal—a delight which I have been putting off from day to day. Could I have cut those leaves in that odious, comfortable hotel at Mundesley? I think not.

After dinner my solitude was broken by a primly silent young couple—lower-middle-class provincials—who sat reading fiction-magazines while I scribbled these pages. At 9.45 they

[1] Sporting scenes etched by Henry Alken (*floruit* 1816–31).

finished their hot milk and sweet biscuits and 'retired to rest'.

My own evening has been alcoholically abstemious. Hence the clarity of my narrative.

September 16 (Maid's Head Hotel, Norwich)

Fine morning after wet night. 10.30–11.30 Blickling Hall (and church). Lunch at Wroxham (tea-shop) after stopping at Oxnead Hall which was a disappointment, though pleasantly situated. (Refilled with petrol in Aylsham; did 203 miles on the last four gallons.)

Weather gusty after lunch; grey and drizzly after 3.30. Stopped at Ranworth church; talked to parson (who had been chaplain at Glamis Castle). View from top of tower. White sails cruising among osiers. Landscape hazy but thirty church-towers visible. Rood-screen interesting antiquarianly, but not aesthetically, as it is very much defaced and faded (St Michael and St George are good). Fine illuminated manuscript in priest's chamber.

Two churches, one burnt, at South Walsham. Went into Yarmouth, and out again, as it looked ghastly, squalid, and tripperish. A holiday-resort of Hell. Tea at Potter Heigham Bridge. Weather very dreary. Got here 6.45. (Seventy-four miles today.)

Am sitting alone in a huge 'writing-room'—recently modernised and utterly insipid.

The Broads are associated in my memory with a sailing-trip in early September 1901 with two masters at my prep-school at Sevenoaks, my two brothers and a boy named J. K. Rooker, who afterwards wrote a book (in French) on Francis Thompson![1]

But the Broads are nothing when seen from a motor. And this afternoon was grey and gusty. All my capacity for enjoyment and assimilation was used up at Blickling, the loveliest country house I've ever seen.

I add a footnote, registering my intense satisfaction in being alone and independent, with all this England to explore. Cobbett on his cob made Rural Rides; why shouldn't I, in my Gwynne, become the Laureate of Landscape Inspection?

If the stability of English character is expressed in its rural

[1] Published in England in 1913.

scenes (rather than in its Industrial Gehennas and Golgothas) neither cinemas, char-à-bancs, nor Newspaper Syndicates can vitiate its heritage.

September 17 (Lamb Hotel, Ely)

Another pleasant guide-bookish day, in grey, gusty weather. (Did sixty-eight miles.) Spent the morning 'doing' the museum and cathedral at Norwich. Of the museum I remember some Great Bustards in a glass case and an eighteenth-century curricle. Also, of course, the Norwich School paintings; but these were not very visible, owing to the bad light, and left an impression that one need not go further than Trafalgar Square to see old Crome[1] at his best. The Cathedral was crypt-like in climate, but very white and cheerful in tone, in spite of the lack of sunshine. But it suffers from the destruction of all its old glass. A rather touching modern memorial to a young girl, by Derwent Wood.[2]

The head waiter at the Maid's Head had the aspect of an ex-quartermaster-sergeant. (In old days he'd have been town-beadle.) He was inclined to bully me, but I assumed hauteur and he became respectful. There was also a very old and doddering waiter who dropped knives and forks, and was garrulous when encouraged; he contributed character to the ancient hostelry which exploits its quaint Chaucerian charms for the benefit of American visitors.

At 3.15 I set off along the straight stretches of the Dereham road, very much blown on by a bracing breeze. D. is sixteen miles from Norwich and I did it in thirty-one minutes, a lapse into 'speed-merchandise' which I have refrained from lately. After passing Dr Jessopp's[3] rectory I turned aside into lanes and went four miles out of my way—very enjoyable—passing a party of partridge-shooters, accompanied by a woman in a tweed skirt (they were all marching solemnly across a stubble-field). The landscape was autumnal, the elms not yet changing colour, but equinoctially besomed by blasts of mild air; most of the

---

[1] John Crome (1768–1821), landscape-painter.
[2] Francis Derwent Wood (1871–1926), sculptor.
[3] The Rev. Augustus Jessopp (1823–1914), schoolmaster and historical writer. Headmaster of King Edward VI's School, Norwich, 1859–79; Rector of Scarning, Norfolk 1879–1911.

harvest in, and men working on the summits of large stacks.
The region I passed through on my way to Castle Acre was
extremely bucolic, lacking even churches; pure Colin Clout
(plus partridge-preservation by gentry). A series of Wilson
Steer[1] water-colours. The Priory at Castle Acre has much charm
and enormous antiquarian interest. But I prefer a complete
cathedral to these relics of monkery. Except for the surroundings, a place like Castle Acre Priory is only old stones to me,
though one appreciates the beauty of a Norman arch when one
sees it in farmyard surroundings. If only cathedrals stood in
green fields, miles from the nearest market-town! What miracles
they'd seem! (St David's is the only one I know.)

Left Castle Acre at 5.30 and hurrooshed to Downham Market
(eighteen miles) in thirty-four minutes. Slowed down after
that. (Lovely fen-effects along the Little Ouse beyond Southery.
But heavily clouded skies.) Got here at 7, just as a soaking
drizzle began (followed by a strange low scarletish strip of
sunset). The Lamb is a small, clerical-atmosphered hotel, very
demure and dowdy, but comfortable. The guests all very genteel
(twenty of them), including two Lieutenant-Colonels; rather
the effect (at dinner) of a seaside boarding-house at a golfing
resort. Two prim maids and a worried, nice-mannered waiter
who looked as if he'd rather have been a clergyman. Drank half
a bottle of Moselle and feel well. Since dinner I've sat in my
bedroom; someone has been playing the piano below—very
audible, and very facile and florid in execution—Schumann's
Träumerei (with trimmings), Grieg (*molto rubato*) and various
waltz-effects with much arpeggio decoration. This music has
relieved the Rural-Dean dowdiness very pleasantly.

I have only £2.10.0 left, so must terminate my tour tomorrow
(724 miles since September 6).

September 18 (54 Tufton Street)
To-day was fine weather. After an hour in Ely Cathedral
(magnificent it is) I drove fast and windily to Cambridge.
Stayed there 1.30–4, drifting around; very empty it seemed, and
even the shops were closed; looked into the Fitzwilliam and
observed my portrait,[2] becomingly re-hung.

[1] Philip Wilson Steer (1860–1942).
[2] By Glyn Philpot, painted in 1917.

Here by 7 (stopping fifty minutes at Ware for tea). (Did exactly *800* miles September 6 to 18.) This evening to Queen's Hall. Holst's *Planets*. Roderick joined me in the middle. Saw Festing-Jones outside. He had been to the *Egyptian Hall* with four Sicilians!

Over £100 has been subscribed for the Bridges Clavichord. Robert Graves sends me a long poem and his book on Dreams.[1]

September 19

To *Back to Methuselah*[2] (Act V) in afternoon. At Court Theatre, with Schuster. Was much impressed. Working at Westminster Abbey poem (rewriting) 6–7.30. (Sent it to *Statesman*, as Squire has kept it seven months at the *Mercury*— *luckily*, as I have polished it up a lot.)

EVENSONG IN WESTMINSTER ABBEY

Out of the pattering flame-reflective street
Into the Abbey move my adagio feet,
Out of the lofty lamp-lit London dusk
Ferrying through vaulted sanctuaries a head
Calm, vesper-tolling, and subdued to shed
Gross thoughts and sabbatise the intemperate husk.

Gazing around, I glimpse the illustrious Dead:
Assembled ancestries of England loom.
Here, on this *Second Sunday after Epiphany*,
Milton and *Purcell* triumph from the tomb;
Spirits aspire on solemn-tongued antiphony,
And from their urns immortal garlands bloom.

Poets, musicians, orators, and Abstractions
Sponsorial, guard the suppliant congregation.
Fame with mum trumpet, posturing ripe attractions,
Sustains her simpering Eighteenth-Century station;
While *Shakespeare*, shy 'mid History's checked polemic,
Muses incognizant of his translation

[1] *The Meaning of Dreams* (1924).
[2] By Bernard Shaw.

Into a lingual culture-epidemic.
Charles Wesley; *Isaac Watts*; each now enjoys
Hymnistic perpetuity from boys
Chanting like scarlet-cassocked seraphim :
Here saintly *Keble* waits his Evening Hymn,
And hearkens, quiet, confident and humble.

John Gay looks glum . . . A clergyman ascends
The pulpit steps; smooths with one hand his hair,
And with the other hand begins to fumble
At manuscript of sermon. We prepare
Patience to listen. But *Disraeli* bends
Forward a little with his sceptic stare.

Time homilizes on. Grave ghosts are gone.
Diction has turned their monuments to stone;
Dogma has sent Antiquity to sleep
With sacrosanct stultiloquential drone.
But cryptical convulsions of the Past
Pervade the benediction's truce and sweep
Out on the organ's fugue-triumphal tone
When hosannatic Handel liberates us at last.[1]

Queen's Hall after a hasty dinner. A second-rate pianist of the helter-skelter variety played Chopin's Andante Spianato and Polonaise. Also there was Beethoven's Eighth Symphony. And Mozart's Divertimento No 10.

September 20
Went to Brighton to stay with Aunt Mozelle. Called on Dolmetsch at Haslemere on the way. Went to Kreisler[2] Concert in evening.

September 21
Took Aunt M. for drive round Ringmer, Isfield etc. 3–5. H. Marrot to tea. Dinner alone with Aunt M.

[1] Published in the *New Statesman* 18 October 1924 and *Lingual Exercises*.
[2] Fritz Kreisler (1875–1962), great Austrian violinist.

September 22

Back to lunch. (Rather exhausted by Aunt M. but conscious of a duty performed.) Dined with Enrico at 120 Maida Vale [*page torn out*].

September 26

Dined with Arnold Bennett at Cadogan Square, the Lynds,[1] H. Griffith,[2] Harriet Cohen,[3] Lord Buckmaster,[4] and Mrs de Beer.

September 27

To *The Great Adventure*[5] (alone) in evening. Driving Turner in Park after lunch. Fine weather. Called at 40 Half Moon Street, saw Roderick (ill) and drove Burton to St John's Wood to see H. Lawrence's house (sale of furniture) and to tea with Christopher Millard.[6]

September 28

Drove (alone) seventy-five miles after lunch. To Luton by St Albans, and back by Welwyn and Barnet. Fine weather. Dined 120 Maida Vale. Gabriel there. Also A. T. Bartholomew (in bed with flu).

September 29

To *The Rat*[7] in evening (alone). Gilbert Wakefield took me behind after to see his wife (Isabel Jeans, who plays a leading part).

Lunched at Club with C. Masterman[8] and W. Roch. M. praised my Wembley poem, which pleased me.

---

[1] Robert Lynd (1879–1949), Irish essayist and critic and his wife Sylvia (1888–1952), poet and novelist.
[2] Hubert Griffith (1896–1953), journalist and playwright.
[3] Pianist (1896–1967).
[4] 1861–1934. Barrister and Liberal M.P. Lord Chancellor 1915–16.
[5] By Arnold Bennett.
[6] Book-collector, admirer and bibliographer of Oscar Wilde, 1872–1927.
[7] By Ivor Novello.
[8] Liberal M.P. and writer (1873–1927).

September 30

To Royal Society of Literature before lunch. Very wet day.
To Queen's Hall in evening (alone). Turners gone to Eastbourne till Friday.

October 1

Dull foggy-inclined day. Lunched with Bennett, Swinnerton[1]
and O. Sitwell at club. (O.S. lunching with A.B.) Saw last two
acts of *Our Betters*[2] after. To Queen's Hall evening. Mitja
Nikisch[3] played Brahms D minor Concerto finely.

October 2

Ivor Novello[4] lunched with me at Savoy.

Dinner with Tomkinson and Henry Head at Oxford and
Cambridge Club.

Talked to Henry Newbolt for an hour at Reform after lunch.
(I.N. had gone to his matinée.)

I have destroyed my diary for the last five days, merely rewriting the details.

October 3

Alone all day. Called on Mrs Hendry at Royal Palace Hotel,
Kensington, but she was out, luckily, so I got off with leaving
seven shillings' worth of carnations. Also sent flowers (eleven
shillings) to Mrs Hardy (who is in a nursing home after her
operation for malignant growth on neck).

Feeling too tired to go to Queen's Hall, but peaceful [*pages
torn out*. A separate note records that he was at Tufton Street
for the whole of October, and on November 1–3 he stayed with
H. G. Wells at Easton Glebe.]

[1] Frank Swinnerton, novelist and critic (1884–1982).
[2] By Somerset Maugham.
[3] Hungarian pianist (1899–1936).
[4] Welsh actor, composer, song-writer and dramatist (1893–1951).

October 13

Was delightfully entertained by the Gosses, although there was a 'domestic crisis'. (The parlour-maid left suddenly and Tessa Gosse had been taken ill with a chill.) E.G. opened the front-door when I arrived, and explained all this in agitated tones, warning me to expect nothing but a boiled egg and some cheese for dinner. But the meal was adequate—almost ample— and E.G. seemed to have been stimulated and genialised by his elder daughter's illness! Still wearing his spectacles with one eye blackened (as he was in the summer) he excited me to almost excessive hobnobberies. Over our cigars I read aloud the list of subscribers to the Bridges Clavichord, and almost every name drew from us a miniature conversation or anecdote.

'I am always so deeply interested to hear who has *refrained* in these affairs!' he gleamed. He told me how when R.B. went to Buckingham Palace as Poet Laureate elect, half-awed and half-arrogant, he said, hoity-toity-ishly to Lord Stamfordham, 'Understand that I don't want any of your Stars and Garters.' Lord S. replied suavely, 'His Majesty will not trouble you, Mr Bridges.' R.B. afterwards told this as an instance of how he'd scored off Lord S.! How alike poets are! Proud and irritable when in contact with pomps and presences and the empty unfamiliar splendours of 'the grand world', secretly shy and outwardly haughty, but how amenable to flattery and blandishment! E.G. told me how a man said to Robbie Ross (at some dinner), 'Can you *stand* Gosse?' R.R. 'Yes. I try to put up with him; for, *like you*, I am deeply indebted to him.'

E.G. described Mrs Asquith (at a dinner) as 'a fossilised butterfly', caressing with her frozen fingers some confused Labour Minister, as she congratulated him on the superb speech he'd made in the House on the previous night. When she'd flitted away, someone asked J. H. Thomas 'Who was that?' J.H.T. 'Don't you know who *that* is? That's Margot the 'arlot!' Poor Margot! The world little knows how innocent she really is!

1925

—◦●◦—

Undigested impressions have their value, and the road
to a true philosophy of life seems to lie in humbly recording
diverse readings of its phenomena as they are forced upon
us by chance and change.
(Hardy, Preface to *Poems of the Past and the Present*, 1901)

We seek to know the moving of each sphere,
And the strange cause of th'ebbs and flows of Nile;
But of that clock, which in our breasts we bear,
The subtle motions we forget the while.

Sir John Davies

'Believe me, I'm so chock-full o' knowledge that I can
hardly get it out o' the bung-'ole o' my 'ead.'

Mr Jorrocks

1925

‑‑‑◦⊙◦‑‑‑

February 19
Ten minutes late, I was convoyed into the luncheon-room at
the Marlborough Club. There I found Sir Edmund Gosse
entertaining Admiral Sir William Pakenham,[1] Walter Sickert,
Philip Guedalla,[2] and Philip Gosse.[3] These ingredients mixed
none too well, and Sir Edmund was all anxiety to set conviviality in motion. When making me known to the Admiral (rubicund, hard-bitten, genial, and unostentatious) he revived the
faded glories of my fox-hunting—'Mr Sassoon is the only living
poet of any eminence who hunts'—whereupon (somewhat confused by the Bohemian proximity of Sickert and the Whistler
tradition) I clumsily blurted out 'I only do it to save my face!'
(an obscure utterance which implied that I have done my little
best to compromise with the Philistines, but was allowed to pass
without comment).

Guedalla, elegantly Semitic, with a fat pearl in his tie, was

[1] 1861–1933. Commander of the Battle Cruiser Fleet 1917–19.
[2] Historian and essayist (1899–1944).
[3] Doctor, writer and naturalist (1879–1959). Son of Sir Edmund.

sedulous in politeness to the Admiral, but out of range of Sickert, with whom he'd fain have discussed Max Beerbohm. Philip Gosse sat silent, as though waiting to be utilised when required. Sickert talked to me in undertones. He began by congratulating me on my poem in the *New Statesman* a few weeks ago ('On Reading the War Diary of a Defunct Ambassador'—it was on the same page as an article about *him*). This caused me to feel that the said poem wouldn't be well received by members of the Marlborough Club. With E.G. there, Sickert made no attempt to shine as a raconteur. He is either first or nowhere. But he told me (I forget how it cropped up) a story about a woman in Paris who was crazily wrought up about the visit of the Czar and Czarina. 'She flung herself into the Seine. When her body was recovered, it was found that her drawers were made of the Russian flag.' This reference to drawers seemed to make the Admiral more at his ease, and the topic was pursued in a series of anecdotes. The Admiral's was about a critical moment in the Battle of Jutland, when his fellow-Admiral broke the tension by remarking, 'I am told that Princess Mary wears pink flannel drawers.'

After lunch we were joined by Admiral Sir Roger Keyes.[1] (E.G. presented Sickert to him as 'Mr Sickert—of the Academy'.) Also Sir George Arthur[2]—a typical court official and amateur of letters, with too ingratiating manners, who hung upon Guedalla's lips, being himself the biographer of Kitchener, whose private secretary he was.

E.G. told a funny story about King Edward lunching with Sir Sidney Lee[3]—something absurd about Shakespeare—imitating King Edward's Germanic intonation adroitly—'King Edward, who seldom trifled with printed matter' etc. The presence of Sickert somehow made me feel antagonistic to the Marlborough Club atmosphere. He is an old friend of E.G's, but I sensed his dislike of the artificiality of the entertainment. Anyhow he left early. At lunch I was complaining to him about the daily papers and their outrageous posters, and about other daily phenomena

---

[1] 1872–1945. Admiral of the Fleet. Created Lord Keyes of Zeebrugge and of Dover 1943.

[2] Prolific author on royal and literary subjects (1860–1946).

[3] Assistant editor of the *Dictionary of National Biography*, biographer of King Edward VII (1859–1926).

which get on my nerves. He said, 'When you get a bit older you'll cease to resent such things. I have lived into an era when "Sorry" and "Don't bother" have replaced the "I beg your pardon" and "Pray don't mention it" to which I was accustomed. One learns to accept the material which life provides. I am continually exasperated by what I see and hear around me, but I manage to adapt myself to the changes.' So perhaps he didn't altogether dislike the urbanities of E.G's club hospitality. One certainly finds good manners at the Marlborough.

March 2 (Hotel Gonnet, Cannes)

Rain beats against the window. Wind howls around the hotel. The walls of my bedroom are papered with perpendicular stripes of black and bilious red. Muffled dance-music goes dum-di-dum downstairs.

In a large looking-glass I see myself, pink and well-fed, seated at a small round table, smoking a pipe, my fountain-pen poised above the paper. All day the weather has been as bad as possible, but I am feeling quite contented, after a dinner which evoked encomiums from Schuster himself. 'The pea-soup—perfect. The blue trout—ambrosial. The orange soufflé—superb!' Thus spoke Schuster; and beckoned the waiter. '*Commandez deux cafés, et chauffez les tasses.*' This was at the Café de Paris, quiet and not overcrowded, with a pleasant little band playing Puccini and Massenet, the pianist interluding a couple of pieces by Debussy. We drank only some light claret ('a nice little Bordeaux') so I am not under the influence of alcohol. My thoughts move in a discreet and undishevelled procession. 'How pleasant,' I think, 'to be authentically *abroad*, with Schuster to arrange everything and order exquisite meals.' (He is a monarch among the *maitres d'hôtel* of Europe.)

March 5 (Eden Hotel, Cap d'Ail)

When writing my journal in foreign hotels, since the function can only be performed in my bedroom, I invariably scribble with the silent assistance of my own reflection in at least one looking-glass. This evening my companion has an air of well-being which is the outcome of a day of unclouded brilliance. All the morning I basked in the hotel garden and saw nothing but the sparkling of the sea. Never before had I understood the significance of the word 'sparkle', as applied to the ocean. 'The fireflies of the sunlight on the sea'. Surely this 'inevitable' line has occurred in the words of some complacent poet? After imbibing the beneficial brightness I went in to luncheon and found old Frankie much pleased because he'd been pacing up and down the terrace with Sir Squire Bancroft, who'd regaled him with reminiscences of every Hamlet he'd ever seen—from Booth to Barrymore. While we were finishing our luncheon (Schuster strongly objects to it being called 'lunch') Bancroft joined us. He seems a dear old chap, but was rather pathetically insistent on the fact that he has outlived his own generation.

Late in the afternoon I climbed to the Middle Corniche. The lower road is an inferno of limousines which make noises like angry wild animals, as they rush round corners with their cargoes of ugly elderly men and overdressed women. Escaping from this, one can soon discover solitude and stillness on rocky paths among dusty olives. And the expanse of ocean is magnificent. This evening it was the colour of a Conder.[1] I watched it fade slowly to the palest lavender, smooth as silk, with a mauve horizon. All the sparkles had vanished, and the effect was as delicate as a fan-painting. I have seldom seen anything more serene and lovely. Re-entering the hotel, I encountered the monocled octogenarian ex-actor-manager. He was pottering along the vast and gloomy corridor which leads to my room. I stopped and exchanged a few remarks with him, but felt shy.

March 6

The sea is sparkling again. Voices murmur pleasantly from the terrace below my window. Since breakfast I have extracted five grey hairs from my brown thatch—a reminder that I shall be forty in eighteen months. People who don't know my age still guess me to be a good deal younger than I am. On such a morning as this no one wants to be snowy-haired and eighty-four, like Bancroft, or parchment-bald and seventy-two, like Schuster. So I have blown my five silver hairs out to the calm

[1] Charles Conder (1868–1909). Painter of fans and water-colours.

blue sea and looked up (in Beeching's[1] *Paradise of English Poetry*) that poem of Peele's which begins:

> His golden locks Time hath to silver turned;
> O Time too swift, O swiftness never ceasing!
> His youth 'gainst time and age hath ever spurned,
> But spurned in vain; youth waneth by increasing:
> Beauty, strength, youth, are flowers but fading seen;
> Duty, faith, love, are roots and ever green.[2]

In the next room Frankie Schuster is putting himself to bed. I listen to him padding to and fro. Then—tweet—tweet—tweet—whistle—chiree—chiree—I hear a tiny shrill piping which stops as abruptly as it started. It is the eighteenth-century *Oiseau Enchanté* which he brought back from Nice this evening. (He paid £14 for it.) The box is charmingly painted with scenes in which a balloon is prominent. This exquisite little toy was unwrapped after dinner, to the delight of Bancroft, who bent his large bronzed and wrinkled face above the diminutive nightingale, exclaiming 'You dear!' while it warbled and agitated its wings. How strange to think that the songster was executing its mechanical recital eighty years before Bancroft was born. One might moralise on the meaning of that automatic cadenza, that epitome of technical ingenuity. One might say that human existence is itself a very small performance, and that few of us achieve the elegance and perfection of that charming toy.

Walking down from the Middle Corniche before dinner, looking at the glitter of lights along the coast, with the lamps of motors creeping up from Monaco and round the hill from Eze, I was inclined to moralise in similar style. I had been trying to tidy up my future, and wondering whether I'll ever write anything on a big scale; and then life suddenly seemed commonplace and restricted, and my own chance of a large achievement dwindled. 'Poor human beings,' I thought, 'groping their ways like the procession of hairy caterpillars I was watching this morning in the hotel garden when Gabriel came up the steps from the station in his smart blue suit with a red flower in his buttonhole.'

[1] Canon H. C. Beeching (1859–1919). This anthology appeared in 1892.
[2] The first stanza of 'A Farewell to Arms' by George Peele (c. 1558–98).

March 8

Since I came in from my walk (along the seaside rocks, nearly to Monaco) I've been ruminating, while cleaning the cover of my *Oxford Dictionary* with a piece of india-rubber. But the rubber has failed to remove the grime of Tufton Street from that brown binding. The thought of Tufton Street is positively repulsive to me, now that I am detached and feeling healthy for the first time since September. Health brings a vague mental discomfort from which I extract a sense of the futility of my existence. I suppose this is not unusual when one approaches forty. To realise that one has outlived the purposeful ignorance of youth, is that the main achievement of a successful maturity? One must try to serve the world in some small way, through the mind. But when my body is healthy my mind feels itself getting worsted by the animal in me. When I am unwell my mind is more athletic.

March 9

A breezy bright day with a few clouds which cause the burnished silver of the sea to be striped like a mackerel. I listen to the dry rustle of the palms and the squeaks of some Argentine children playing on the terrace. A few pages of Proust have made me wonder whether insignificant episodes aren't the most significant, in such a record as this. For instance, the most memorable event yesterday was, perhaps, the fact that Schuster changed a £10 cheque for me at the smart Beaulieu restaurant. The franc was at 94 last week, but he only brought me 850 francs. So the restaurant has done me out of about 50 francs. Another 'event' was that I finished yesterday evening with a wrangle about Wordsworth, of whom Gabriel spoke disrespectfully. Picking up my anthology, he remarked that 'Peele Castle' is a ridiculous poem, whereupon I rebuked him ferociously. 'One *must* be serious about something; and I happen to be serious about Wordsworth', and so on. Utterly absurdsworth, of course! But I went to bed morose, without saying good-night. Another 'significant' detail of these days is my being without a watch (which I associate with my inability to converse in French).

March 15 (Dominion Hotel, Avignon)

'A day of divine impressions', Schuster called it. But for me it was a day of bolted delicacies and wasted opportunities. I have 'seen' the Pope's Palace, Les Baux, Arles, Les Saintes Maries, Aigues-Mortes, and Nîmes. A busy day, in fact. But I mustn't grumble. Better a succession of snapshots than nothing at all. And the weather wasn't suitable for saunterings and lingerings. A starving cold wind, dust, and glaring sunshine made everything hard and colourless, shrivelling up one's sensuous-recording apparatus. Aigues-Mortes, for instance, should be visited toward the end of a still autumnal afternoon, 'where the afternoon light slept in the dreamiest, sweetest way', as Henry James described it. (I have been sweetening my impressions by reading his *Little Tour in France*.) Clothing the dry bones of to-day in that mantle of trained and temperate observation, I have envied H.J. his autumn travels, thirty years ago, envied him even his slow trains and crawling kilometres in horse-drawn carriages. For we have crowded into nine hours what should have been spread over a week. We 'did' the Palace of the Popes in ten minutes. From a window I heard a bird piping in the gardens and longed to be alone for an hour, watching the landscape and the roofs of Avignon smoking in Sunday morning sunshine, with snow-sprinkled mountains in the distance. But the Rolls-Royce was inexorable, and there wasn't a minute to spare for the perspectives of History. The salt marshes near Aigues-Mortes were enchanting, and the approach to Nîmes, in the low rays of a clear sunset. But we were raising no end of dust, and Schuster was busy with his *Baedeker*. He had seen most of the places before, and his indigestion has been bad lately. And Anzie was feeling the stress of driving so far over bad roads. So I made the best of it, hoarding up anything I could collect from the rush of cinematographic sightseeing.

March 26

Dined 17 Hanover Terrace. E.G. and Sylvia there—he at his best. Asked me a lot about Ralph Hodgson. Told me he is writing an article about Robert Graves's *Poetic Unreason*, and doing it with a real desire to give R.G. a leg up. A contrast to Turner telling me recently that he'd asked Virginia Woolf to write an 'attack' on Gosse in the *Calendar* (Edgell Rickword's 'advanced' magazine). I pointed out that this would be an outrage—knowing that E.G. would be deeply hurt—additionally, since V.W's father, Leslie Stephen, was a helpful friend to him. Why do they want to be 'attacking' everyone? (I have heard V.W. being a bit catty about E.G., but can't believe she would do it.)[1]

March 29 (54 Tufton Street)

This is one of those typical Tufton Street nights which I dread so much when I am away from London. O, the solitude of these nocturnal hours of inability to work or read or do anything except brood by the fire, turning at last to add a sterile page to this diary. It is a sort of voluntary insomnia, wherein my brain becomes more and more active, spinning its useless webs of disgruntled introspection. I try to read Edith Sitwell's *Sleeping Beauty*. Fail. Then try to write a little poetry of my own, self-consoling and mechanical. Of course it ends in a crumpled sheet of paper and a few extra flames in my small fire. Then I try to read Mottram's war-novel.[2] But that only routs out a muddle of morose memories from the lumber-room of my own war-experience. I am not exactly restless. Only condemned to a wakefulness in which I function with the dregs of my vitality.

I hear Turner turning over in bed; the creak of his bed, above my head. And the thought of him adds to my dreariness, since his existence now seems to me so dreary and frustrated. I go creeping downstairs and boil a kettle of water in the cheerless little kitchen. Make a cup of chocolate and fill a stone hot-water bottle. And return to my stuffy little room—telling myself that, after all, I have a fire to sit by, and a red-shaded reading lamp, and a vase of fading freesias.

March 30

Perhaps because I performed my dutiful pilgrimage to Pentonville this afternoon (I was there 6–8), perhaps because

---

[1] She wrote nicely about him when Evan Charteris's *Life and Letters* was published. S.S.

[2] *The Spanish Farm* (1925) by R. H. Mottram (1883–1971).

I have moved my writing-desk across the room and 'general-posted' the pictures, I am feeling a bit more hopeful this evening. Neither the bigamist Yorkshire farmer nor the scout-master who became 'over-enthusiastic' about some of his troop, can be described as stimulating talkers. But I have a sense of having helped them in their solitude. Both will be free in five weeks; I shall then only have one 'star man' (first offender) left, and of him I can't say that he is much of a man, in spite of his star. I am now (under a new system) allotted prisoners to visit as they arrive. They all seem to be hardened cases who take prison as part of their routine.

To-day, after lunching alone, I went to stare at the site of Devonshire House. Nothing survives now except the cellars. By the end of the year an enormous building will have been erected and the ducal house will be a demolished memory. Lansdowne House looks rather forlornly across its garden, as if expecting to share the fate of its neighbour. The last few days have been very grey, though rainless; no sign of spring yet, except an occasional daffodil in the Park.

March 31

Cheered up by the arrival of a large wooden box containing *Lingual Exercises*, I went off to lunch at the Reform carrying a couple of specimens. 'Delivering these by hand will make a nice little afternoon walk', I thought. Each copy has its own card-board slip-case. To ensure there being no error in delivery, I inscribed each case with the recipient's initials. 'It would never do for Gosse to get a copy inscribed *Henry and Ruth Head*', I thought, 'and it would be almost as bad if the Heads found their names condensed into Edmund Gosse.' The mere notion of such a mistake appalled me. I remembered how Henry—my kind and sagacious mentor—once said to me, 'I should like to write *the book of the year*, so that I could cut Gosse.' (The only time I've heard him speak bitterly of anyone.)

I knew the reason; for the remark was preceded by his story of how Gosse asked himself to dine with them in order to meet the poet Verhaeren[1] (pronounced *Vah-har-ren* in throaty tenor tones) who was staying with them on, I think, his first visit to London; and how, after a very agreeable evening (though

[1] Emile Verhaeren, Belgian poet (1855–1916).

Henry mentioned that Gosse's French was not good) E.G.,
when H. was seeing him out into Montagu Square, made his
extraordinary remark, 'What a pity it is that Verhaeren doesn't
know the right people!' Thinking aloud half a minute too soon.
And not easy to find excuse for. A remark which H.H. can't
forget—naturally. Yet, much as I love the Heads, I do realise
what E.G. felt. He had wanted to talk to the eminent Belgian
poet alone. And I can imagine how dear Ruth got on his nerves
with her loquacities. I remembered also an episode which I
heard of from Alec Ross.[1] He was dining at Hanover Terrace
and the Heads were there (previous, no doubt, to the Verhaeren
evening). Ruth, chatty and exuberant, upset her wine-glass and
only saved it from spilling by dexterity. 'How lucky!' she
exclaimed to E.G., who chillingly replied 'Yes, indeed. Most
providential.' Poor Ruth looked crushed; and Henry, of course,
would have been furious at such rudeness.

E.G. did once mention the Heads to me. It was a good example
of his peculiar disingenuousness. One fine May afternoon in
1923 I was sitting with him, after tea on the balcony at 17
Hanover Terrace. He had just received Robert Nichols's new
book *Fantastica* (which he described as pretentious bosh).
There was a letter with it (from Tokyo) pompous and ex-
planatory. He read it aloud, and then exclaimed, 'Really, it is as
though Shakespeare were writing to an insect!' (An experience
which *I'd* often endured from R.N.) One of the tales was
dedicated to E.G. The next one was 'To Henry and Ruth
Head'. Fluttering the pages impatiently, he inquired, 'Who *are*
Henry and Ruth Head?' Obviously I couldn't say, '*You* know
jolly well who they are! What price Verhaeren?' I could only
explain, with inward embarrassment, that Dr Head was Bob
N's most valued friend and medical adviser. To which E.G.
replied, 'Ah, yes. Very worthy people, I believe.' So this little
comedy of incompatibilities between my friends has been in
progress for the last four or five years, rendered more comic by
my being such an unconcealing character. For when with the
Heads, my delightful times at Hanover Terrace feel almost like
a guilty secret. And my dining-out activities seem to be mainly
restricted to the Gosses and the Heads.

But I must return to this afternoon. My plan was as follows.

[1] Alexander Galt Ross (1861–1927). Elder brother of Robbie.

I would sneak up to Gosse's door, pop the slip-case into the letter-box, and then toddle away to Montagu Square and have tea with the 'worthy people', whom I've rather neglected lately. My new book would be quite an exciting event for them (as it is for me).

It was quiet grey weather. Spring was in the air. Thrushes were singing confidently in Regent's Park, and young men were sculling their skiffs on the canal. Seeing the present as the past is a favourite trick of mine; and here, surely was a little incident which could acquire a certain retrospective charm and significance. Might not Sir Edmund himself, in some future reincarnation, refer to this very hour of my existence in a graceful essay called 'A Twentieth-Century Diarist'? 'Among the innumerable clarified immediacies of intimate experience which he has preserved so adroitly in his journals there is one that I can never read without emotion. It is that passage in which we observe the poet—now in his thirty-ninth year but still quivering with youthful ardours—carrying the first copy of his *Lingual Exercises* to Edmund Gosse, the agèd and eminent littérateur toward whom he had always looked for advice and encouragement. We watch him, on that quiet grey afternoon of early spring, hastening across the Regent's Park, and we share his eager and tremulous anxiety lest the verses on which he had lavished such toil might fail to win the hallmark of the great critic's approval. A copy of the rare little volume lies before me now, in its faded leaf-brown buckram binding, and its delicately ingenious cadences can still be read with moderate enjoyment. But it was by his diaries that the author would compel the attention of posterity, though of course, all innocently unaware . . .'

Meanwhile I was feeling happy; and in my hand I carefully carried the large envelope containing those two inaugural copies. Entering Hanover Terrace, I extracted one, scrutinised the monogram ⒺⒼ on the slip-case, went up the iron steps and along the arcade, and, not wishing to be observed, passed the dining-room window quickly. I then pushed the case through the front door. Plop! it dropped modestly into the letter-box. My watch said 4.20. I had delivered the first copy to its most appropriate recipient.

Emerging into Baker Street—with a left-hand glance at the burnt-out ruins of Madame Tussaud's Exhibition—I boarded a bus. Sitting in the bus, I thought 'I'll have another squint at the title-page'. Luxuriously I drew the slim volume from its case (marked ⊞). Yes; it looked as elegantly anonymous as ever, with its quotation from Psalm 131, 'I am not high-minded; I have no proud looks. I do not exercise myself in great matters which are too high for me.' Nice, too, that the whole production had only cost me £35, and that every copy would be given away by me. Turning the page, my heart stood still and I went cold all over. For there, below '99 copies printed February 1925', the words *Edmund Gosse* confronted me in my neat calligraphy. 'Jesus wept!' I exclaimed, jumping off the bus without waiting for it to slow down and bounding on to another which was going toward Hanover Terrace at express speed. The idea of E.G. inspecting that copy was too catastrophic to be dwelt on. Skulking along to No. 17 a few minutes later, I inserted a forlorn hope arm elbow-deep in the letter-box. Too late! My fingers groped in vain. I rang the bell, with just a hope that he hadn't yet returned from his club. Parlour-maid appeared. 'Is Sir Edmund in?' '*Yes*, sir.' (Parker's voice had never sounded more emphatic.) 'Sir Edmund has been unwell.' She went upstairs with my nonplussed name. 'Henry and Ruth Head. O hell!' I stood in the hall gazing gloomily at Sir Edmund's umbrella. Then Sylvia Gosse appeared on the stairs. 'O do come up! Father'll be so glad to see you. He's had a cold and is staying in.' Sylvia was a great relief. She has such a sense of humour, and a keen eye for her father's idiosyncracies. Much amused by my explanation of the dilemma, she took charge of the 'real copy', slipped into E.G's bedroom ahead of me, and skilfully substituted the right volume for the wrong one, which was lying uncasedly at his elbow. Wrapped in a fawn-coloured dressing-gown, he was in an arm-chair with his back to the window. With slightly dishevelled hair and the one dark glass to his spectacles, he looked old and forlorn. Always before I had seen him spruce and alert. After a little preliminary talk, I picked up *Lingual Exercises*—a modest and casual gesture. 'So *this* is *your* book, my dear Siegfried! I am indeed delighted. But' (with a puzzled air) 'I had been assuming

hat it was by *Ruth and Henry Head*. I could discover no other
indication of the authorship!' Barefacedly I opened the book and
showed him his name. 'Dear me; how very extraordinary!
What could have made me imagine such a thing?' Then, of
course, I capitulated, and explained that a mistake had been
made. 'And Sylvia changed them . . . legerdemain!' he exclaimed. That was all. The 'worthy people' weren't mentioned
again. Soon afterwards, just as I was pouring out the tea, Jack
Squire turned up. E.G. brightened, and gave us a detailed and
amusing account of his work as Librarian of the House of Lords,
where for ten years he contrived to spend £3000 a year on
books, the cost being charged to the Board of Works as for
pens, ink, and blotting-paper'. He thus converted the dull and
obsolete library into a good one; although, he confessed, 'the
noble lords but seldom referred to the shelves'. Squire looked
slightly ill at ease as he sat there. He is devoted to E.G., but
evidently cannot be *entirely* candid in his presence.

April 4

To-day I went sixteen miles out of London, to watch the
Bar Point-to-Point Races at Northaw. This was a fortuitous
outing. I was induced to go by Judge Sturges, who pressed a
Paddock Ticket on me at the Reform Club last night. After
sleeping badly—awake till daylight—I felt in need of fresh air,
and the day was a good mixture of cloud, sunshine, and shrewd
wind. In the Paddock I bumped into a former brother-officer—
named *Stable*! He was all dressed up for a ride in the first race,
and very excited. 'Last time I saw you, you came down to
Battalion Headquarters with a head punched in your hole!' he
exclaimed. (He meant to say 'a hole punched in your head'.)
He finished fourth in a field of six very moderate fourteen-stone
hunters. Among the six was a ponderous chestnut, owned by
my friend Sturges. The chestnut had come all the way from
Nuneaton for the contest. After surmounting four fences it shed
its jockey, a hard-bitten K.C. named Reeve. Lonely, and unaided
by human control, it travelled as far as the water-jump, where
it decided that honour (and His Honour Judge Sturges) was
satisfied, and by now it is on its way home to Nuneaton (to

spend the summer in a grass field). Stimulated by a glass o'
port, at the Judge's car, I forsook the crowd and watched the
Open Race from a distant part of the course. Men in coloured
jerseys and silk jackets urging their horses from field to field
reminded me of my own race-riding efforts two years ago, and
I felt half-regretful that the literary life debars me from com-
peting any more. But the feeling evaporated, and I set off to
Potter's Bar without waiting for the next race. Had an egg and
a cup of tea there, caught a suburban train, and by six o'clock I
was walking past the pelicans in St James's Park. Those ungainly birds were flapping their wings on their island with a
certain sunset grandeur. The Pegasus Club Point-to-Point did
not interest them, or I'd have been pleased to tell them that
Skylark had won the Heavyweight Race, after a ding-dong
struggle up the straight with—was it Dutch Courage?

Not having been on a race-course for two years, I felt the
queerness of my present existence, as compared with the life I
led before the war, when point-to-points were as important as
anything else in my retarded career. I know well enough that
horsemanship is less important than the art of poetry, but my
love of horses is deeply rooted, and I had an exiled feeling.
Viewed from the detachment of to-day, the sportsmen and the
countrified people in their comfortable clothes produced an
impression of contentment which I envied.

To-night I am haunted by memories, evoked by the hunt-
servants I saw this afternoon, red-faced and scarlet-coated,
sitting on grey horses on the green hill where they were
'keeping the course'. They evoked memorial ghosts of half-
forgotten health and happiness, reviving my youth and raw
inexperience, and the charm of a world seen vaguely through
the irrational magic of animal sensations.

Dining at the club I was joined by Chalmers Mitchell, the
white-haired but not old-faced Director of the Zoological
Gardens. His excuse for joining me was that he couldn't read a
book because his oculist had applied some drug to his eyes,
which caused them to function, till tomorrow, dimly. (While
he told me this, I remembered that Sir R. Cruise, the King's
Oculist, was riding in the Open Race at Northaw.) Mitchell
is—or pretends to be—somewhat cynical. But he talks well, in
a deliberate, quizzical style which makes me feel a blunderer.

Ie has been reading the whole of Wordsworth and finds no
ıerit there, except in a dozen poems which, he admits, are
bove criticism. (A dozen immortal poems ought to be enough
ɔr one author, I thought.)[1] He went on to deplore the neglect
f John Davidson[2] by contemporary taste, and considers Max
Seerbohm very much over-rated. Mitchell is a man who creates
feeling of disappointment, and does it on purpose. Even when
peaking of poor Davidson he said, 'Of course he was a fool, a
ounder, and a pedant.' But he rewarded me by referring
ffectionately to Robbie Ross (who introduced me to him in
hat same room, eight years ago).

When I told him I'd been to the Bar Point-to-Point, he
xclaimed, contemptuous and surprised, 'What on earth made
ou do that?' and strolled away without waiting for my ex-
ɔlanation. I wonder whether he is fond of animals. Afterwards
read a story by de la Mare (in the *London Mercury*) about a
arrot possessed by a devil and an angel.[3]

April 9 (The Hut, Bray)

To-day seemed like an exodus from the long winter. My
wenty nights in London have almost made me forget that I
vent across France and back in March. After lunch I set off in
ny little car, driving it for the first time since January 8. I drove
ut of town with a real sense of escape. Strolling on the lawn
ɔefore dinner, with the leafless elms and poplars reflected in a
wilight river, surrounded by the warbling of birds, a soothing
ense of my days here last summer returned to me, almost with
. sense of regret, although I wasn't often aware of being happy
t the time. And now I sit linking up to-night with the last time
was here, six months ago. The house is a little strange, in its
ıntidiness of alterations and additions—a new wing built on
ınd electric light installed. Tick-tock, tick-tock, goes the busy
ıttle clock on the mantelpiece. Comfort pervades me as I warm
ny feet by the fire. The night is very still; leafless trees that
nove not a twig, and the moon a blur of white in a hazy sky.

On another occasion C.M. said 'One of A. E. Housman's poems is worth all that
Bridges has ever written.' S.S.
Scottish poet (1857–1909).
'Pretty Poll', included in de la Mare's *The Connoisseur and Other Stories* (1926).

Nothing to be heard but a peewit along the river-meadows and
the surge of a distant train. 'Everyone drowsy; only the clock
are alert.' Old Frankie snoring downstairs, his knitting of .
wool rug ended for this evening. Anzie and Wendela reposing
after their exertions in London. Mr Spring, the Aberdeer
terrier, done with the barking and sniffing of the day. Only
myself (and the clocks) alert.

April 10

An easy day which has made me feel more vegetable than
intellectual. Sunshine soaked into me and soft straight rain
showered down at intervals, sprinkling the gardens as though
every drop were one of next week's daisies. After a succulent
luncheon (including cold lobster and hot prune-pie) I played
the piano and strolled about idly. Then drove Schuster to Lady
Annesley's, and after listening to her amusing chatter in her
'dinky' little house near Maidenhead, went on to Taplow to
see the de la Mares in their new house, which they moved into
six weeks ago. Colin[1] greeted me, pale and queer-eyed, with
lock of dark hair on his forehead, charming as ever. His parents
were having tea at Taplow Court, but came in before I left. The
house is pleasantly old-fashioned, red brick, with an arbutus
leaning over the narrow front-gate. This evening I've done
nothing but sit by the fire, chattering fat-headedly and watching
Schuster knit his wool mat, while Anzie reclined contentedly on
a sofa with his Wendela. What else could I expect to be doing
Anyhow I played a little Brahms and Bach before going to bed
and so the day ends. How different from London, where each
day is struggled through in semi-solitude. At dinner I put
corked-up bottle of claret by the fire, left it too long, picked i
up boiling hot, shook it facetiously, and it exploded with a lou
pop! No damage done, except to the floor.

I must remember this Good Friday with gratitude. Waking
after a sound sleep to watch the soft spring sunshine flooding i
on a chair with my blue jersey hanging across it; waking to
hear the birds singing their escape from winter. I must remem
ber the white pigeons fluttering lazily from one apple-tree t

[1] Walter de la Mare's younger son.

another, and Anzie paddling his canoe across to the island, with the two dogs sitting solemnly beside him. And de la Mare's cheery farewell as he stood under the arbutus with Colin in the twilight. All this I *shall* remember some day, when I am turning over my old diaries. And I shall know then, with a pang, that I *was* happy.

April 11 (Hill Hall, Theydon Mount)

Why am I here, and how did I get here? I am here because I am here and because Mrs Charles Hunter[1] invited me (promising the presence of Max Beerbohm as a bait). Schuster drove me here in his two-seater this afternoon, in 'brilliant holiday weather'. Hill Hall (as all the best people know) is two miles from Epping, and only fifteen from London. It is a beautiful Elizabethan plus William-and-Mary mansion in a large park on a ridge. Poor Mrs Hunter, whose cash comes from coal-mines, is entertaining her last house-party before selling the house. The absence of Max is a regrettable feature of the party. Elizabeth Bibesco[2]—expected for dinner only—arrived with her luggage and ousted me from the bedroom which I'd been allotted. She told me that she 'found my beautiful blue pyjamas under her pillow'. I did not tell her what I found on the writing-table of this small room (which she must have rejected as too small while I was out in the park before dinner). What I found was the manuscript of a short story by her (for which she'd evidently utilised someone's letters to her). I skimmed through it and gave it to one of the butlers (there are two, both resembling ex-prime ministers). Unaccustomed as I am to this sort of hospitality, I went down to dinner feeling rather shy and hostile. We had arrived at tea-time but I escaped soon afterwards and rambled about the green park inspecting the mellow pink-and-white mansion from various angles until the scarlet disc of the sun dipped behind Epping Forest and the squawking peacocks flapped up into the cedars for a snooze. In the dusk pheasants ejaculated and blackbirds warbled. Everything was county-family-ish and imbued with high-toned prosperity. Three large obese shooting-dogs lolloped around the house,

[1] Mary (1857–1931), wife of Charles Hunter. Sister of Dame Ethel Smyth.
[2] Novelist daughter of H. H. Asquith, married to Prince Antoine Bibesco.

and church-bells tolled for Easter evensong. Under a red-brick wall pink with peach-blossom there was a 'fine show' of daffodils. Strolling around I made up my mind to get all I could from this environment without putting myself to an atom of inconvenience. But I remembered that Robbie Ross used to stay here a good deal, which caused me to feel well-disposed toward Mr. Hunter (elderly and gold-haired, in gardening gauntlets).

There were a dozen of us at dinner, at two tables, in an exquisite room—gilt and painted Venetian walls and ceiling superimposed on the original Elizabethan structure. The party included Cyril Scott[1] (the composer) and his wife, and Mrs. Annie Swynnerton (the aged A.R.A.).[2] After a dinner of salmon and asparagus and turkey and soufflé and champagne and port and brandy and a fine cigar (and conversation which made me feel an intellectual colossus) we adjourned to the noble galleried hall and listened to the piano-playing of Cyril Scott—an agreeable *réchauffé* of Debussy, Ravel, Scriabin, Strauss, Albeniz, (and Scott). After this feast of tone-colour, everyone except Princess Bibesco seemed to have had enough social and aesthetic exercise. The elders faded away to bed, leaving E.B. to lecture the young men on American tennis-champions, and air her epigrams. *She* is a champion eater and drinker.

I am now entrenched in a bedroom furnished with an ancient painted writing-table, and two ancient painted Italian cupboards, and hung with half-a-dozen Japanese colour-prints, all probably very valuable.

April 12

Hill Hall is certainly a delightful house to stay in. Leaning out of my window this morning I watched two peacocks trailing their plumage on the upper branches of an immense cedar, while a swan ferried its reflection across an Elizabethan fish-pond unruffled by wind and guarded by stone statues stained green with damp. In the afternoon the weather turned wet, but I browsed pleasantly in the library, overlooked by the Smyth family-portraits. I became quite friendly with poor purblind

[1] Composer, librettist and author (1879–1970).
[2] Died 1933.

Mrs Swynnerton, mainly by telling her that Hamo Thornycroft is my uncle. She spoke bitterly against Sickert's work, but I pleased her by saying that my mother has often spoken admiringly about 'The Sense of Sight' (Mrs Swynnerton's best known picture). Ironical, this, because she really is almost blind. At dinner Mrs Hunter (a jolly old Jingo) said to Elizabeth Bibesco, 'The only thing I can't forgive your father is that he wouldn't introduce conscription during the war.' After dinner Scott played a Wagner pot-pourri in his beautiful boudoir-exotic style. Elizabeth Bibesco (rather tipsy in tight white satin) rather spoilt the effect by sitting down to the piano and giving us a few bits of Brahms (while Scott looked as sour as a quince).

April 15 (The Hut, Bray)

Thankful to be here again instead of at 54 Tufton Street (which always seems extra grim after staying somewhere comfortable).

Yesterday morning Mrs Hunter motored off to London to spend the day with her old friend J.S. Sargent.[1] She took with her a letter from Schuster, asking Sargent to subscribe to the Fauré Memorial Concert on June 9 (which concert Schuster is organising with his usual melodophilic energy). Coming in this evening I glanced casually at the *Evening Standard* lying on a table and saw a large headline, 'Mr Sargent Dies in his Sleep. Famous Artist Passes Away To-day'. Schuster, who had been busy all the afternoon hanging engravings and water-colours from his (late) London house expressed heartfelt regret. He'd known Sargent for forty years. But such departures aren't allowed to trouble him long, and I drove him to Lady Annesley's dinner-party without being aware of any depression. I dined at Skindles Hotel and went up to the de la Mares afterwards. De la Mare was amused when I told him how Mrs Hunter said to Schuster—about me—'From reading his war-poems I should never have thought he was such a charming man.'

Picked up Schuster on my way home, and found him in festive surroundings—a jazz-band playing, and young men in white waistcoats smoothing their sleek hair and pulling on their white gloves.

[1] American painter, especially of portraits (1856–1925).

Last night I dreamt that I was going to have a growth cut out of my insides by Henry Head. I kept insisting that he must get me sewn up again quick, as I had to ride in a point-to-point at 5.30. I can remember feeling doubtful whether I should emerge from the anaesthetic in time for the race.

April 16

Very windy weather. Drove Schuster to Marlow, to a party given by General Sir George Higginson. '*Dancing: 4 to 8*.' The General will be ninety-nine in two months. He was spoken to by King George IV, while out in the Park with his nurse. (He was three-and-a-half at the time, and thinks he remembers it.) He was shaking hands with his guests in the garden—a sort of ceremonial parade. Schuster went up and made a little con-gratulatory speech, almost *too* polite and ingratiating! The General was very brisk, and when the dancing had started I saw him go across the room and give some special instructions to the jazz-band. This was keeping the game alive indeed! I didn't dance, but sat in a side-room reading Arnold Bennett's first novel, *A Man from the North*, which seemed pretty poor stuff.

April 17

To London for the afternoon. Went to private view of Max's Exhibition at Leicester Galleries. Called for letters at Tufton Street. Two about *Lingual Exercises*. One from Max Gate. T.H. thinks the book an advance on my previous poems (and Mrs T.H. supplements this by writing that he said 'Really these are *very* good', when she read them to him). T.E. Lawrence quotes what T.H. said to him: 'Somebody wrote to me that they weren't as good as the old Sassoon poetry; but I thought they were good; very good indeed. Better than the war-poetry and the American poems. I liked them very much.' This is very reassuring.

April 18 (after putting the clock on for 'summer time')

Haven't been outside the garden-gate all day. Weeded the

lawn for a couple of hours after lunch. Mrs Stevenson[1] staying here. Her husband is in the Embassy at Sofia, where they blew up the Cathedral two days ago. This evening Schuster received a cheque from Sargent, dated the day of his death and sent on by his sister. (It was his subscription— £6.6.0—to the Fauré concert.) So he can meet Fauré in the next world with a clear conscience.

April 21 (54 Tufton Street)

Life is built of trivial happenings; when one looks back along the avenue of months or years, one sees the foliage, not the separate leaves. To-day's leaves seem narratable to-night because I am mentally vigorous. Yet I began the day jaded and rheumy-eyed, after lying awake till 5 a.m.

Talking to Meiklejohn at the club after lunch didn't raise my intellectual temperature. As usual he grumbled along in his Treasury official style. Talking about *Lingual Exercises*, he said: 'Yes, they're quite good. I must read them again; it won't take long. And one sometimes gets more out of a second reading of poetry.' Meekly I replied, 'Yes; I think the workmanship is quite competent.' M. only discovers merit in authors when they've been dead fifty years. When dead two thousand years they are beyond criticism. (In two thousand years I shan't be there at all.)

Setting out for my walk in the Park, I remembered my photograph in this month's *Vogue* (a journal which I ordinarily despise). Having purchased a copy and admired my physiognomy, I tucked it under my arm and sunned myself in Hyde Park. The bright flower-beds, the pale green froth of foliage, and the shadows of trees on prosperous greensward—these obvious things made a charming background for the people who sat or sauntered in the late afternoon light. But I was meditating, most of the time, not about eternal verities and austerities, but about my own photograph in a fashion journal. What a conceited superficial ass the man must be, thinks my invisible reader. (For there *must* be one, or I shouldn't be writing these pages so punctiliously.) Worse still, I can remember wondering

[1] Wendela's sister Helen, who was married to Ralph Stevenson (1895–1977), diplomat and later Ambassador. He was knighted in 1946.

whether people will be impressed by the suffering aspect of the countenance. Lapsing a degree lower, I speculated as to the number of *Vogue* readers who might—after perusing the care-worn countenance—order a copy of my *Selected Poems*.[1] Vanity of vanities! But why should I feel ashamed to confess it? Such small episodes can help to stimulate me.

During dinner at the Reform I was reading *The Prisoners of War*, a painful but interesting play.[2] At page fifteen, I was joined by Jack Huntingdon.[3] I showed him the book, explaining that the hero is a tormented homosexual officer, which led me to dilate rather rashly on the subject of dealing with that theme in literature. 'Some day I shall write my autobiography,' I said, adding that I am accumulating material in my diaries. Was this wise, I wonder? For when one starts talking about a thing so nebulous as an unwritten autobiography, there is a danger that one may talk about it until it is too late to put anything on paper. Anyhow the conversation reminded me that a lot of these pages are probably worthless and woolly-headed—a mere jungle of insignificant grumblings. And the people who populate my pages—are they interesting or important? Possibly their *literary* importance is irrelevant. But I should like to be certain as to which of the 'characters' in my personal panorama are organically essential to my mind-life. Robert Graves, for instance. He and Nancy had asked me to go and see them this evening. After dinner I went. They are staying with his sisters, who live somewhere off St John's Wood Road. And there I found Robert, uncouth and charming, affectionate and impulsive, complaining that London upsets his nerves. And there was his younger brother Charles, who is 'assistant news-editor' of the *Sunday Express* and boasts that he has scribbled two thousand words a day for the last four years—a horrible achievement! And there was Nancy, queer and uncouth, concealing her shyness behind a mask of sharp-tongued reserve. The two sisters were friendly, but I bore the brunt, doing my best to 'make things go' by telling them anything that came into my head. There was also a black-and-tan collie puppy named Rufty, which R. and N. had brought with them from Islip. Rufty lay languidly

[1] Published on 23 April 1925.
[2] By J. R. Ackerley (1896–1967). Published in 1925.
[3] The fifteenth Earl of Huntingdon, artist (b. 1901).

on a camp-bed. Robert's four children were also in the house'
supposedly asleep.

April 22

Dumped down on this post-midnight shore of solitude, I feel
depressed, but not so deflated as to be incapable of recording
another day. After writing last night's entry I finished *Prisoners
of War*. I so seldom read anything even remotely connected
with 'the subject nearest my heart' that almost any work of that
kind causes a peculiar emotional disturbance in me. And all
to-day I have carried about with me an inward sense of home-
sickness for that land where I would be—that Elysium, forever
deluding me with its mirage in the desert of my frustrated and
distorted desires. I know that real happiness cannot be created
by any sensual Elysium. But even a ramshackle Elysium is
alluring, when the discredited oasis beckons me toward its dis-
enchanted groves, though I know that the reality would leave
me desolate and dissatisfied. But enough of that.

I went to 40 Half Moon Street for tea, and the homely good-
nature of Nellie Burton was a help. Burton was feeling bright;
her cosy room was full of tulips and roses, given her by the
amiable theosophist who occupies her 'best suite'. And she'd
'been on the bust and bought six silk jumpers' (for her bust!);
with each jumper, she explained, she'd wear a different bead-
necklace. 'When I change my necklace it brings me luck,' she
said, helping herself to another doughnut and putting three
lumps of sugar in her second cup of tea. She was wearing one of
the new jumpers, bright scarlet, and waiting for the evening
paper which would tell her what had won the City and Suburban.
She likes to have a small bet now and again. Portly N.B. is
always worth writing about, but I despair of ever being able to
describe her adequately. Her humanity is Shakespearean in its
proportions. She is a sort of female Mr Jorrocks. Schuster dined
with me at the Reform and we went to Queen's Hall to hear an
indifferent performance of Elgar's oratorio *The Kingdom*. But
the music soothed me, and I came home feeling that the day had
been got through fairly well.

The bus I got into at Piccadilly Circus was one of those which
the London General Omnibus Company calls 'pirates'. These

shabby buses are always slow starters, since they hope to pick up as many passengers as possible. At Trafalgar Square several people got in and then got out again, irritated by the dallying demeanour of the 'pirate'. I felt impatient myself, and was about to get out. Then I noticed the face of the conductor. He was a tired middle-aged man with a gentle diffident expression. I saw that he was sadly aware of his vehicle's lack of prestige. He stood—one hand on the bell-string—with a patient humble look which made me sympathetic. So I remained where I was, meditating on the humanising effect of the episode. And I was rewarded, for the old bus went down Whitehall full gallop. I watched the grey-haired man gently collecting the pennies; he smiled charmingly at two poorly-dressed little boys, and I was glad to be healed by such simplicity. Strange that one can get a moral lesson from a motor omnibus.

April 23 [S.S's *Selected Poems* published]

Last night (after doing my diary) I sat up till 5 a.m. writing thirty-nine lines of semi-satirical verse. Was awakened at 8 by the telephone bell ringing persistently. No one answered it. No doubt it was someone trying to ring up Victoria Station, which they do quite often, owing to an unlucky similarity of the numbers. Lunching at the club, I saw C. F. G. Masterman—that famous political failure—who stopped at my table to tell me that my Wembley poem (in *Lingual Exercises*) is 'one of the great poems of the century'.[1] I sincerely hope that he is right, but mustn't be too sanguine! I also met Meiklejohn, who conveyed to me an offer from the Medici Publishing Society. Would I go to Australia next winter and write a descriptive booklet (20,000 words); £60 and all expenses paid. I can't write such stuff, but might have accepted if it had been anywhere but Australia. Turner's native land attracts me even less than this room in his house, so I must try and find some less economical means of escape. After tea I went to Pentonville. Dining at the club I was joined by H. G. Wells, who treated me to the best claret and talked with his usual vigour and friendliness. He said that Conrad's books are very much *over-written*, which is probably true; I wish H.G. took as much trouble in finishing his own books, all the same.

[1] See pp. 117–19.

April 24

I am a diffident and dallying diarist to-night. My evening
ended too early, when, after two enjoyable hours of dinner and
discussion, Robert Graves left the Reform at exactly nine o'clock.
He only had to go up to Apple Tree Yard (three minutes' walk)
but his wife was awaiting him and he'd invited Paul Nash[1] to
join them; to have gone with R.G. would, I felt, have upset my
evening's equilibrium, for I wanted to take those two hours
away undimmed by any 'afterwards' of perfunctory sociability.
So I was left, high and dry and slightly flushed with Burgundy,
and the rest of the evening has been solitary and unsatisfactory.
I came home to play the piano, but hadn't struck three chords
before the Turners returned and smashed up that consolation,
for I was embarking on my favourite emotional rendering of
Elgar's Violin Concerto. Turner went upstairs at once—complaining of having caught a chill—but I was unable to continue
the Concerto because he hates it, and after fumbling a page of
Bach I abandoned the instrument in semi-disgruntlement. I can
no longer conceal the fact that I've lost touch with Turner.
Everything he says, does, and is, irritates me. (Unfortunately he
seems unaware of this.) I suppose my feeling is caused by my
dislike of living here and the impossibility of leaving. This
afternoon I went to the Zoo, having arranged to meet the
Graves family there. I found the children awaiting their turn for
a ride on the camel. Nancy was pushing the baby in an odd little
folding perambulator. R.G., as usual, was being gentle and
patient with the children. It always touches my heart when I see
him with them. They are countrified little creatures, chubby and
frolicsome. William Nicholson and his son Ben[2] (and wife)
joined us, and after a long stare at the monkey house,[3] we went
into the Aquarium, which Robert enjoyed immensely, in spite
of his parental responsibilities. Then they all crowded into the
tea-house and there I left them to it.

Nancy is quite friendly with me, but I always feel awkward
with her. It was quite a concession on her part when she allowed
Robert to dine with me.

[1] Painter (1899–1946).
[2] Painter (1894–1982). O.M. 1968.
[3] This monkey house visit, combined with some volumes of 'Curious Characters'
which I gave him [Graves] last Xmas, caused him to write *The Marmosite's
Miscellany*. S.S.

April 29

The last two hours have been used for writing to Bob Nichols
(in California). He wrote, acknowledging his copy of *Lingual
Exercises*, on seven large saffron sheets, signing himself 'yours
in the name of Poetry and the words I WILL'. Of my poems he
says, 'I get a good deal of pleasure out of them, though whether
I am an "Advanced Vocabularian" or no I cannot say. Personally
I am infernally tired of all known vocabularies. For me the
principal thing is to have the courage to be what one wills . . . I
am fundamentally interested only in heroic literature.' Then he
goes off into a lecture on why Shelley is a 'world poet' and who
isn't. Tennyson, Rossetti, Swinburne, Matthew Arnold, and
Browning aren't. Leopardi, Turgenev, and Rimbaud are! He is
'tired of this dropsied age and its regrets'. 'I am for going
straight for the big problems, chief of which is Creationism
versus Possessionism.' 'All that England has been in the past
means nothing to me if it is not a foretelling of what England
may be in the future . . . We need a creative and co-operative
Commonwealth of Empire.' 'I want an enterprising England,
highly technical, highly imaginative, determined, elastic—an
England, in short, that shall initiate the Modern Age as
opposed to mere Modernism.' Such a letter speaks for itself!
'In short' . . . He might well have added 'In short, I am writing
to you as if you are a Mass Meeting.' However I contrived to
reply without being unkind in my plea for a more humanised
medium of epistolary communication.

April 30

Talking (or being talked to) by Clifford Sharp[1] after my club
dinner, I put out one of my modest antennae in search of
reassurance about the art of keeping a journal. But the editor of
the *New Statesman* pooh-poohed the idea of any modern diary
being important as literature. 'Pepys is the only existing
masterpiece; there *are* no other diaries. And Pepys is great
because he was that rarest thing, a man who could write and
was at the same time a simple-minded man.' This rather dashed
me, though he doesn't know that I am a diarist, and is probably
unaware that I am somewhat simple-minded. I'd merely

[1] Journalist (1883–1935). First editor of the *New Statesman* (1913–31).

suggested that a modern diary might be more interesting to posterity than most modern novels.

So I withdrew my snail-like sensory feeler, and he went on with his orotund survey of the landscape of literature. Sharp is one of those men whose mental monarchy exists mainly when he is writing his weekly article. When he brings this editorial omniscience into club conversation one feels that he is only assuming a toga of factitious importance. In appearance he is a rather shoddy imitation of a rather bounderish Roman Emperor. He is an able journalist and editor. But when pronouncing finalities on famous authors he seems a bit of a windbag. Reinforced by the 'double brandy' which he occasionally consults, he goes god-like from reputation to reputation with sanction or censure, while I sit meekly at his elbow, now and again applying conversational aids in a chameleonic spirit. 'I differed from him only to delude', as some eighteenth-century coupleteer might have put it. While he was deploring the aridity of contemporary poetry, I inwardly wondered whether he would mention *Lingual Exercises,* which I sent him three weeks ago, several of the pieces having appeared in his paper. Had he forgotten about it, or was he masking his embarrassed inability to say anything at all? Luckily I said nothing, for at the ultimate moment, when he had his hat on and was entangled in his overcoat in a twilight punctuated by hat-pegs and umbrella-handles, he 'O, by the way'-ed me about 'the little book you sent me', thereby revealing that he hadn't read it (some day he will sell it for several pounds). 'Do you want it reviewed?' he asked. 'O, no. I only sent it round to my friends. Most of it was only written for my own amusement. There's no point in reviewing it,' I replied, with effrontery. He looked quite non-plussed.

May 1

The sky was cumbered with dark clouds when I walked across Hyde Park this afternoon (after dropping in to Wigmore Hall to hear Dohnányi[1] play Beethoven's Op. III Sonata). The May Day Labour Demonstrations weren't impressive, numerically. Nor were they impressive in their human texture. For 'the

[1] Hungarian composer and pianist (1877–1960).

Workers' were, most of them, at work, and the proceedings were a *Daily Herald* day-out. From a cart the shrill voice of Mrs Ayrton Gould[1] was urging something or other to about a hundred apathetic and unintelligent-looking people. No doubt she was 'urging' something absolutely essential for the emancipation of the workers. A brass-band was tootling 'The Red Flag'. A few hundred persons were imbibing the stentorian utterances of a pot-bellied man in a bowler hat. He, without economy or variety of gesture, was denouncing Sir Alfred Mond[2] and 'seven-day shifts, seven-day shifts, seven-day shifts, till they drop down dead, and all this is happening now, my friends, is happening a few miles from Swansea. I say it again—seven-day shifts, seven-day shifts, and let them arrest me if they dare!' Above his head someone was exalting a crudely painted banner on which was the face of Lenin. Women and children had been conveyed from the East End in waggons to enjoy these May Day delights. The waggons were drawn up along Park Lane. Rain had fallen heavily during the afternoon and the wind was northerly and cold. As I went out at Hyde Park Corner I could hear the sound of remote cheering. It seemed rather pathetic. What chance have these people and their crudely 'agitating' orators against Mond and Mammon? To-morrow the *Daily Herald* will be full of it. Messages of 'fraternity' will have been conveyed to brother-workers in France, Germany, and the Slovaks and Slovenes. And Mond will go on with his industrial enterprises and his orchid-growing.

May 2 (Chilswell)

The Poet Laureate is an early rooster. I've already been in my bedroom half an hour, wondering whether I shall be asleep by 4 a.m. Meanwhile I can smoke a couple of pipes and fill a few more pages. Tennyson may have been 'a sort of Apollo'—as FitzGerald said of him at Cambridge—but I am sure he never looked more bard-like than Bridges did when I arrived this evening and he stood in the late sunlight, waving me into the

---

[1] Labour activist (d. 1950). Wife of Gerald Gould (1885–1936), poet and critic, and mother of Michael Ayrton (1921–75), artist and writer.

[2] 1868–1930. Industrialist and former Liberal M.P. Chairman of I.C.I. Made a Baronet 1910, first Lord Melchett 1928.

shed where my little car is housed. Silver-grey, gaunt and genial, he towered over me with his wide-brimmed grey hat on the back of his head and his hair hanging over his forehead in Olympian locks. Gruff, gentle, and glad to see me, he led me into the house. Not only gentle, but gentlemanly; for he is an old English gentleman of the Victorian type; no one was ever more English than Bridges.

As we entered the house he pulled some papers out of his pocket and dropped them into a large leather wallet which was lying on a chair in the hall. 'You've caught me reading Proust', he remarked, which mystified me until I realised that he'd said 'proofs'. (He has written a biographical introduction to some posthumous work by Henry Bradley,[1] and is being rather important about the proofs. There was something boyish about the way he mentioned them.) 'I shall be busy on Monday morning, reading proofs', he said again, later in the evening. Showing me my room, he said, 'Masefield has just returned from Rome' which reminded him that his own father and mother went to Rome in their own carriage.

Ralph Hodgson once spent a day here. 'It went like lightning', he told me. I can't exactly say that about this evening, friendly though it was, with dear Mrs Bridges being discreet and helpful. Naturally I felt a little over-anxious to give them the best of what I have to give, and was never quite sure that my efforts would find favour with the Laureate. But my less felicitous openings were brushed aside, and he always seemed to be talking about things which interested him. We were most at our ease about cricket! He is proud of his former prowess as a batsman, and even spoke of the game in the *present* tense. When I said that my cricket had been cramped by nervousness in matches, he exclaimed, 'When I go in, the one thing I can't believe is that there is anyone in the world who can get me out!' He added that he 'once hit the ball out of the ground on all four sides of the wicket in one innings'. I could only retaliate by telling him how my *bowling* was once hit over some houses by F. G. J. Ford, a famous left-handed batsman of the Nineties.

[1] Philologist and lexicographer (1845–1923). Editor of the *Oxford English Dictionary*. Bridges's memoir was privately printed in 1926, published in Bradley's *Collected Papers* (1928) and then in Bridges's posthumous *Three Friends* (1932).

I asked his opinion of Sir Walter Scott's poetry. R.B: 'No better than Macaulay's, except for a few lyrics.' But he admires *Redgauntlet*. (Andrew Lang told him that it contains more corrections, in the manuscript, than any other novel by Scott.) Andrew Lang was rather early in the world's history for me, so I mentioned H. G. Wells (in connection with Bertrand Russell, whom R.B. knows and, rather unexpectedly, likes). R.B: 'Wells is a very nice chap. I once thought of something very good; but I found that Wells had said it already.' His prejudice against Hardy cropped up once, but died away quickly. We were talking about Masefield's little theatre. R.B: 'They did a play by Hardy and another by Sturge Moore in the same evening. I heard that Sturge Moore's was good, but Hardy's was *very bad and very dull*.' Much embarrassed, I remarked that I'd also heard that *The Queen of Cornwall* isn't very interesting (which was true; I haven't read it). After dinner we sat close to a log-fire. He smoked a pipe, grumbling a bit because there were only two matches in the only available box. These soon went, and we relied on 'spills'. Handing me a tin of Bird's-eye tobacco, he inquired whether I could say what it smelt of. After a terrific sniff I guessed 'quince'. R.B: 'Very *nearly* right. I put a slice of American pippin-skin in to moisten it.' 'Robert has a very delicate sense of smell,' said Mrs Bridges, in her polite little voice, adding, 'He is sometimes awakened at night by a smell!' 'How nice, to be awakened at night by the smell of jasmine!' I said, and then felt rather fatuous. Soon afterwards he asked her to play the clavichord, which she did, carrying a lamp into the dining-room where that eightieth-birthday Tribute stands. He exclaimed delightedly while she played Byrd and Purcell, quite skilfully, and I inwardly congratulated myself on having been responsible for the advent of the exquisite instrument. Sitting in his arm-chair, he hangs his long legs out in every direction—they seemed almost long enough to touch the ceiling. He does everything with them except tie them round his neck. His slight and intermittent stammer contributes to the effect of charming naturalness. During the evening he broached two subjects—phonetics and philosophy—on which I was unable to produce any response.

May 3

My mental portrait of R.B. has been amplified and clarified by this happy and stimulating Sunday. At 8 o'clock in the morning he looked in at my door; with a towel round his head and wearing a long bath-gown, he looked like an Oriental potentate. 'The bathroom's empty!' (I'd only had four hours sleep but felt fairly fresh.) It was a fine morning and as he said he wanted to be alone ('reading proofs') I wandered in the fields, glad to be detached and meditative. By mid-day he was out of the house and calling me lustily. Then I went down to Balliol to fetch Peter Quennell[1] and brought him up for luncheon. (P.Q. hadn't met R.B. and I wanted to bring them together, P.Q. being so young and promising.)

R.B. liked him very much, and P.Q., who behaved charmingly, seemed properly impressed. He is sixty years younger than R.B., who talked to him as though they were contemporaries. He is the same with me; never a suggestion of patronage or speaking *ex cathedra*. He contradicts, and asserts opinions pugnaciously, but always with a gruff way of implying 'That's my notion. Now I want to hear yours.'

He remarked to P.Q. that 'a great deal of *Paradise Lost* depends entirely for its effect on the metrical arrangement. Printed as prose it would make no effect.' He doesn't like Landor. 'Pretentious stuff.' (I doubt whether this would be his finally considered judgment.) He doesn't like Spenser's *Faerie Queene* (which has always bored me a good deal) but thinks 'Sweet Thames run softly' a successful poem. (He put two stanzas of it in *The Spirit of Man*.[2]) He is 'not interested in the future', he said. That I don't believe. Anyhow I wish I knew as much as he does about the past. 'Dante had curly hair and a black beard.' That was news to me. Schubert, he said, was 'a great composer in spite of his comparative ignorance of musical counterpoint'. Surely there are, also, poets who are great in spite of their ignorance of prosody. I bow to R.B's insistence on the importance of the theory of poetic technique. But I have an idea that *emotional content* is equally essential to a really great poem. R.B: 'There is no verse-form, in England, suitable for writing narrative. Blank verse is no good, and all stanza forms

[1] Poet, biographer and critic (born 1905).
[2] Bridges's wartime anthology (1916).

soon get monotonous. The speech cadence can't be sufficiently varied. But (with a look of lively secrecy) *I believe I've discovered a new form.*' (This was in the garden.) S.S. (trying to create a topic): 'Very few poets seem to be interested in the way their poems are *printed.*' R.B: 'Why should they be? They aren't interested in the way they *write* their poems' (goes on playing patience—this was after dinner).

After luncheon I drove P.Q. back to Balliol, and went on to Garsington, where I conversed with Ottoline for half-an-hour. Got back here at 5. It was a wet afternoon and evening. R.B. had been reading Bertrand Russell's little (popular) book *What I Believe*, which I'd given him. He thinks most of it 'rubbish', and sticks to his guns about 'the aristocratic ideal being the best one'. 'You can't reform the world by beginning at the bottom. You must start at the top and work downwards.' He added, 'Considering what it started from, the world has done extraordinarily well and is making steady progress.' 'Human wireless communication is underdeveloped. I often learn more of a man by sitting silent with him.'

Only one thing to-day which I'd wish unsaid. At dinner (probably he was getting tired with so much talking) he reiterated the anti-Hardy motif. R.B. (out of the blue): 'I can see no merit in Hardy's poetry.' And (with emphasis) 'I am not alone in my opinion.' Mrs B. (timidly to me): 'What do *you* think?' S.S. (desperate, but loyal to Max Gate): 'I find the *content* of his poems interesting, and I think some of them very beautiful.' The subject was then dropped.

Intellectually R.B. appears to be still in his prime. (Hodgson said the same.) He hasn't lost the capacity to *enjoy*. He devoured B. Russell's book with the gusto of an undergraduate, and dis- agreed with undergraduate vehemence. He lives *in the present*— surely a very rare quality in an octogenarian. After I'd come up to bed, he poked his head in at the door and exclaimed, 'If you're reading Russell's book I'll give you a text from Blake. "Damn braces; bless relaxes!" ' 'Bless Bridges' was my text for to-day.

May 5 (54 Tufton Street)

Yesterday, after breakfast, R.B. read me several manuscript poems, including two humorous ones which Mrs B. mildly

deplored. I asked him about Gerard Hopkins, but he didn't
respond very freely, and soon got out a book of manuscript
Psalm Chants, with his own 'pointings'. He sang several of
these, in a tenor voice, with great gusto and occasional exclamations of satisfaction at the way his system brought out the
'speech-rhythms'. It was all a mystery to me, but I nodded and
acquiesced for all I was worth. He said : 'I lectured about all this
to a hundred organists for two hours in London.' But that
morning fireside scene has become blurred in my mind, and I
can only remember his large hands (with black-and-white
mittens) and his showing me the fixture-card of The Band of
Brothers (the best amateur cricket club in Kent) which had
arrived by the morning post. 'How I wish I could have one
year's cricket again!' he exclaimed. 'Cricket brings out all the
devil in a man!'

He speaks disrespectfully of most modern verse. (Housman
and Hodgson excepted.) W. H. Davies is 'very poor stuff' and
Binyon 'never succeeds'.

'I've always regarded poetry as an Art. It's no use unless you
can do something *new*. People paint water-colours which are
admired by their relations—the world's full of such stuff.
What's the use of it—poetry or water-colours? No one will
praise my new poems when I print them. But I'd rather have
their blame than their praise.' (Naughty old Poet Laureate!)
He flings these remarks out impatiently while he paces along
the flagged path in front of the house.

One might say that *method* has become more important to
him than material; but I infer that he is suffering from the fact
that the passage of time makes natural poetry more and more
difficult to write. Personally, I desire spontaneity in poetry; and
how it blossoms in R.B.'s *Shorter Poems*.[1] He is a great man; and
below his ephemeral behaviour there is a noble and gentle concern for the welfare of all that is finest in life. After lunch I discovered that he shares my delight in W. K. Haselden's drawings
(in the *Daily Mirror*), and has actually been to see W.K.H. At
2.30 I departed. R.B. standing by the gate, having gone ahead
to open it for me, his wide grey hat tilted back, and wearing his
gardening gauntlets. I remember his face as a mingling of
melancholy and sweetness. Mrs B. said, 'You have been kind

[1] Published in 1890.

to us, because you don't remind us that we are old.' 'I've enjoyed your visit very much,' said R.B. as I buzzed through the gate. I shouted over my shoulder, 'We got on jolly well, didn't we?' And it was true.

From Chilswell I went down to Oxford. I had arranged to visit Robert and Nancy Graves at Islip, so I purchased a pound of jam roll, a pound of chocolates, and Russell's *What I Believe*. At World's End I found Robert busy with the baby; the other three children were at the lane-end, playing with some village children. Nancy was upstairs resting; and there was a Mrs Mallory staying with them (wife of Mallory who perished in the Mount Everest Expedition last year[1]). My offerings were well received, and Nancy was amiable. After tea R. and I rambled along the bank of the Cherwell; R. picked a big bunch of cowslips, and we sat in a pollard-willow. I talked rather incoherently, trying to adapt myself to R.G. I couldn't say much about Chilswell, because Bridges isn't altogether approved of by Robert, who picks holes in R.B's poems. It was rather an unsatisfactory conversation, and it ended in a rainstorm.

I left at 7 and stayed the night at Garsington. The Morrells have taken a house in Chelsea for the summer (having let the Manor House to an American lady) and were on the eve of departure. The house is full of newly-arrived furniture and pictures from old Mrs Morrell's[2] house in Oxford. Philip Morrell gave me an amusing account of the family ill-feeling which has been aroused by the problem of dividing up the old lady's effects. 'Who shall have father's old silver inkstand?' etc. Apparently P's sisters almost came to blows, and he admitted that 'feeling ran very high' all round. Ottoline showed me last Sunday's *Observer*, containing a column-review of my *Selected Poems* by J. C. Squire. This sent me to bed in a glow of self-esteem! However hard I try to suppress my craving for 'recognition', the desire is there and flourishes on such fodder. Gilbert Spencer (the painter)[3] came in for dinner. 'Good old Gil.' Rubicund and charmingly simple as ever.

---

[1] George Leigh Mallory (1886–1924).
[2] She was the subject of S.S's poem 'To an Old Lady Dead'.
[3] 1893–1979.

May 9 (Easton Glebe)

How pleasant it is—to get into a small car and drive away from London on a fine Saturday afternoon. As one gets nearer open country, one slows down to watch half-a-minute of local cricket. By the time the bowler has started to deliver his next ball one is out of sight. Easton Park is an ideal destination. At the lodge-gate one turns into the untidy deer-dotted park, with its rooks and rabbits and derelict-looking old trees; half-a-mile across the green levels there is H.G's cosy house, demure and Jane Austenish (H.G. at home is described in detail elsewhere). This week-end wasn't noteworthy.

May 13 (54 Tufton Street)

When feeling bored lately I have reminded myself that 'my days are dedicated to the art of poetry'. Thus I try to escape the feeling of futility, which is accentuated when H.G. and Arnold Bennett urge me to write novels.

This morning there seemed nothing to be done with the day, which was warm and sunny—a perfection of weather, making London seem a city of peace and prosperity. I spent the morning having a Turkish Bath in Jermyn Street! And after lunch I went to the Royal Academy to be amused and amazed by its hordes of typical old ladies, all solemnly marking their catalogues. These people purchase poets after they (the poets) have died and are safe in padded leather bindings.

May 14

Elysian weather, so I sought the nearest Arcadia, which is Kew. Got there at noon. Lunched off cold lamb and rhubarb tart in the umbrageous back-garden of a restaurant on Kew Green. The talkative seedily-evening-dressed waiters in those places are quite a feature—one of the things which one will regret when they have disappeared! Lay on my back under a beech until 4, reading *The Times Literary Supplement* and listening to the birds and the cries of children picking daisies. Then strolled around, inspecting the bluebells—which were at their best—sniffing gorse, and dipping my nose into every blossoming bough. Tea at Kew Green, and then round the gardens again.

At 6.15, while I was reviewing the bluebells, I was hailed by Gosse, who was walking very lame (with Nellie, and Philip Gosse and his wife). This was a delightful finish to my sunlit solitude and I thoroughly enjoyed half-an-hour's saunter and chat with E.G. and N.G. (though I was sorry to see how aged E.G. looked in the evening light). Dined alone, reading Blunden's *Masks of Time*.[1]

May 15

Fine weather again. Rang up Nellie Burton at lunch-time and offered to take her for a drive. I was well rewarded by her delight in every moment of the outing—from the moment when she caused the little car to sag heavily under her embarking weight to the moment when, four hours later, she stepped out again and inserted her key in the door of 40 Half Moon Street ('once', she often remarks, 'the 'ouse where 'Azlitt[2] lived'). Burton has a passion for chestnut trees ('like Christmas trees with candles in them', she exclaimed). After admiring those in Kew Gardens we went to Richmond and through Bushey Park to have tea at 'Ampton Court. After tea we strolled on the greensward and admired more chestnuts. The flower-beds exhausted all N.B's superlatives ('Ow I do love flowers! They're my children'). And Burton heard the cuckoo (which she ' 'adn't done for years' —heaven knows how). She was in her very best form, mispronouncing the names of the flowers, dipping wildly into English history with references to the associations of Hampton Court Palace, and remembering how she saw a white blackbird in the wistaria last time she was there. 'I do love the tapestries of the Seven Deadly Sins, don't you?' she ejaculated, her voluminous face brimming over with good-humour. (She meant the Mantegna frescoes.) She had a comment for everything we passed on the way home. Pope's Villa, Teddington Cemetery ('where Lord Roberts's mother was buried'), the Albert Hall ('Kensington Gas Works, they call it') 'and so on and such forth', as she says, finishing with Rotten Row, where 'the dear little children' were cantering along on their ponies. It was most

[1] Poems published in a limited edition (1925).
[2] William Hazlitt (1778–1830), essayist.

refreshing, and I ended up exhausted, but aware that I'd given vast pleasure to one of my best friends. I am coming to the conclusion that the best hobby one can have is to devote one's spare time and energy to brightening up one's friends. To do that properly, one must live simply and avoid owning things.

May 16

To-day has contained its 'good deed'. At 11.30 I set off in the car, to pay an 'Enoch Arden' visit to Paddock Wood. I hadn't seen my mother for several months. She seldom comes to London, and it isn't possible for me to stay at Weirleigh, all the rooms being occupied by my brother and his family. Going there 'for the day' is a depressing performance, as I can't see Mother alone, and don't much want to see my brother and his family. I had lunch at the Angel at Tonbridge. After lunch I strolled in to the county ground, where I made so many small scores in the past. How small and unimportant the pavilion now appeared! Once it was the Mecca of my ambitions as a cricketer. The Tonbridge team were sitting about, waiting for the Penshurst eleven to arrive. The photograph of 'Tonbridge Cricket Week 1897' still hanging on the wall, thronged with once familiar local figures. Although expecting to remain unidentified, I was greeted by the skipper of the Tonbridge team (whose name I'd unaccountably forgotten). He asked whether I'd 'come over for a game' (to play for Penshurst?) After a few minutes I slipped away from the unchanged familiarities of 'the Angel Ground'. It must be twelve years since I last had a game there.

Got to Weirleigh at 3. Left the car surreptitiously at the garden-gate down the road. Tom Homewood happened to be passing, on his way back from Maidstone with his carrier's van. He has done it ever since I can remember, but goes only three days a week now. His pleasant bearded face seemed unaltered, except for grey hairs. How does he find it worthwhile to steer his plodding old horse eleven miles to Maidstone in these days of motor-buses?[1] I went up the garden; under the cedar-tree I found my youngest nephew—aged five—digging with a small wooden spade. He stared at me solemnly, not knowing me for

[1] He is now, temporarily, immortal [as John Homeward] in my *Memoirs*. S.S.

his uncle. Then I stole up the stairs to the studio, my old writing-room, and still full of my books. There I found Mother dozing in an arm-chair, with her feet up and *The Times* on her knees. My brother was away at Brenchley cricket-ground and his wife somewhere in the house, so I had three peaceful hours alone with Mother. We remained in the studio and had tea, assisted by a placid, smoke-coloured Persian cat. Visiting Weirleigh is like revisiting the past. There was a sense of unreality about my intrusion to-day, with the widespread landscape dreaming in early summer sunshine, and no incongruities to mar the completeness of the picture. Mother, as usual, gave me a heartache, with her tired, undaunted face, and her impulsive, disconnected, intolerant comments on modern art and literature (and modern manners). And of course she insisted on my having an egg with my tea.

We went down the garden, and she gathered a large bunch of narcissus (they are scenting my room now) and then I said good-bye to her at the ramshackle gate under the lilac-bushes, where the old red may-tree used to lean across the fence; and I slipped down the hill and back to London in an evening radiance of Elysian gold. I halted for a while on Crockham Hill. Birds were warbling in the hot sunset glare and some gipsy-vans were camped among the gorse. All around the green country looked as though the world was all happiness, and life all promise.

Thus I end this three months' diary hopefully. The tranquillity of to-night is broken only by the tipsy singing and gramophone cacophonies of a 'party' which is taking place down the street, in one of the impoverished houses—last remnant of the slum which once was Tufton Street.

I brought back with me Mother's water-colour of 'The Sower'. I can remember the early spring day when she did it, and can visualise the actual field in which her model (a local Abraham named Larkin) was working. Twenty-eight years ago she painted the picture. And now it hangs above my desk. Lifting my eyes from this page, I see that figure of hope and fertility, striding nobly across the land with a vague blue valley behind him. Perhaps that picture is a good omen for my future.

May 18

A sultry afternoon. The opera season opens to-night with *Rosenkavalier*. Schuster has, I think, bought a ticket for me; but I'm not certain, as he doesn't mention it in his letter (received this morning) and merely asks why I haven't been to Bray during the fine weather. Probably he has refrained from sending me the ticket, for fear that I give it to someone he doesn't want to sit next to. So I shall pay him out by not putting on evening dress. The thought of that smart crowd of 'society people'—all there because it's a social event—irritates me, and makes me want to be different from them! A form of snobbishness, no doubt. Bought Virginia Woolf's new novel[1] this afternoon, and sat in Hyde Park without reading a word (staring morosely at Sir Philip Sassoon's Park Lane mansion).

After consuming half a lobster at Scott's in Piccadilly Circus, I rolled up at Covent Garden, and gloomily watched the fashionable and cultured crowd shoving its way through the swing-doors—from sultry exterior to still more sultry interior. Being the only individual not in evening dress, I felt 'a certain psychological satisfaction', whatever that may be, but I had compromised slightly by putting on my new dark-blue flannel suit, so I wasn't actually ill-dressed. I wish I could understand why I enjoy adopting the attitude of a sort of social and slightly sinister Enoch Arden.

Anyhow Schuster soon came bustling in at the swing-door (which I'd taken to holding open with my foot—neither old Frankie nor anyone else had time to thank me). Under his arm he was carrying a heavily-framed autograph letter of Jean de Reszke's, which he is lending to the Opera House Museum. It transpired that he'd enclosed my ticket with his note, but it had escaped my notice (a sign that I was in a bad temper this morning). However, Schuster is well-known at the box-office, and got me in quite easily. *Rosenkavalier* is always enjoyable. During the second interval I bumped into Arnold Bennett and sat with him in a corner. A.B. is a very humanising influence. Afterwards Schuster hurried me away to the Savoy Grill Room for supper, and then shuffled off to catch the midnight train back to Maidenhead—astonishing septuagenarian!

[1] *Mrs Dalloway* (1925).

Noël Coward, now a celebrated playwright and earning £1000 a week, was sitting quite near me, with a friend. I avoided recognising him, because he has been ridiculing Edith Sitwell again, in a volume of silly parodies,[1] and this annoys me, though I am not 'on visiting terms' with the Sitwells. My situation was complicated by the fact that Sacheverell was actually sitting quite near Coward. (I could see both tables by turning my head a couple of inches to left and right.) Sacheverell was alone with a dark young lady. While I sipped coffee I peeped at him, and decided (partly because he looked so charming, but chiefly as an anti-Coward gesture) to go across and greet him. This I did, with some trepidation, and was most warmly greeted, though I hadn't spoken to him since October 1921. He introduced me to his friend, a Miss Doble.[2]

May 19

Dining at the Reform, I listened to a couple of clergymen in the smoking-room. One of them was ninety-four, a wonderful old chap from Oxford. Both were deaf, so I could follow their conversation easily! The ninety-four-year-old one was deploring the decay of Classical Education, the condition of the Church, Socialism, and so on. 'My brother-in-law', he quavered resolutely, 'will be ninety in September. He is lukewarm, *very* lukewarm' (about the condition of the Church). His septuagenarian host agreed with everything he uttered, and looked exactly like Mr Harding (of Barchester).[3]

May 21

For some reason I am fresh and alert, although to-day has been exacting, and I slept atrociously last night. I had two vivid 'surface dreams' in which I was in a state of poetic afflatus and quite confident that I was really doing 'the big stuff' at last. The second afflatus concerned a poem about driving a motor-car in a snowstorm, and the only extant line is 'And there the ship lay with her funnel'. Freud would assert that this signified some-

---

[1] *Chelsea Buns* by Hernia Whittlebot (1925).
[2] Whom he afterwards married. S.S.
[3] In Trollope's *The Warden* etc.

thing sexual. But he would be wrong, I think. The line arose from my needing a rhyme to 'tunnel'. But perhaps 'tunnel' is sexual too!

From 1 to 6 I was with Mother. I called at her club, with the car, and drove her to the Heads', where we lunched well and she got on beautifully with that couple of middle-aged angels. They, too, were charmed by Mother, and I had a pleasantly creative feeling, as I always do when I am 'bringing together' people who are dear to me, and who were intended by nature to become known to one another. More and more I want to weave this texture (or context) of my friends into a tapestry of human understanding. It is like someone building a house and furnishing it slowly and wisely. My friends are my house. I have no other refuge on earth.

After lunch I drove Mother round the Park, and we visited the bird sanctuary, where she was temporarily infuriated by the Epstein sculpture[1] (which I refrained from arguing about). The Park caused Mother to remember how she used to play there every day when she was a child. Then I took her to tea at 40 Half Moon Street, where Nellie Burton had made her famous meringues. Mother ate two. As we were departing, the Sitwell brothers arrived. I was amiable, and Osbert gave me a little glass globe containing a toy gold-fish. Mother and I went on to the Royal Academy, always a big event for her. She didn't seem overtired when she returned to Kent by the seven o'clock train. Her face left me with the usual heartache.

May 22

As I was going to bed last night (at 3 a.m.) I heard Turner come in. As usual, he went straight upstairs; and, as usual, poor Delphine was awake, and they carried on a conversation for more than an hour, before he went to his own room. It is queer, how detached I have become from their domestic life. But for several months I have been uneasy about their relationship, though I've been hoping that 'the dark lady' of last winter has been dropped. But in such matters I can only remain aloof and pretend to know nothing.

[1] Rima, the memorial to W. H. Hudson (1841–1922), commissioned by the Royal Society for the Protection of Birds and unveiled in 1925.

This evening I dressed up in tail-coat and white waistcoat and took Ottoline to *Rosenkavalier*. Turner was there also, so I took them both to the Savoy for supper, and my Tufton Street antipathy to Turner evaporated in the course of conversation (as most of my secret antagonisms do, when I am in human contact with them). But Turner is too individual and independent for me. I feel that he is always refusing to be woven into the tapestry and is contemptuous of most of its ingredients. (Ottoline is, at present, one of the few friends we have in common.) My inevitable reconciliation with the Sitwells won't make things any easier, for Osbert and Turner have always disliked one another cordially. It is all like a jigsaw puzzle which refuses to fit together, an assembly of incompatibilities, unified only by my interest in them all.

May 23 (The Hut, Bray)

To-day began with a page of appreciative criticism of *Lingual Exercises* by Desmond MacCarthy[1] in the *New Statesman*. I didn't intend the book to be reviewed, but can't complain about this one.

After lunch I got the car from the garage in Queen Anne's Gate, and was about to set off from Tufton Street, when Romer Wilson[2] arrived, looking haggard and distressed; and no wonder, since her husband is in St Thomas's Hospital with typhoid fever and has only to-day recovered consciousness. I remained for over an hour, trying to distract her attention from the trouble. She is a sort of half-genius, with something big about her, though her writing is often rather pretentiously 'powerful', and her manners are too 'new womanish' for my taste.

The sky was crowded with rainy clouds as I drove sedately down here. Found everything as usual. Honeysuckle-bush by the gate in full flower; Schuster reading the evening paper on the verandah; the two dogs (Aberdeen and long-haired Sheep) romping on the lush lawn; birds singing, lilac blooming, river-reaches gleaming rather wistfully; butler laying the table for

---

[1] Literary and dramatic critic (1877–1952). Knighted 1951.
[2] Novelist (1891–1930). Author of *The Death of Society* (1921). In 1923 she married Edward J. O'Brien (1890–1941), American author and editor.

dinner. I felt vaguely soothed by being here again. But the talk at dinner was vapid and trivial. (Wendela's sister is here, plump and empty-headed and smart.) After dinner they played Mah Jong, and then went off to a 'small dance' at Lady Anneseley's, leaving old Frankie and self. The rain began to drop down on the garden, and when I played *Rosenkavalier* it seemed to have lost its charm; and MacCarthy's article no longer made me feel famous. I was haunted by Romer Wilson's unhappy, harassed face. And Schuster was an old opera-goer shuffling off to bed with nothing much to look forward to on the morrow. Perhaps The Hut is losing its charm. Everything here is so soft and succulent and richly-sauced, and life is converted into a cosy parlour-game.

May 24

A quiet morning, with an hour's lawn-weeding, and a tiresome lunch. A Mrs Brougham-White and a Mr Otis Taylor came—the latter a South American in the film business—horribly cosmopolitan—cultured, with a sallow repulsive face. Otis was the exact name for him. At 4.15 I set off in the car—to Taplow Court.[1] Ottoline is staying there, and asked me to go there for tea and 'help her to feel less out of it'. Nobody in when I arrived. The solemn butler said 'her ladyship is on the water', and directed me to the boat-house (which I avoided, and wandered under the magnificent cedars, listening to the sound of the weir below). On my return I was greeted by Ottoline in the hall, introduced to Lady Desborough, led into a room full of people, and introduced to Sir Philip Sassoon. He looks a bit of a bounder, but has a remarkable face. I was introduced to Lord Balfour[2] and several titled dowagers—old Lady Wemyss,[3] Lady Kenmare,[4] etc. Sat down at a long table, between Ottoline and Lady Desborough, with Lord B. on Lady D's left. About twenty people at the table. I felt very shy and self-conscious. Lady D. made conversation hectically, asking whether I wrote at night or by day, and did I alter my poems much afterwards. I

[1] The home of Lord and Lady Desborough.
[2] Conservative politician and writer (1848–1930). Prime Minister 1902–5.
[3] Mary (née Wyndham), wife of the eleventh Earl of Wemyss.
[4] Elizabeth (née Baring), wife of the fifth Earl of Kenmare.

explained my methods ponderously, and Lord B. joined in, very amiably. He is plump and pink-faced under his white hair, and wore white flannel trousers (had been on the river and was about to play tennis). His face looked prim and lacks nobility.

Conditions were impossible for conversation, with Lady D. pouring out cups of tea all the time and a terrific cackle going on all round us. After tea I discovered Eddie Marsh in an adjoining room, playing Mah Jong with Mrs Lindsay[1] and Desmond MacCarthy. I thanked D.M. for writing so nicely about me in the *Statesman*, and he replied, 'They all say I didn't praise you nearly enough.' ('They', I suppose meant E.M., who is enthusiastic about *Lingual Exercises*.) After that I drifted to another room and sat listening to a feeble conversation between P. Sassoon, Lady Londonderry[2] and Lord Hugh Cecil[3] (a soft-looking man). Ottoline joined us, with her camera, and sat down opposite P.S. and took photographs of him. O.M. in her out-of-date picture-hat and pale brocade dress looked like her portrait by Conder—very charming. (She said afterwards 'I felt so out of it in my faded finery, among all those people who were so odious to me during the War.') Soon afterwards we escaped from that too-prosperous house-party and went down to de la Mare's, which was like coming to life again.

Back here for dinner, I didn't say anything about the people at Taplow Court. It seemed absurd to mention all those swells (though Schuster would have been thrilled).

But it was fun to see such a menagerie of well-known folk (and to know that they were interested in ME). Tomorrow morning they'll be thinking about something else, forgetting my poems, which Eddie Marsh simply raves about. Anyhow they can't read them, because *Lingual Exercises* isn't for sale. Let them go to Hatchard's and try, damn their aristocratic eyes!

[1] Norah (d. 1948), wife of Harry Lindsay (1866–1939), uncle of Lady Diana Cooper.

[2] Edith Helen (1879–1959), daughter of the first Viscount Chaplin and wife of the seventh Marquess of Londonderry. Political hostess and author.

[3] 1869–1956. Fifth son of the third Marquess of Salisbury. Conservative M.P. 1895–1906. Provost of Eton 1936–44. Created Baron Quickswood 1941.

May 26 (54 Tufton Street)

This evening I went (alone) to Covent Garden and heard Strauss's *Elektra* for the first time. I found its savagery very satisfactory, as I am rather fed up with 'idealised Greece'.

Sophoclean and Aeschylean Greeks were probably every bit as barbaric as Hofmannsthal suggests.[1] Afterwards I broke the spell of the music by calling at 40 Half Moon Street. (Burton had rung up, wanting to see me about Max Meyerfeld's arrival from Berlin, which is imminent.) She was in festive mood, having been to see 'Lord French's[2] Funeral Procession' before dinner. She made me drink two glasses of champagne, which I now regret, as I am feeling muddle-headed.[3]

At the club to-day I sat after lunch with Arnold Bennett, Swinnerton, and Walter Roch. They were talking about dreams; rather stupidly, I described my dream about writing poetry and only remembering one line—'And there the ship lay with her funnel'. A.B. murmured something inaudible, and when Swinnerton inquired what he'd said, replied 'I only made a joke —a small one, but rather good.' When urged to repeat the masterpiece, he remarked, 'I said it was a *hermaphrodite brig.*'

I laughed mechanically, but the other two didn't see the joke, or pretended not to. A.B. looked at me and said, '*He* doesn't see it, really.' And I didn't. When A.B. had gone, I asked the other two what he'd meant. They looked embarrassed, and Roch said, 'A.B. was tired to-day. I suppose he meant that you didn't know whether the ship was "it" or "her".' This was kindly put. I have just looked up the phrase in Webster and find that 'hermaphrodite brig' signifies a ship having characters of two kinds of craft. No doubt they all think me much simpler than I am. But I ought to know better than to narrate my dreams in my club.

June 9 (80° in the shade)

I went to the Fauré Memorial Concert at Wigmore Hall in the afternoon. From my seat in the front row of the gallery I

---

[1] Hugo von Hofmannsthal (1874–1929), poet, wrote the libretti of *Elektra, Der Rosenkavalier* and other operas by Richard Strauss.

[2] Field-Marshal Sir John French (1852–1925), first Earl of Ypres.

[3] On another occasion she turned on a little French musical box as I entered the room—to celebrate my arrival. S.S.

observed Schuster in his frock-coat, bowing over the hands of
the French, Italian, and Austrian Ambassadors. Schuster in a
flower-garden of richly-attired elderly dames of wealth and
distinction—to whom he'd sold 160 seats at a guinea each.
Schuster shouting 'Bravi' at the end of each item. Schuster
enraptured by the familiar cadences of 'Soir', 'Clair de Lune' etc.
An exquisite concert of almost too refined music.

July 4 (The Hut, Bray)

It is a long time since I allowed myself sixteen days' vacation
from my damned diary; and now that those two weeks have disappeared into 'dateless oblivion and divine repose' there seems
little enough in their evasive remoteness, and any diverting
details are beyond recapture, according to their custom. On
June 22 the hot weather turned chilly and grey but remained
rainless. (The rainfall for June was 1/450th of an inch.) On
June 28 it turned to gold again, and so I stayed on here from
day to day, weeding my patch of lawn under the willows by the
music-room, and lumbering through pages and pages of *The
Ring*, with occasional excursions into *Meistersinger* and Beethoven Sonatas. I read very little except the daily papers, never
missing a line of the cricket news. The Open Golf Championship
has had its days, and Jim Barnes has carried the Cup to America
from Prestwick. I have written, late at night, three or four
negligible lyrics. This place seems to lull me away from all
mental activity. Nellie Melba and the Dean of Windsor have
been here, and the Morrells came to lunch to meet Melba. (The
vulgar old woman stayed the week-end.) On June 28 Schuster
gave one of his famous musical parties. André Mangeot's
quartet played Fauré and Ravel in the garden music-room to a
midge-pestered audience (most of them were outside under the
apple-trees). Elizabeth Bibesco was there, and Prince Blucher,
and a bevy of dowagers. Dear Miss Schuster came, dignified in
pale grey; I gave her my copy of Virginia Woolf's *The Common
Reader*, which has since delighted her.

The lotus-eating idleness here is getting on my nerves.
Schuster always refusing any intellectual fare which isn't
'amusing'; Anzie hearty and kindly, but more and more occupied

with money and motors. Wendela and her painting the only 'serious' element in the ménage, which costs £150 a month in food and drink for three people, six servants, and an occasional guest. Last night I went to town for the evening, and drove home rather ferociously. Going too fast round the hairpin corner beyond Runnymede, I skidded, pulled a back-tyre off, and spent three-quarters of an hour in the dark under the trees changing the wheel. (The jack was too low, and I had to supplement it with *Dorothy Wordsworth's Journal*.) This little midnight adventure rather cheered me up. It is so seldom, in my padded and protected existence, that anything happens to remind me, even faintly, of the gipsying uncertainties of the War. To-day has been quiet. Anzie and Wendela in town, and old Frankie pottering about his Leeds china and loose music. (Thirty-six cases of Leeds china from his Old Queen Street house have been unpacked and are being arranged in his new room.) So the summer slips away, with nothing ahead of me that I seem likely to get any stimulus from. An almost full yellow moon glints behind the rare American Lime on the lawn (the one Schuster calls 'Lady Tree'); a train throbs away toward Reading. (The sound of a train, a few miles away, on a summer night—why does it always give me a 'tears, idle tears'[1] feeling?) The night is perfect; the place, perfection. Peace. I am alone with the tiny tick of my watch on the table; alone with a vase of red and white sweet-peas. Schuster complains of 'indigestion pains', and goes to London four days a week to make them worse. He can't rest from his pursuit of pleasure, poor old boy. And I lose shillings steadily to Anzie at 'crazy croquet', and save several pounds a week by living on Schuster's faultless food. Is this futility? Or only 'an ordered existence'?

(From June 19 to 21 the house was full, so I slept at the hotel on Monkey Island—a journey of 250 yards up the backwater in Anzie's canoe. Uncomfortable as it was, compared with this, I preferred it, for I had a slight sense of detachment.)

July 5
'*Saturday, March 27, 1802.* A divine morning. At breakfast William wrote part of an ode . . . We sate all day in the

[1] Tennyson, *The Princess*, canto IV.

orchard.' Thus wrote Dorothy Wordsworth. A page or two of
her Journal has soothed me at the end of a depressed and
irritating day. After being harassed by the sunlit cackle of
Schuster's acquaintances, I felt as though I were back with old
friends again, when I read Dorothy's words—as though
Robert Graves (in the old Army days) had dropped into my
room for a talk about poetry.

As I'm always grumbling, the Schusterian existence is
vitiated by lack of serious foundations. Its froth-de-luxe conceals
nothing but materialism and refusal to face life with courage. It
is based on selfishness and social insincerity. Therefore I am
less and less able to appreciate the diversions provided—the
'character parts' who come to lunch, the delicious food, the
delightful riverside garden, the faultless taste in furniture, the
singing of Debussy and Fauré songs by Blanche Marchesi[1] etc.

I long to escape into austerity and solitude; to be back with
Rivers at Cambridge. To-night the moon is round and golden,
and the garden quiet as Elysium. I feel like a prisoner. But I
must remain here a few more days, since there is nothing for me
to do in London.

July 7

Schuster has been complaining because his gardener doesn't
produce as many flowers as the gardener of his neighbour,
Colonel Something, to whom he went for tea to-day. And he is
always fussing about his belongings. Always something lost.
'Stolen, of course!'—and then it turns up again! This grudging
ownership of things is a lesson to me.

General Smuts says that the next Ice Age will probably come
in about ten thousand years, and will be followed by a higher
type of humanity. South Africa is already getting cooler, he says.
The information leaves me cold.

July 8

On June 7 I scribbled irritably in my diary 'I seem to avoid
the Turners more and more, and this house never gives me any
feeling of homely welcome. I have lost sympathetic contact with

[1] Italian singer and teacher (1863–1940).

Turner and the sound of his voice about the house (in which all sounds are audible) exasperates me.' On July 4 I wrote 'I saw Turner yesterday at Tufton Street and we talked for half-an-hour, so pleasantly that my secret antagonism to him seemed rather grotesque.' On July 5 'Last night I read Turner's platonic dialogue on Art, which he has lent me, in typescript. It contains an odious travesty of Ottoline, who is described as a sort of Jezebel, whereas I see her as an essentially simple soul under her superficial decoration of aesthetic and intellectual interests.'

On Monday I returned the dialogue with a note urging him to cut out a phrase about 'Lady Caraway's eagerly offered embraces' before he shows it to Ottoline. I added that I wouldn't advise him, as I'd 'no hope that he would avail himself of my advice'.

This evening he replies. 'I expect Ottoline to be intelligent enough to know that one cannot write fiction without embellishments, extensions, and ornamentations of one's original models. I did not attempt to make a portrait of her. She is merely the starting-point of a speculation.'

I have now written, telling him that he is deceiving himself; that he has used the material nearest to his hand; that the 'portrait' is offensively recognisable (except that he has multiplied her pug-dogs by seven and inserted some zebras!) and that the Morrells will be hurt, and O.M's enemies delighted, if he prints it. I felt inclined to add that it will be 'the starting-point'—not of a 'speculation'—but of his being permanently cut by the Morrells, whose hospitality has been such a help and enjoyment to him for nearly five years. I am only making this effort to save the feelings of Ottoline (and Delphine). I have lost all faith in Turner, as a writer. He seems to have become an imitator of Aldous Huxley's sophisticated aridities, without any of Huxley's educated clarity. Turner is a poet, imaginative and rather incoherent. This dialogue is neatly written but worthless. If he prints it he will accentuate my hostility to him.

In his last book of 'verse'—*The Seven Days of the Sun*—he showed that he is catching all the fashionable maladies of the cultured small-fry who chatter and argue in sophisticated coteries, and write books about one another.

July 10

A busy day in town. It may well be asked 'What do I consider a "busy day" '. Well, I left here at 11.30, in mild, cloudy weather; drove Schuster to Chelsea, where I dropped him. (He was going to look at some Leeds china in some shop or other, and then going on to some luncheon-party or other.)

I myself went doggedly on to Tufton Street, where I unloaded a bundle of soiled linen, and abstracted a cheque from my chequebook. Then I cruised to the City; at my bank in Old Broad Street I filled in the cheque and received a £10 note and five £5 notes (for my motor-tour which begins next Monday). It always seems a mystery and a miracle when my bank pays me money which I've done nothing to earn.

Stuffing the notes—no, folding them affectionately and placing them in my pocket-book—I re-entered my 'little bus' and sailed past St Paul's to lunch at my club, where I was hailed by Richmond Temple and introduced to a Mr Raphael Herman of Los Angeles. Mr H. was almost blind and very deaf, spoke with a German-American intonation, is very rich, and is over here for a Peace Congress, toward which he has contributed a lot of money. He trotted out the usual clichés, and seemed worthy but of limited intelligence.

R.T., in his florid way, introduced me as 'our most famous pacifist poet'. Raphael murmured 'Of course', but I suspect that my name and poetical status were novelties for him. At 3 o'clock, leaving my car outside the club, I sallied forth on foot. Bought a pipe and half a pound of tobacco. Then had my hair cut in Curzon Street. Was there till 4.30 and purchased some lavender-water. Next I consumed an ice (pineapple) and two sponge-cakes at Gunter's in Berkeley Square. On my way back to the car I called at Sotheran's and bought and inscribed a copy of my *Selected Poems*, to be sent to Raphael (the Peacemaker) at the Hotel Cecil. For myself I bought Muirhead's *England* (for motor tour) price sixteen shillings.

Back at Tufton Street I became excessively 'busy'. Dealt with my seven days' accumulation of letters (only three of which required immediate answers) including a refusal to stay the week-end at Taplow Court. Turner was out, but I could hear Delphine tapping on her typewriter. (A recent accomplishment.) Then—smoking my new pipe all the time—I packed shirts, socks, etc. for the tour. Mustn't forget field-glasses, maps, *Oxford Dictionary*, and spare jersey (for Gabriel, who always neglects to take adequate clothing). Starting off again, with a clean sheet, at 7.30, I put a (Gunter's) peppermint in my mouth; crunch, crunch; and a back-tooth broke in half, revealing (via looking-glass in bath-room, hastily consulted) a mass of metal stopping. No pain, however. Discarded segment of tooth looked aged and quite unfit for social purposes. (Taplow Court!) Dined alone at club, reading Shaw's excellent article on Massingham.[1]

At Tufton Street I'd found a note from Robert Graves, saying that he is in town (with Nancy and no children) till Tuesday. He must have rung me up, mentally, last night, for I spent an hour writing to him; as this was nicely done, I felt absolved from actual conversation, so came back to Bray without calling at Apple Tree Yard, as I ought to have done. Left the club at 9.30, and drove serenely into the rosy-clouded remnants of sunset. Very lovely were the clouds, as I buzzed up St James's Street, and the twilight roses lasted till I was beyond the new road which skirts Brentford. 'Home' at 10.40, passing the merry-go-rounds and swings of Bray Fair. Gosh, what a 'busy day'!

July 11

While weeding the lawn before dinner, in Elysian weather, I was thinking about Communism. For once in a way I really did seem to be *thinking*, instead of ruminating, meditating, or wool-gathering from one reverie to another. But it is all blurred now, after a rich dinner, and champagne, and the small talk of Mrs Charles Hunter and Madame 'Lala' Vandervelde. But although I have idled the best of the summer away in lotus-life here, and accomplished nothing since I stayed with Mrs Hunter at Easter, I have learned a little about *Capitalism*. It is merely this—that to own anything beyond one's reasonable requirements is an occupation in itself. For 'good old Anzie' a Rolls-Royce is a requirement. He returned this afternoon with a new one, worth £300. But I don't object to people owning things, though I

[1] In *H.W.M.*, a commemorative volume edited by his son H. J. Massingham (1925).

believe that possessions interfere with spiritual freedom. Ownership can be sterile or creative. All ownership is anti-social unless shared freely and ungrudgingly. (E. M. Forster once said something similar to me, but I couldn't realise the truth of it then.) You may say that for me to be staying in Frankie's perfect house is a temporary justification of his expenditure. But he doesn't entertain creatively; his charming hospitality is merely an exchange of commodities. He doesn't give me a creative background, because he doesn't care whether I work or not. All he wants is my 'creative companionship'— for his own amusement. This sounds ungrateful, for he is genuinely fond of me. But it is a circumstantially accurate statement. Frankie is frivolous.

Before coming up to bed, I paddled up the river alone, and watched the fireworks sputter and rain brilliant sparks beyond the dark willows while I listened to the music of the weir. Drifting back, I saw one star ahead of me in a moonless sky, and the heavy-foliaged elms reflected in windless water.

Left Bray on Monday, July 13. Gabriel joined me at Maidenhead station. Blazing hot day. Stayed at White Hart, Salisbury. Blandford Tuesday, Exeter Wednesday.

July 17 (Ship Hotel, East Looe)

I had intended to write many pages about my travels, but have failed to do so; and now, on the fifth day, in the tranquillity of this homely little inn on a narrow street, after reading fifty pages of *Moll Flanders*,[1] I can remember only a few things clearly. A very vivid green oak by the bridge at Hurstbourne Priors at the end of a blazing hot Monday afternoon; that oak foliage will probably survive in remembrance when a multitude of other memories have gone careering down the winds of my autumnal years. Of Dartmoor, sombre on a sunless day, I can make only one momentary picture. Two sunburnt young women pushing bicycles up a long slope while I traversed Devon, Somerset, and Dorset through field-glasses. While I brought them near me by this optical aid, their voices came close up and I diagnosed them as 'Cambridge' by their earnest discourse. A trifling episode, but it comes to mind without being whistled

[1] By Daniel Defoe, published in 1722.

for. Why an oak and two cyclists—out of the incessantly observed details I've gobbled since Monday?

Perhaps I shall also remember—from to-day—five boys on one bicycle, in the street below my window. They wobbled, with much laughter, and collapsed after a short zigzag. Later on, as I strolled along the little sandy bay, the same quintet came running through the twilight, down to the sea, in dark blue bathing-suits. Their gaiety made me sad.

July 20 (Fowey Hotel, Fowey)

Did nothing before lunch except inspect Fowey Church. (Gabriel was sketching it.) Drove to Falmouth after lunch and bought a pair of flannel trousers. (Mine had suddenly contracted two large holes in the seat.) New ones cost 19/6, so I saved £3/4/6, as my tailor charges £4/4/0 and they look just the same. How pleasant it is to be moving from place to place, never knowing what the next will look like! To be on the road, accumulating a few good books, and enjoying them as I never enjoy a book at Tufton Street or in Schuster's Retreat from Reality on the river. Motoring mildly from hotel to hotel—not a romantic or adventurous experience! But it reminds me that I am a wanderer by temperament; uncertainty about the future is my elixir. (I have been relishing the hand-to-mouth atmosphere of *Moll Flanders*.) I am always dreading that my life will become an affair of comfortable certainties. At such moments I fall back on the 'adventures of the spirit' idea. I suppose one can be mentally adventurous in a villa at Bournemouth, or a mansion in Park Lane. Thus I meditate, watching the lights of little sailing-ships in the harbour, and the lights in the little houses of the steep village across the dark water. The sea washes and softly crashes against the rocks; and my healthy red face puffs its pipe in the wardrobe looking-glass. Heaven preserve me from complacent acceptance of an easy way of life, and keep my thoughts on the road to unexplored countries.

July 23 (Mullion Cove)

The car is showing signs of wear-and-tear, and I've been thinking how much I should enjoy a new one next year. But I see no chance of being able to afford the £250. Anyhow the rooms *here* are only 4/– a day. Mine is a cell-like place looking on to the garage-yard, and I'm writing on the dressing-table. The *Daily Sketch* announces that Sir Victor Sassoon is spending £100,000 on a private race-course at Poona. (I have been drinking water at meals, to balance Gabriel's large whiskys.)

July 31 (54 Tufton Street)

Here again after six weeks' absence (from my bedroom). And very dreary it is, as a place to return to. Anyhow I've driven exactly a thousand miles since July 13, and had a very happy time. Yet I feel nothing has been achieved except that I need a hair-cut and have spent £50. (*An hour later*) Things are now worse! Among my letters I find one from Ottoline, asking whether I can assist the Turners with money. She has been attempting to solve the problem of Turner and the 'dark lady'. (I didn't know that the problem existed—to a serious degree.) She says that Turner and Delphine must go away, so as to give him a chance of forgetting Miss N. But they can't afford to, and £200 would make it easy.

August 1

I am alone here. The Turners have gone to Eastbourne till Tuesday. This is a relief, as I don't know what to say to either of them. This morning I talked to them as if nothing were wrong. Delphine merely said, in her pathetic treble voice, 'Walter has been having emotional trouble.' Personally I think it is about time for Delphine to treat *herself* to a little 'emotional trouble'. I rang up Ottoline, who thinks that the danger of W. going off with Miss N. is averted 'for the time being'. She said it has been quite like a Pirandello play. She arranged a meeting between Delphine and Miss N.! (This seems to me a bit thick.) Miss N. said to D. 'I only want to know what the truth is.' D. replied, with her usual splendid simplicity, 'There *is* no truth.' She was right. None of their 'discussions' can alter the fact.

This evening a huge bunch of carnations arrived for W. There was a card attached. 'Get well soon, darling.' (W. is supposed to be suffering from one of his gastric attacks.) I destroyed the card. The flowers will be faded by the time he returns. This afternoon I doped my disquietude by going to Ibsen's *Wild Duck* at the St James's. Hjalmar, with his histrionics, was a warning to me, not to behave like that myself. Hedvig's 'I don't understand what is happening' made me think of poor Delphine.

August 2

After lunching with the Morrells I am in full possession of the details of the upheaval in Turnerdom. The details are, that W. has been seeing Miss N. almost every day since last November. That he began by concealing the fact that he is married (surely Miss N. could have found that out?) and led her to suppose that he is quite well off, and spent a lot of money on entertaining her. (He only earns £30 a month.) Meanwhile Delphine has been denying herself everything, and eating almost nothing. When Miss N. learnt that he is married, she seems to have encouraged him to apply for a divorce, on the ground of nullity. O.M. says 'she is a hard, matter-of-fact little thing, with a good deal of charm. A sort of pocket-Venus.' Her parents are very rich.

O.M. was 'called in' (by W. and Miss N.) about two weeks ago, and endless discussions have taken place. For months W. has been on the point of going off with Miss N., but always changed his mind. O.M. showed me a letter W. wrote her from Sutton Veny (where he was staying with the Nicholsons and 'trying to make up his mind') in which he asked her to break it to Delphine about the 'nullity suit'. In this letter he says that he expects *me* to provide for D. and will 'never forgive his friends if they fail to rally round her'. Then Miss N. came here with O.M. and told poor D. that her marriage is 'an incomplete relationship'. I can't imagine how D's patience has endured it all.

Turner has evidently confused and misled both Miss N. and D. But the main element in his behaviour has, apparently, been indecision. When 'discussing' with O.M. he 'stood up for Delphine'. When alone with Miss N. he bewailed the incompleteness of his marriage. (Would he want to marry Miss N. if she had no money?) Now Miss N. is going to France for a time. I would like to see the affair as ludicrous, but I am too fond of D. for that to be possible. I feel that W. has treated her with unpardonable cruelty. I'd have respected him more if he'd 'gone off' in a decisive way. But all this 'discussing' makes me doubt the strength of his feelings. Strong passion doesn't act in that way. While talking to the Morrells, I kept on wondering what they'd think if they could read W's dialogue, with its insulting caricature of O.M.

August 9

All that really 'happened' was—on August 5 O.M. sent me a note (by Turner, who'd been 'discussing' with her again, blast him!) saying that if the Turners had a small car they'd be quite happy. Next day I gave Delphine an envelope containing a cheque for £75, and a note saying that another £50 would be forthcoming soon. I made it clear that I was doing this for her, and not for him. On August 7 (when I happened to be alone with her for a few minutes) she began to thank me. 'It is too wonderful about the car' she said, adding 'Are you sure it isn't too much for you?' S.S. 'I am doing it for *you*. You mustn't say any more about it,' and went on to mumble something about her having had a terrible time. She made excuses for W.—'He hasn't enough to occupy his mind,' she said—poor soul!

Miss N. writes to W. every day from Deauville. 'But' (said Ottoline) 'Walter's face fell when I told him that Miss N's father has cut her out of his will.'

My diary records that I felt wretched all that week, and had a bad sore-throat. On August 9, to-day, I have felt extremely morose. My cold is much worse—an event which affects me strongly though the world is not interested. Turner has bought a Bean car (secondhand) and D. is very pleased. I suppose I ought to feel pleased also. But I don't!

August 10

Went to *Sun-Up*, a Kentucky Mountain peasant play; remarkably acted by the chief character, an old woman who smokes a pipe.[1] When I imagine myself writing for the theatre I am appalled and repelled by the crudity of stage-effects as compared with the swift and subtle dramas of the visualising mind. *Sun-Up* was nothing at all, judged by the standard of the *written word* in

[1] Lucille La Verne (1875–1945), American actress.

good literature. It was *good drama*, depending on effective business and competent actors in an unusual setting. It was never dull and often intensely moving. Crude emotions were presented, but peasants aren't subtle. Poetry seems out of place in the theatre. Shakespeare's greatest effects are made without the aid of poetry, I think.

Anyhow the emotions of the theatre restored me to comparative serenity, and the morose self-lacerations of the daytime disappeared. (My daylight feelings had amounted to hatred of myself and everyone I could think of. I wanted to slam every door of my soul against everyone and lock myself in until further notice.) I shall be alone here for a fortnight after August 13, which will be the greatest of luxuries.

August 11

Another solitary day. I received a letter from Heinemann's, objecting to my wanting 400 lines from *Selected Poems* for the 'Sixpenny Poets' edition.[1] They say it will spoil the sales. I replied (during a violent thunderstorm) that I have no intention of altering my selection for the Sixpenny edition. This made me feel as if I'd done something strong. The alternative would be to print nothing but my new poems in the Sixpenny. This would infuriate Heinemann's. At present I am in the mood to be objectionable to everyone, myself included. How different I felt a fortnight ago. The sun came out after lunch, and I sat in Hyde Park till 5.30. Everything looked lovely; a Borzoi dog capered around on the grass with a brown French poodle, while the band played Mendelssohn's Wedding March brassily. But I felt ill and morose, and the sunlight only made my head ache. After dinner was a different story. Thank God for the Proms! Haydn, Mozart, and Mendelssohn (a piano concerto this time, and a very melodious one) made me feel quite happy and calm. I sat in the gallery and saw no one I knew.

August 13

At 11.15 this morning the Turners went off in their car, to stay with the Nicholsons, near Warminster. Turner was in a

[1] One of the Augustan Books of Modern Poetry, published by Ernest Benn at sixpence. The S.S. volume appeared in March 1926.

stew, as he's only had three driving lessons. He has become a member of the Automobile Association, which, in my hearing, he referred to as 'the Ack Ack'. (He told Ottoline last week that he already knew how to drive; but he always 'knows' everything before he knows the first thing about it.) Watching him swerve round the corner into Smith Square, I wondered whether they'll ever arrive at Warminster. But it was pleasant to see D. looking happy and excited (in her reticent way).

August 17

A blazing hot day which has bequeathed me a headache. I had no plans when the day began, but was feeling better than I'd done for ten days. At 11.30 Robert Graves arrived unexpectedly. He and Nancy are staying at Apple Tree Yard for two weeks. R.G. looked worried, and at once began to talk about Turner. (R.G. had come from Sutton Veny, where the T's are staying.) Apparently when W. Nicholson told R.G. that the T's were 'coming down in a car', R.G. said 'How on earth have they got a car? I suppose S.S. gave it them.' W.N. replied that that couldn't be the case because Turner had told him, quite lately, that he was earning £1000 a year and making very successful investments. And Turner had said that 'S.S. was very mean, and never helped anyone unless it helped him to dominate them.' Turner had talked of me with great dislike and had expressed a strong desire that I should cease to live in his house. He also complained that I annoyed him by playing his piano. The piano belongs to me, and T. has had the use of my thirty volumes of bound music. He used the piano—his playing is atrocious—whenever he wanted to, whereas I could only use it when he happened to be out of the house.

R.G. 'explained' that Turner realises that he has been behaving badly, and is 'trying to compensate his self-respect' by persuading himself that I have behaved worse. I spent most of the day with R.G. In the afternoon we went to Lord's. In the evening he gave me the proofs of his new poem, *The Marmosite's Miscellany*, which I read with pleasure.

1925

August 18

Cooler again. Slept badly. Headache till 3 a.m. and then terrifying dreams. To-day I drove R. and N. to Kew. We stayed there all the afternoon. I have relieved my feelings about Turner by carrying all my music up to my room. (I would carry the piano up too, if I could!) That made me feel better. A sop for my possessive affection for inanimate objects. Dined alone and went to Queen's Hall. (Mozart's evergreen G. minor symphony.)

August 19

R.G. being in town is a perfect godsend for getting me through the days. (An ungracious way of putting it, but true.) The fact that he was indirectly involved in the Turner crisis is a help, because I can safely let off steam to him about it. Nancy, of course, dislikes Turner, who is providing her with an ideal example of the way husbands maltreat their wives—which has always been her staple grievance against the world.

To-day I lunched at Apple Tree Yard (precious little to eat, as usual) and then accompanied R.G. to the Broadcasting Headquarters, where he underwent a voice-test. Miss Mary Somerville,[1] the lady in charge, made me read a poem (Blunden's 'Almswomen') which I did unwillingly and with intentional bad diction. We then called at Heinemann's for some new books for R.G. to 'talk about' to the 'listeners-in'. While we were alone in the waiting-room I 'presented' R.G. with the Loeb Library edition of Petronius, and thus got even with the firm for being tiresome about my sixpenny selection! When I got home the Turners had just arrived from Sutton Veny. D. said 'Walter is a splendid driver already', which I doubt. (I heard afterwards that he drove all the way to Warminster in *second gear* and arrived with the engine red-hot.)

Dined at Apple Tree Yard and took R.G. to Queen's Hall. Getting off the bus in Langham Place, we saw that Turner had been sitting just in front of us. (He looked slightly ashamed of himself.)

[1] 1897–1963. Director of Schools Broadcasting, B.B.C., 1929–47. Controller of Talks Division 1950–5.

August 20

The Turners have gone to Essex for a week. I took Robert Graves to tea with Burton. He left at 6, and I stayed on, jawing to her about my worries. She told me that she heard, some time ago (from Alec Ross's niece, Mrs Lucas) that Turner had told Romer Wilson that my being here prevented them ever going away when they wanted to. (In 1923 I rented the house from them when they went to Italy, and last year I gave Turner £50 with which to go for his summer holiday.) After all this I shall certainly leave Tufton Street at the end of the year.

A fortnight ago my eye was attracted by a small oil-painting in a shop-window in St James's Street. The shop was shut, so I couldn't ask about it. To-day as I passed the shop, the memory of it drew me like a magnet, so I went in and a ginger-haired Jew produced the picture. It is a market scene (Masham, in Yorkshire) by Julius Caesar Ibbetson,[1] whose name is new to me. Dated 1801, it is as fresh as when he painted it. It is, I'm sure, a little masterpiece which would hold its own in the Dutch Room at the National Gallery. The price was £75, but the man knocked off £5. (I arranged to pay £30, and 'the rest at my convenience'.) As I've only got £100 to live on till December 1, this seems irrational. 'Dash it, I can overdraw £50,' I thought. The picture is like a poem by Blunden, and the idea of its being my own gives me intense satisfaction. Query; was this self-indulgence? I bought it, anyhow.

August 22

Feeling tired. (Awake till 6 a.m. on August 21.) Showery afternoon. Sat in Dutch Rooms at National Gallery 3–4. Read Emily Dickinson's poems here 5–6. Then walked along by the river to Chelsea and dined with the Morrells, who are back from Devon and Dorset. They took me to Queen's Hall for an hour. Heard Bach's G. minor Organ Fantasia and Fugue played (badly) by Salisbury Cathedral organist.

Back here by 10. Felt so tired that I lay on my bed and fell asleep for four hours. Have just had a cup of chocolate and am wondering what to do with myself. The night is very still; the air cool and fresh and the sky clear. My Ibbetson picture is now

[1] Yorkshire painter (1759–1817).

at the Morrells'. O.M. is getting it re-framed for me, and applauded my taste in buying it.

August 23

Took Robert Graves to 17 Hanover Square. Very pleasant chat with E.G. His Golden Wedding was on August 13. Today I gave him a little Battersea enamel box which I bought at Penzance. On it a motto, 'Until the end I am your friend'.

August 24

Before dinner O.M. rang up to say she'd seen some rooms in Mecklenburg Square, which she wants me to look at tomorrow. I am now in lively hope that November will find me installed in my own snuggery.

There was a vociferous skreeling of starlings as I walked across St James's Park to dinner, and the lawns were vivid green, even in the damp grey twilight. Gazing along the lake, with its steely sheen bordered by bowery foliage and the pelicans white and motionless on their rock, I wondered whether a lovelier evening scene could be found in any other (capital) city. I shall miss that meal-ward walk when I'm living in Bloomsbury, but I shan't miss much else of my life here.

August 25

Weather grey and chilly. Feeling low, and coughing again. Lunched at Vale Avenue. O. and P. Morrell took me to Mecklenburg Square to look at some rooms. No. 21 was too large and too dear (£250 a year). No. 41 sounded more suitable (£150 a year) but we couldn't see it. I arranged to go there tomorrow, and shall take it, unless it is utterly impossible. Dined this evening with the Gosses. E.G's jolly talk made me feel much better.

August 26

But E.G's dinner couldn't make me sleep last night. I lay wondering whether 41 Mecklenburg Square would prove possible as a refuge. At 3.45 a.m. I got up and stumbled down to the kitchen to heat myself some milk. As I sat sipping this, with one elbow on Turner's writing-desk, my gaze was caught and held by a startling apparition on the sofa. Even an overcoat and a stick can achieve dramatic intensity when given their 4 a.m. opportunity in an empty house, and the coat and stick on Turner's shabby old sofa did indeed catch me napping (or rather they caught me 'preternaturally wide-awake'). I am sure that my mouth was agape as I stared at the inexplicable visitors, who seemed to stare back at me with sinister effrontery. For half-a-minute, perhaps, Messrs Coat and Stick, Conspirators, held the stage and were uniquely emphatic. They almost scared me. 'Now who the hell are you?' I thought (perhaps out loud). 'You weren't here three hours ago, when I closed the piano and blew out the candles (after playing a Suite of Handel's) and I've been wide awake upstairs ever since?' But coat and stick soon lost their dramatic prestige. I 'spotted' the coat as being Turner's (the stick was a new one). He must have come in very quietly, some time after 1.30 a.m. When I awoke this morning he'd departed.

Before lunch I went to Mecklenburg Square, and was shown the rooms by the woman who lives in them. They are clean and pleasant (on the ground floor, which I don't quite like). The sitting-room is twice the size of both my rooms here combined. I decided to take them.

Lunched at Vale Avenue. O.M. had an interview with Miss N. before lunch. Turner spent yesterday evening with Miss N. which explains the coat and stick visit. He seems to intend to go on philandering with her affections, and told her that he hopes to see her every day next winter.

My great-aunt Mozelle writes, 'Tomorrow we go to Foxwarren Park. I always like being there. They have a huge aviary and parrot-house, and also wallabies, kangaroos, cranes, etc and two dear little girls.'

August 27

This is the twenty-eighth night in succession that I've 'slept' here. I shall say good-bye to August 1925 without regret! The only satisfaction it has provided has been my talks with R.G.

(who went away in a hurry this morning, to look after his children at Sutton Veny, their temporary nurse having fallen downstairs and been removed to hospital). He was in a nervy state when I saw him off at Paddington at 12.30. Then I lunched with Nancy at Apple Tree Yard. Her Swedish masseuse, Miss Haltman, was there; also another woman, whose name I didn't catch. Miss H. is ugly, intelligent, kind, and humorous—not a bad mixture. I tried to be bright, but felt the reverse, after a bad night plus the rush and fussation of seeing R. off. After lunch I restored my shattered health at the hairdresser's, and emerged sleek and smooth, to call on Miss Burton. (Dined with the Morrells and went to a crook play and supper at the Trocadero, with a cabaret-ballet—all this for Julian Morrell's benefit—not for mine!) Since then I have been skimming a new *Miscellany of American Poetry*. The seventeen authors (the play to-night was called *No. 17*[1]) seem to have had nothing to write about. Such titles as 'Sea Holly', 'Whale', 'Swallows', 'Bug-Spots', 'Sea Surface Full of Clouds' (ninety lines about it!) suggest poverty of subject-matter. Even Vachel Lindsay[2] has become dull, though his 'Elegy on a Good Printer' is one of the few poems with any human interest. Contrived and concocted emotion; mediocre workmanship; automatic writing in verse; irony without 'bite'. Such is this Miscellany.

August 28

Awake till 4 last night. Constance Collier rang up and asked me to spend this evening with her. After a solitary day in sunshine I called for her at 7.45. She doesn't dine, so we went and sat in the Tivoli Cinema till 11! The main item was a fatuous film called *Drusilla with a Million*—the worst Yankee sob-stuff I ever saw. But we laughed at it. Had supper at the Savoy Grill, which was almost deserted and quite peaceful. Constance has been staying with 'the Bendirs'. (Bendir is head of Ladbrooke's, the bookmakers.) He has rented Clovelly Court for six weeks, and invited Sir Charles Hartopp (an aged and dyspeptic rake) and similar celebrities. Poor Constance has returned feeling unwell, after the rich food, late hours, racing talk, and million-

[1] By J. Jefferson Farjeon (1883–1955).
[2] American poet (1879–1931).

aire ennui of the entertainment. As usual, she urged me to write more—'write a modern play in verse', etc. She can't understand that poetry is composed subconsciously and only emerges after (apparently idle) periods of incubation, and doesn't realise that a poet can do twelve months' work in a few days.

August 29

Turner has an article in today's *New Statesman* called 'The Passing of the Pianoforte'. He considers that the pianoforte is an obsolete instrument. 'More pianofortes have rusted away in the British Isles than have ever been worn out with practice, and in the house in which I am writing this there stands a pianoforte made by Broadwood which had not been opened for years until I opened it the other day and found that it was useless for playing on until it had been tuned.' What otiose English he writes! He might have added that he found that *he* was useless for playing on it until he'd learned how to play. I shall now play on my Broadwood for a bit. (The Turners are back to-day, but still out.)

August 31 (Highcliffe, Lyme Regis)

With intensest relief I escaped from that poisoned house this morning. I'd left the car outside, and I was away by 5.45. Was at Guildford in an hour, and well along the Hog's Back by the time the first pale gold rays were touching the foliage of oaks and beeches. I seemed to be driving away from all the miseries of the past month. Was at Winchester by 8 (sixty-six miles). On by Romsey to Salisbury. (Had an altercation with a man driving some pigs, near Romsey.) Breakfasted at the White Hart at Salisbury. Left Salisbury at 11.30. Stopped to look at the gateway of Wilton House. Lunched at Shaftesbury, after a détour to inspect Tisbury. Tisbury Tithe Barn is 188 feet long (says Muirhead) and the finest in England. Tisbury is also the birthplace of Sir John Davies (1569–1626), the poet who wrote:

> For why should we the busy soul believe,
> When boldly she concludes of that, and this,
> When of herself she can no judgment give,
> Nor how, nor whence, nor where, nor what she is?[1]

[1] From his poem 'Knowledge and Reason'.

In the church I noted that Sir John 'bequeathed £100 to the poor of the parish, for binding apprentices'. Left Shaftesbury at 2.30. All the golden afternoon I was threading Dorset lanes. I went across to High Stoy (avoiding Sturminster and Sherborne) and along the glorious ridge by Evershot to Beaminster and Bridport. (At Bridport I'd done 172 miles, and had still a few drops of petrol left, out of the four gallons I started with.) Tea there, and arrived here at 6.30. The Heads were out walking, but their butler-factotum made me welcome to this delightful old-fashioned house which belongs to the Lister family. What an antiseptic it is for me at this moment! I must try and capture its atmosphere, which attracts me greatly.

Spent a typical evening, chattering away to the Heads, for whom my affection increases with the years, saddened only by Henry's increasing inactivity. Through dark trees the moon is silvering the sea—a Birket Foster, Tennyson effect. I am here for a week. There is a grand piano and I've brought some Bach. Peaceful days of mellow fruitfulness—150 miles from Tufton Street.

I don't feel tired or sleepy, though I only slept three hours last night. No words can recover the loveliness of the landscapes I've seen since sunrise.

September 2

Motored to Max Gate with R. and H. There 3.30–5.30. I talk such a lot here that it is difficult to write anything about it. And when I'm alone I am vaguely oppressed by sadness about Henry's illness, which makes my scribblings seem trivial. He works for two hours every morning, reading proofs of his great work on *Aphasia*.[1]

September 4

We went to tea at Racedown. W. and D. Wordsworth left here 128 years ago; the present occupants are the Pinneys (whose ancestor lent it to the Wordsworths). General Pinney's wife is Henry Head's sister. I served in Pinney's (33rd) Division in France, but was never spoken to by him then, as I wasn't

[1] *Aphasia and Kindred Disorders of Speech* (2 vols, 1926).

under him long. To-day we got on very well. Fox-hunting, cricket, and infantry warfare were our points of contact and I exploited all three fully. (H.H. looked quite astonished, and must have thought me a bit of a chameleon.) The General cordially invited me to look them up any time I am passing that way and probably thinks me 'quite a decent young feller'. Lady P. showed me the inventory book of household effects, dated 1795, with Wordsworth's manuscript notes in it. T. Hardy came to Racedown on August 19 and was much interested by it. The General remarked, 'My wife is getting quite poet-proud!' (a variation of 'house-proud').

September 5

After tea I drove R.H. to Mapperton—a Tudor and seventeenth-century house near Beaminster. We went owing to the 'good offices' of Lady Pinney. Arrived in rain at 6.15, feeling rather like intruders. The owner, Mrs Labouchere, received us. We sat for half an hour in the drawing-room, indulging in very constricted conversation with Lady Kenyon (very stout wife of the Head of the British Museum) and a Mr Lynch. Then Mrs Labouchere showed us the house, which she bought in 1919 'from the Henry Comptons, who'd had it 150 years' (a remarkable example of longevity, if the H.C's had it all the time). Mrs L. is a vague, invalidish lady, fragile and refined; she talks with her teeth clenched and adores Mapperton. She seemed anaemically gratified by our ejaculations of admiration for the beautiful plaster ceilings etc. (In the drawing-room R.H. and I had nearly disgraced ourselves— Lady Kenyon somehow caused us to get a fit of the giggles.) The gardens also elicited our encomiums. It is a perfect place— too perfect to live in I imagine, unless one could be content to spend one's life admiring it. We had a rollicking drive home, through grass-grown lanes which landed us, unexpectedly, outside Racedown, which led to jokes about 'supposing we broke down here and had to ask for assistance'—how the Pinneys would disapprove of R.H. gallivanting about the country and keeping Henry waiting for his dinner etc.—undutiful wife that she is! The rain had stopped while we were at Mapperton, and now the west showed a ragged array of purple and yellow clouds. Back, at express speed, by 8.15—to be welcomed by a glimpse, through dining-room window, of H.H. lamp-lit and benign, just starting his dinner.

It is surprising, how gay we three contrive to be, under the shadow of H's encroaching paralysis—slow but inevitable.

It makes me sanely aware of the triviality of my own 'troubles'. When with Henry I feel as if I'd just left Cambridge! But I shall be thirty-nine next Thursday, and am only twenty-four years his junior (and immeasurably younger in experience and sagacity).

September 6

My last night at Highcliffe. After a quiet forenoon, we went (in a hired car) to Netherton Hall, and stayed there five hours. Only Mr and Mrs Granville-Barker[1] there, plus three dogs— Alsatian, Aberdeen, and black Chow. Everything agreeable. (I'd only met them once before.) G-B. is charming; would pass for thirty-five (but is ten years older). Has the look of a man who lives too easily. His thick red-brown hair shows no grey, but his face is too fleshy and his eyes lack liveliness. (Perhaps he is unwell? He was said to be 'on a diet'. What *does* it matter, anyway!) Mrs G-B. is cultivated and exquisitely dressed. The house and garden are perfect, and so is the butler. I remember G-B. with a green-and-rose-coloured parakeet in his hand; he cordially dislikes Swinburne, and never allows his wife to be left behind in an intellectual discussion. Politely he waits for her to 'catch up'. I also remember a specimen of my 'slowness in the uptake' (when with 'perfect-mannered people'). After luncheon —the ladies having left us—I was leaving the dining-room with G-B., Henry being somewhere in the offing. G-B. delicately indicated the way to the lavatory. 'No thanks,' I murmured. G-B. looked at me with what appeared to be an intense express-ion and said '*Is Head all right?*' Clumsily I replied 'No; not at all'—thinking that G-B. had asked about his health. But it was only his 'polite' way of indicating the lavatory. Showing us 'the place', G-B. looked very much the country gentleman, in his light brown plus-four suit. It was a sunny day, and the gardens were ideally early-autumnal and Sunday-afternoonish.

[1] Harley Granville-Barker (1877–1946). Actor, theatrical director, playwright and critic. His second wife Helen Huntington, American author, died in 1950.

September 7 (Hare and Hounds Inn, Shepton Mallet)

Left Highcliffe at 11.45 in fine weather. The Heads (with Pratt, their admirable ex-butler, who has been looking after them during their holiday) were rather a forlorn little group outside the creeper-clad house, but my week with them has been perfect.

Got to Max Gate by 1 and stayed till 5. T.H. was very sprightly, and once again amazed me by his vigour of mind and body. After lunch an emissary arrived from Edward Carpenter,[1] who is at Bournemouth, asking if E.C. might call on T.H. next Wednesday. (An interesting octogenarian encounter; T.H. seemed vague about E.C. and his writings.) T.H. is busy with the proofs of his new poems[2]—279 pages, surely a record for a man of eighty-five. After much charming consultation of maps— by T.H.—with regard to my route hither—I left them waving cheerily outside the gate, with dog Wessie in close and tousled attendance. I came by Maiden Newton, Evershot, Batscomb. I went up Batscomb Hill by mistake, and found myself going along the ridge I travelled a week ago; then, I remember, I noted the *long shadows* of some low bushes on the slope; this time the sky was overcast. I turned down a precipitous and rugged lane which took me past Batscomb Church, a derelict-looking little yew-guarded edifice under the hill. The place will haunt me—there has seemed to be some queer, sad attraction about it both times I've passed that way.

Leaving Melbury Bubb on the left, I went through Chetmole, and Ryme Intrinseca (a name which has often signalled to me from the map). These remote Dorset villages and their linking lanes are a delight to me as I buzz along in my little boat-like bus. Near Chetmole I passed a homeward-trudging labourer who might have been T.H's Giles Winterborne[3]—a tall, youngish, bearded man with a tool-bag on his back, a figure often drawn by black-and-white artists fifty years ago. So here I sit, in this old-fashioned hotel (T.H. once stayed here, he said) with only a pair of candles to light my page. This morning I received a letter from Delphine. It is direct and honest, like everything she does and says. (I wish I could believe that

[1] Social reformer, writer and poet (1844–1929).
[2] *Human Shows Far Phantasies* (1925).
[3] In *The Woodlanders* (1887).

Turner is worthy of such a woman.) But the letter can speak for itself.

My very dear Siegfried, Ottoline has told me about your plans. I think you are quite right to want to live more comfortably than is possible for you here, and I more than realise that our feeling and affection for you should in no way interfere with your doing so. But Ottoline tells me that the reason is that you are so deeply hurt at things Walter said about you to Robert Graves. Now I know that with your delicate and sensitive nature it is difficult for you not to take it too much to heart, but you surely must know by this time how things W. *says* are merely a curious form of cerebral activity that have no relation at all to him as a human being. I know that you have—and quite rightly— felt displeased with W. for some time past, but don't you think that people often go through a period of apparent disintegration in their lives, and it is at these times that exceptional demands of tolerance and sympathy are made on their most intimate friends. After all, I and all his friends would have deserted him long ago, were it not that one is convinced that the quality of his real self is something fine and worth-while. As for R.G., I am furious with him. I think one of the saddest things in life is the dis- illusion one suffers about people like Robert G. It is incredible that he should turn out to be so clumsy and literal-minded as to repeat things W. said, out of their context—or can it be that he deliberately delights in destroying the relationship between you and W? I do hope you will not think that I have set out to make excuses for Walter. No one would admit more than I do, how difficult or impossible he often is—but I do want to try to make you believe in the absolute genuineness of his feeling for you, which after all is that which matters most. I am miserable that you should have been hurt in this way. I am also worried because I cannot tell W. about R.G. It would shock and astonish him so much.   Delphine

I haven't the energy to copy out my reply, which is to the effect that I will do my best to forget the recent troubles and help her with the difficult job of making Walter behave less irresponsibly.

On September 8, my thirty-ninth birthday, I left Shepton Mallet at 10.45, lunched at Bath, reached Painswick at 5.15, was greeted outside the Beacon House Hotel by Schuster and Adrian Boult, dined in Gloucester with them, heard Elgar's *Apostles*, and had supper with George Villiers[1] and his mother (Mrs Leigh) at their house in Painswick.

September 9 (Beacon House Hotel)

A surfeit of British music to-day. Parry's *Job* (Boult, who drives us to and from Gloucester in his British car, which he calls 'the hearse', considers *Job* a 'very great work'). Parry's *Job*, I repeat, tested my patience, but did little else for me. Walford Davies[2] and Vaughan Williams—not much livelier. After lunch, Ethel Smyth's[3] *Kyrie and Gloria*—grandiose and flavourless. Then Holst's new Motet (Henry Vaughan's 'Body and Soul') which sounded singular but not impressive. Finally Elgar's A flat Symphony, which was rather scrappily performed under the baton of the composer. (Billy Read, the leader of the orchestra, said afterwards to Schuster that 'something went wrong with the scherzo after Elgar had got rattled in the first movement'.) How musical I am! Read was at Dr Brewer's. Boult took us there to tea. (Brewer is the Cathedral organist, and conducts most of the works at the Festival.) After a bit, Elgar came up the stairs, looking very broad, in a smart fawn overcoat and a rainbow tie. The Canterbury Cathedral organist, whose name I couldn't quite catch, chaffed him about his gorgeous tie. 'It's a *club tie*; I have to wear it,' answered Elgar abruptly, and passed on with a 'We are not amused' air. But why he *has* to wear it will never be known! He greeted me cordially, by my Christian name, and began to discuss motoring. (He once asked me to take him for a tour of the Cathedrals in my car—offering to pay all expenses.) He has recently acquired

---

[1] Second son of the seventh Earl of Jersey (1883–1969).
[2] Organist and composer (1869–1941). Knighted 1922. Master of the King's Music 1934–41.
[3] Composer and writer (1858–1944). D.B.E. 1922.

a car, which he drives himself. 'A man ran into me yesterday,' he said.

Afterwards, when Boult and I were waiting for Schuster outside the Cathedral, B. said he is losing faith in all Elgar's works except *The Kingdom*, the Second Symphony, *The Enigma Variations*, and 'the Fiddle Concerto'. 'I thought *The Apostles* sounded awful last night!' he added. I can only say that most of Elgar's music excites me emotionally. How sad if it is spurious emotion! In that case Hans Richter[1] was wrong, when he announced (at Manchester in 1908) that Elgar is 'the greatest man since Beethoven'—a dictum often quoted by Schuster when his hero's merits are being questioned by the unconverted.

September 10
Music all day, but nothing 'to write home about' till the evening, when I enjoyed Verdi's Requiem to the full. (Was sitting at the end of a row and could lean comfortably against the wooden barrier, instead of being squashed as before.) The music seemed to 'come from another world', as the saying goes; a sort of dramatic panorama of emotions, which left me with a strong suspicion that Verdi has 'got Elgar skinned'.

Outside the cathedral I watched the crowd of gold-eyed motors buzzing away, and the pattering troops of people filing away under the dark sky and the lit windows of the nave. All this seemed quite strange and exciting, and there was a sort of suspension of all my mental activity, a complete calm, too satisfied to be excited, though an intense excitement underlay the tranquillity. The '*Libera me, libera me*', *spoken* at the end of the Requiem, seemed to echo on and on—a tremendously simple stroke of genius, crowning a masterpiece of baroque imagination.

September 11 (54 Tufton Street)
Boult bolted off to Birmingham before breakfast, and Schuster made for Maidenhead at 9.30. Personally I quitted Painswick at eleven, and drove quietly along, enjoying the autumnal sun-

[1] Hungarian conductor (1843–1916). Conducted the Hallé orchestra 1900–11.

shine. Lunched at Wantage. Stopped at Pangbourne for half an hour, and sat on the weir listening to the water. Tea at Maidenhead (at Skindles, which was delightfully deserted) reading an article on 'The Future of Poetry' in the *Times Literary Supplement*. 'Poetic production', says the writer, 'depends on an inborn capacity. Or, to speak more exactly, it depends upon a convergence of two factors—the right mind co-operating with the widest experience, and then freely expressing itself.' Why can't *I* think of things like that? I couldn't do it to save my life. But I've never claimed that I am a clever man.

At Tufton Street I find a letter from my solicitors, enclosing a cheque for £450 (result of selling out capital). This is for furnishing my new rooms, and making a fresh start in life. But the lady at 41 Mecklenburg Square writes that she wants me to pay £80 for the fittings (worth about £20) and will let the rooms to someone else unless she hears from me by September 10 (yesterday). So I've chucked the letter away and shall try for something cheaper.

September 15

I spent the week-end at the Hut, very peacefully as no one came, except Lionel Holland for lunch on Sunday, and he is a nice man. The weather was 'autumnal-age-of-gold'—a type I prefer to anything else in the year. Came up after tea on Monday, and took Delphine to *The Prisoners of War*, which was painful but impressive. It was strange, to watch, on the stage, the sort of behaviour which I've mildly indulged in myself, when 'attracted by an incompatible object'. Delphine said little, but understood and appreciated.

To-day Arnold Bennett and E. M. Forster were lunching together at the Reform. (Heaven knows why, I'd written to A.B. last night, congratulating him on his very sensible article on 'My Religion' which appeared in the *Daily Express*.) He was very genial, but condemned *The Prisoners of War* as 'no good at all, and quite untrue to life'. E.M.F. disagreed, and called it 'a fine thing'. Feeling certain that E.M.F's opinion was the correct one, I went off and bought a new tobacco-pouch. Then called on Miss Burton, but she was just off, in her best hat (a very large one), to Wembley, to see 'The Military Tattoo'.

On September 16 I left Tufton Street at 6.45 a.m. Breakfast
at Oxford. Left at 11.30, after having a shave and buying
De Quincey's *Literary Criticism*. Lunched at Tewkesbury, and
got to Malvern at 4. There I picked up my clerical friend, Cyril
Tomkinson, who had asked me to take him for a few days'
motoring. We went to Hereford. Next night at Welshpool.
Then two nights at Bettys-y-Coed. C.T's incessant chatter
made me drive carelessly. A few miles before Bettys-y-Coed I
failed to slow down on a steep hill and ran into a flock of sheep,
killing one and knocking the shepherd over. He was a lanky, red-
haired barbarian with a weak face and watery blue eyes. He
couldn't speak a word of English, and was wildly excited. I gave
him £2.10.0, and felt rather upset. C.T. never turned a hair. In
the evenings C.T. ploughs through *The Three Musketeers*, while
I peruse De Quincey.

Stayed a night at Bridgnorth. Lunched at Stratford-on-Avon.

About six miles from Dunstable one of the front tyres flew off
and went bowling on ahead of us. Stayed the night at Dunstable.
C.T. is about my age but grey-haired. Very talkative and excit-
able; walks with short brisk steps and gesticulates a lot. Very
'high-church', and much concerned with cassocks, confessionals,
and 'Our Lady'. At Bettys-y-Coed, he was too insistent about
'being called early to go to Mass' (why not *go*, and say less
about it?). Talks mainly about things which *have* happened—
'A man named Blank who I once went to Switzerland with'—
followed by some diffuse anecdote. But enjoyed himself vastly,
and I feel I've done a good deed. I am fond of the little man, in
spite of his irritating mannerisms. Wales was rather wet.

September 23
At Queen's Hall, Geoffrey Whitworth was sitting just behind
me. He mentioned Turner's having smashed up his motor last
week, and seemed surprised that I didn't know about it. (I hear
now that the accident wasn't serious, and the car is insured.)

September 24
Wrote a poem called 'All-Souls' Day' last night (1–3 a.m.).
Was wakened at 8 by loud knockings of the postman, and went
down to take in some parcels. This is a Tufton Street detail.

Delphine is paid £2 a week by O'Brien (Romer Wilson's
husband) who edits a Short Story Annual Directory. D. has to
read and make lists of innumerable magazine 'short stories'. The
magazines arrive in shoals. I felt jaded, but joyful when I
remembered the reason (the poem I'd written).

ALL-SOULS' DAY

Close-wrapped in living thought I stand
Where death and daybreak divide the land—
Death and daybreak on either hand
For exit and for entry;
While shapes like wind-blown shadows pass,
Lost and lamenting, 'Alas, alas,
This body is only shrivelling grass,
And the soul a starlit sentry
Who guards, and as he comes and goes,
Points now to daybreak's burning rose,
And now toward worldhood's charnel close
Leans with regretless warning' . . .
    I hear them thus—O thus I hear
My doomed companions crowding near,
Until my faith, absolved from fear,
Sings out into the morning,
And tells them how we travel far,
From life to life, from star to star;
Exult, unknowing what we are;
And quell the obscene derision
Of demon-haunters in our heart
Who work for worms and have no part
In Thee, O ultimate power, who art
Our victory and our vision.[1]

September 25

My Ibbetson picture arrived at 6 in its new frame. I called
Delphine up to look at it. 'How *rich* it is!' she said (the exact
epithet for its glowing twilight atmosphere crowded with
beautifully arranged figures). I drew her into a discussion of

[1] Published in the *London Mercury* December 1925, then in *The Heart's Journey.*

the future—the first time I've talked openly to her about W. In extenuation of W's irresponsible utterances about me (and her) she reminded me how he once said, before a lot of people, that if his mother were to drop down dead he wouldn't feel any emotion of regret (a remark quite incongruous with his real feeling for his mother).

Our conversation made me realise how tolerant and sorely tried Delphine has been. Not a touch of bitterness. I think she dreads my dropping W. altogether.

September 26

Went to 40 Half Moon Street 10–11.30 this evening. Burton produced a bottle of Sparkling Pommard (red) and some Tunbridge Wells wafers. She is going to 'find me a lovely little flat somewhere'. We talked about 'the Italian Royal Wedding', and she told me how she 'once tidied up the old Kaiserin's hair at Friedrichshof'! She has just been to Dieppe for a few days and is full of beans.

September 28

Pleasant weather, brisk and still. Strolled up Bond Street after lunch. It is being re-laid and free from traffic—almost like a foot-way—making one realise how delightful the streets would be without buses and cars.

Pausing to stare at a Bechstein Grand in a window, I went in and inquired the price. I left the shop having bought the piano for £226. Next week the 'McKenna Duties' come into operation, and German pianos will be 33% dearer. So I have saved something by my extravagance. (I shall give my seventeen-year-old Broadwood to Gabriel.)

Before dinner to-day I forced myself to go down and talk to Turner and got on quite easily—by discussing Robert Graves's long poem in *The Calendar*.[1] W. told me he has recently written a poem of seven hundred lines in rhymed couplets. It was called *Marigold*, and appeared in *The Calendar* and then in a limited edition. Talking to him like that (though I avoided meeting his eyes) it seemed incredible that he has been so tiresome.

[1] *The Marmosite's Miscellany.*

September 30

In the Reform Club (after lunch) I discovered E. M. Forster in the morning-room. He was perusing his bank-book pensively. He said 'Making such a lot of money makes me feel heavy'. (*A Passage to India* had been selling largely, both in England and America.)

October 1

Hazy sunshine and autumnal stillness. At 3.30 I went with Burton to inspect flats in South Kensington. Decided to take 39 Queen's Gate—two good rooms on ground floor of an imposingly porticoed house. One room very large, but dark. (£150 a year plus 'service'.) N.B. is determined to buy me arm-chairs, grandfather clocks and tallboys galore (none of which I want).

October 3 (11.30 p.m.; after putting the clock back an hour for 'winter')

Met E.M.F. by accident at Queen's Hall. He came back here for an hour afterwards. After a bit Turner came in, and began, with typical tactlessness, to advise E.M.F. *never to get a car*! 'It is the most exhausting and unpleasant form of recreation.' (Expensive, too, for me!)

As he sat there, it suddenly struck me that he looked rather dotty. E.M.F. wriggled unhappily on the sofa, bored by Turner's long-winded style of talking. Once one loses faith in his over-emphasis and *final* pronouncements, the whole thing seems absurd. I don't see E.M.F. often enough. No one is more sympathetic, wise, and witty about the surface-subtleties of human existence. He said 'The trouble about Turner seems to be that he lives like he writes—confused improvising which develops into huge grotesque patterns.'

October 6 (Midnight striking. I shan't be sorry to say good-bye to 'Big Ben'!)

The weather continues its autumnal afterthoughts of summer —soft hazy sunshine, tarnished gold above banks of mist. This afternoon I bought Gosse's *Silhouettes*,[1] and read one—about

[1] A collection of articles and reviews (1925).

Branwell Brontë—on a chair facing Park Lane. Then I plodded
round the Serpentine, wishing that some of the younger writers
who 'dismiss Gosse as no good' could give me half the enjoyment he does.

There is a silly parody of 'Everyone Sang' in *Punch* this week
called 'Mr (full name) refuses to sing in public'. I seem to be
creating a reputation for literary aloofness.

Last night at 4 a.m. a stray tabby cat came mewing outside
the door. I went out and gave it a saucer of milk. It was so
grateful and delighted that I went to bed sadly, remembering
its anxious little face peering in at a chink of the front gate,
whither I'd unwillingly conducted it.

October 10

On Thursday I drove down to Abinger Hammer and stayed
two nights with E. M. Forster. Lowes Dickinson[1] also there.
On Friday we went to tea with the R. C. Trevelyans[2] at Leith
Hill. A very happy visit. L.D. is charming.

I have a letter from Glen Byam Shaw,[3] to whom I sent a funny
postcard when I was at Painswick. He says he wants to see me,
which pleases me, as he is a nice boy.

October 12

Have just copied out two more of Dryden's Epistles, and have
now done 549 lines (out of 1096) in my best calligraphy (in a
small folio manuscript-book—an old binding refilled with good
paper). I began this patient toil ten days ago, and although it is
only a pastime (or kill-time) I am hoping that it may improve
the clarity of my style. (*Later*) In the last three-quarters of an
hour I have read Flaubert's *Un Coeur Simple,* in an American
translation which I found among Delphine's 'O'Brien books', of
which she makes lists. Last summer I began it in French, at
Schuster's, but didn't progress far. Now I have polished it off at

[1] Goldsworthy Lowes Dickinson (1862–1932), philosophical writer and essayist.
E. M. Forster's memoir of him appeared in 1934.
[2] Robert Calverley Trevelyan (1872–1951), poet. Brother of G. M. Trevelyan.
[3] Actor and theatrical director, born 1904, whom S.S. had met towards the end of
1924. He remained a great friend for the rest of S.S's life, and *The Weald of Youth*
(1942) is dedicated to him.

a sitting, murmuring 'What a masterpiece!' After one perusal, one refers to such a work, for the rest of one's life, as if one were as familiar with its subtleties as the man who wrote it.

October 13

Sachie Sitwell was married yesterday in Paris. This morning's papers full of photographs of the family.

Turner has just come home at 2 a.m. Delphine, as usual, waiting up for him. I hear them talking above my head, and listen with smouldering anger. My dislike of him seems to deepen. Have just copied another 117 lines of Dryden.

October 14

The rooms at 39 Queen's Gate have proved too expensive. (£175 plus £90 for compulsory 'service'—surely this is a lot for two unfurnished rooms.) This afternoon I went to look at a flat in Lexham Gardens. The keys had to be got from the agents, so I contented myself with a peep through the letter-aperture; an expensive and unattractive place. I left feeling rather hopeless about my domiciliary future, which is becoming an urgent problem. (Turner thinks he can let this house by November.)

October 15

This morning Turner asked me to have lunch with him. I assented—not too graciously—and he came to the Reform Club. We began with evasions, which I intended to sustain, but he compelled me to discuss 'the problem of his life' (his favourite subject). We sat in the gallery till 3.30. He told me that Miss N. is in London and pulling at him all the time (but no longer relying on him to go off with her). Turner realises the value of Delphine; he also realises the intrinsic worth of Miss N. Talks, unconvincingly, about his craving to produce children, but says nothing about the financial stability which Miss N. would provide. T's apparent ingenuousness was very disarming. He really seems to enjoy talking for hours about his most private affairs. He asserted that his literary earnings for

the past eighteen months have been about £1500 (double what
I thought). But if this is true, why did he allow me to give him
£50 for his holiday in August 1924? (He told me then that he
had no money for a holiday.)

October 19

Stayed the week-end at Garsington. Lytton Strachey there.
Duchess of Marlborough came to tea on Sunday, bringing the
Duchesse de Clermont-Tonnerre who has written a book about
Proust,[1] and talked intensely to Lytton. After they'd left I asked
him what her book on Proust is like. L.S. (with a slight tremor
of his shoulders) 'A footling sort of book'. (I mention this
because it is the only occasion on which I've heard him give 'a
straight answer to a straight question'!) David Cecil to dinner.
I played poker all the evening with him and Lytton and Philip
Morrell and Julian (lost ninepence). L.S. was very jolly.

Came back this afternoon, in cold rain, and dined with
Schuster at Pagani's. (L.S.O. Concert—including Respighi's
Pines of Rome, with a gramophone record of a nightingale.
Nothing original in it except the nightingale.) Brentano (New
York) writes me a preposterous letter, offering to publish me
there 'for a few volumes, *starting in*, let us say, with a volume
on our spring list' etc.

October 20

Glen Byam Shaw to dinner. Very successful evening. He
seems nice and straightforward, full of charm and good sense.
He came back here 10–12, and I showed him various books and
manuscripts. He left me with a feeling of peace. He goes to
Oxford next week, for a six-weeks season with Fagan's[2]
repertory company.[3]

October 21

Robert Graves writes that he is hoping to get the Cairo
professorship (£1500 a year) but needs money at the moment.

[1] *Robert de Montesquiou et Marcel Proust* (1925).
[2] J. B. Fagan, dramatist and impresario (1873–1933).
[3] 4 May 1931. My best friend ever since. S.S.

Sent him £10. Dined with the Heads. Since then I've been trying to eliminate books from my shelves. Selected about 120 volumes, which Sotheran's will take. (Worth about £30—to Sotheran's.) It is always a sort of perverse pleasure to me—to lighten myself of imaginary encumbrances. Many of the books are those which I formerly believed to be indispensable. Anyhow they are piled up on the sofa, and soon I'll be rid of them.

October 22

Another mild rainy day. This evening I went alone to *The Sea-Gull*,[1] which stimulated me very much. Margot (Asquith) talked to me in an interval.

Before dinner I received a very nice letter from Glen Byam Shaw. He says 'You can help me so much if you will only waste (from your point of view) your time with me. Most stage people are bloody, and I don't want to get like them, although I love acting and everything to do with the theatre more than anything else.' His letter is in reply to a reticent one I sent him, with a copy of *Lingual Exercises*. He seems to think that I can obtain the flat he told me about—at the top of a house in Campden Hill Square. (It belongs to Harold Speed,[2] an artist who is a friend of the Byam Shaws.)

(Odd, that I should have seen *The Sea-Gull* that day, as it is one of Glen's favourite plays, in which he afterwards acted with considerable success.)

October 23

Finished copying out Dryden's Epistles this evening.

October 24

A happy evening with Glen.

October 26

A dark rainy afternoon, very mild. I went to inspect 23 Campden Hill Square. Mr Speed greeted me effusively, and led me straight in to his large studio, where he showed me all his

[1] By Chekhov.
[2] Painter, chiefly of portraits and frescoes (1872–1957).

recent work. (Landscapes of the Lake District, competent and conventional.) One was a scene of rocks, with a stream. 'I think I shall *throw in a few nymphs*', he remarked breezily. He said he'd only seen a few of my poems, and mentioned that he is 'about to do a portrait of Sir Edward—that is to say *Viscount*—Grey', to which I replied 'What an interesting subject!' (and wondered when he would show me *the flat*). Speed is about fifty—a bearded specimen of the artist as typically delineated in *Punch* jokes. He talks all the time, without expecting or wanting any response. While he was 'admitting that he has strong views about modern art' (puffing a pipe and wearing a blue smock) I suffered gradations of boredom and exhaustion. He told me that 'Barrie wrote *Peter Pan* in this house', and I responded with exclamations of gratified interest. In return I could only contribute the information that Sir Hamo Thornycroft is my uncle—'You probably know him?' 'O yes; what an energetic chap he is; wonderful man for his age.' ('Blast his impudence,' I thought, thinking also how polite and miserable Uncle Hamo would be when in close contact with a bumptious man like Speed.)

Speed then gave me a short lecture on portrait-painting, while displaying some of his own portraits. 'The dullest subject for a portrait is a good-looking young man,' he announced. This pained me internally. Finally he took me upstairs and the flat turned out to be exactly what I want (except that it has gas-fires). Speed informed me that he had the rooms converted into a flat when the Labour Government came in. 'I was afraid they'd force people to *let* spare rooms in their houses, like they did in Italy and Germany. One has to be careful about these Socialist tactics.' I felt inclined to tell him that he's got a Socialist tenant after all.

The flat costs £150 a year. Glen's house is only three minutes away.

November 6
Went to Oxford to see Glen as Bentley in Shaw's *Misalliance*.

November 7

Dined with Gosse at the Marlborough Club. I was the youngest of a party which was—Lord Dunedin;[1] J. M. Barrie; Professor Legouis;[2] M. Saurat;[3] Dean Inge;[4] and Desmond MacCarthy. It was most enjoyable. The Dean (who had come from Bishop Auckland) had a touch of lumbago and was hard of hearing. Gosse was charming and told his best Hall Caine stories. I sat next to Barrie, who was positively garrulous. We talked mostly about Max Gate. After dinner I was deputed by E.G. to 'tell Professor Legouis all about the younger generation of English poets'. (Prof. L. is head of the English Literature department of the Sorbonne, and has translated *Paradise Lost* into French.) He was very gracious, and looked like a diplomat in a Sardou drama—pointed grey beard and red rosette in buttonhole. I came home completely convivialised, to find a letter from J. C. Squire, to whom I'd sent my new poem ('All-Souls' Day') for the *Mercury*. 'The poem is very beautiful and powerful. There is a strange stirring in all you do now. When you put your poems together there will be general amazement. May I say that I don't think *anybody* is doing such work as you are now.' This is very gratifying. I only hope he is right.

November 10

Went to Easton Glebe on Saturday and stayed till to-day. J. M. Keynes there. H. G. Wells was very jolly.

November 11

Alone all day, except 9.30–11.30, when I was with the Heads, which got me through the evening very happily.

[1] Andrew Graham Murray (1849–1942), first and last Viscount Dunedin. Former Conservative M.P. Lord Justice General of Scotland.

[2] Emile Legouis (1861–1937).

[3] Denis Saurat (1890–1958). Author and Director of the Institut Français in London.

[4] W. R. Inge (1860–1954). Dean of St Paul's 1911–34. Classical scholar and trenchant writer. His criticism of popular illusions caused him to be known as 'the Gloomy Dean'.

November 13–15

Stayed at Oxford (at the Randolph). Saw two performances of *Ghosts*.[1] Glen as Oswald was surprisingly good. I had no idea that he has so much talent. On Saturday afternoon I gave him a lesson in driving the car, which pleased him greatly. He makes me feel as if I were his own age. (I was eighteen years and three months old when he was born.) On Sunday and Monday afternoons I was out at Islip with the Graves family.

November 17

A quiet and dutiful day. Lunched with Mother at her club and listened to her lively simplicities till 4. She then went to see her sister (Mrs Donaldson—Auntie Fattie) at 2 Melbury Road, where I joined her at 5.30. Several of my cousins there. They are such good people, and made me feel a brute for neglecting them. (They never refer to my long absences.) Saw Mother off at Charing Cross at 7.30. As usual she was mainly concerned about the thickness (or thinness) of my top-coat, and urged me to imbibe cod-liver-oil—'the best thing for keeping off colds'.

November 18

To-day I *have* got a cold, and a headache too. Lunched with Squire, at the Rainbow in Fleet Street—the sort of pothouse meal I detest—two sausages, a roll and butter, and some very cold beer. Squire drank four whisky-and-sodas, and has grown whiskers and a moustache. With his large spectacles, he looks like some sort of woolly amiable animal. Robert Lynd and J. B. Morton[2] there. The talk wasn't interesting—mostly about T. E. Lawrence, to which subject J.C.S. added nothing that I didn't already know. (He hasn't seen T.E.L. for four years.) Schuster dined with me at the Reform—paying special attention to the thick soup (for which, it seems, the Reform is famous). I was feeling so unwell that I declined to dress up and accompany him to 'Madame Crommelin's musical party in Tite Street'. However he insisted on taking me to the Coliseum to see the Russian

[1] By Ibsen.
[2] Author of many books (1893–1979). Famous as the inimitable Beachcomber of the *Daily Express*.

Ballet (*Zéphyr et Flore*[1]—very inappropriate to my shivering state of health).

November 21

Awake till 6.30 a.m. last night. After lunch to-day I had a pleasant Saturday afternoon walk in the City, exploring narrow streets along the river. It was a quiet sunless day and the streets were almost empty. Bells were tolling in St Dunstan's, Billingsgate. Flags (stuck out for the cancelled Guildhall Banquet yesterday) were at half-mast for the Queen Mother[2] (who has had a 'press' of incredible journalese mawkishness). On my way home I entered St Paul's. A service was going on (camping out in the nave, owing to the repairing of the Dome). The Dead March in *Saul* was played, but it didn't sound impressive. This evening I went to *A Doll's House*[3] at the Playhouse.

November 23

Wrote a poem last night (11–2). 'To a Room' (*this* room), not a bad poem, I believe.[4] Awake till 6 a.m.—brain too busy. Lunched alone; called to inquire after Constance, and found her having tea with Haidée Wright (one of the few good actresses). Stayed 5–7, and got on well. (H.W. being there made it easy to avoid mentioning Ivor Novello, who has gone to Bristol.) C. very amusing, though in pain with her arm. H.W. is a little grey woman; intelligent (and had never heard of my poems). Dined alone and back here by 9.30.

November 24

Went to Lener Quartet 6–7.30 (Schubert and Borodin). Lunch and dinner alone.

---

[1] Produced by Leonide Massine, music by Vladimir Dukelsky, costumes and décor by Georges Braque.
[2] Queen Alexandra (born 1844), widow of King Edward VII.
[3] By Ibsen.
[4] See *Diaries 1920–1922*, p.18.

November 25

Lunched with Tomkinson at Oxford and Cambridge Club. He had been 'taking a retreat' at a theological college, exploiting his own and the students' emotions. I suppose this is unavoidable; it is his substitution for sex. He ought to have been an actor. Went to see Constance 6–6.30. Dined alone. Began *Jean Christophe*[1] with enjoyment. Very cold day. Have begun sorting out my irrelevant belongings—letters etc.

November 26

Saw no one. To Queen's Hall 9.15–10.30. Heard Isolde Menges[2] play Brahms's Violin Concerto; also Strauss's *Don Juan* (Bruno Walter). Cold and rather foggy. Rather crazy letter from H. E. Palmer, who has dedicated his new poems 'To the Ghosts of John Masefield and Siegfried Sassoon'.[3] He says he 'intends no offence'; (I doubt whether he knows *what* he intends!) He is *almost* a fine poet and has flashes of real inspiration.

November 27

Snow this morning. Queen Alexandra's coffin is in the Abbey tonight. Long queues of people filing in at this moment. Dined alone; reading *Jean Christophe* after.

November 28

Positively for the last time I enter up my diary at 54 Tufton Street. So ends a domiciliary period of five years three months (since I returned from America) of which not less than two-thirds has been spent here. My book of satirical verse, which I began seriously to accumulate in September 1920, is finished, so I've no cause to complain. Did nothing today except see

---

[1] A *roman-fleuve* (1904–12), ten volumes in French, four in English, about a musician, by French author Romain Rolland (1866–1944). He was awarded the Nobel Prize for Literature in 1915.

[2] Violinist (1893–1976).

[3] *Songs of Salvation, Sin, and Satire* (1925) by Herbert E. Palmer (1880–1961).

Constance 4–5.30 (she goes away for a month tomorrow), and hear Lener Quartet play Brahms 5.45–7.45.

Have been packing all the evening. Am going to stay with Meiklejohn at 22 Connaught Square tomorrow, till Tuesday or Wednesday.

November 29–December 4	22 Connaught Square
December 5	Oxford
December 6–7	Garsington
December 8	23 Campden Hill Square

December 9 (23 Campden Hill Square)

A gap of twelve days in my diary, since I left 54 Tufton Street for ever. I am disinclined to continue the diary, perhaps because I am feeling contented.

November 29–December 4 I stayed with Meiklejohn at 22 Connaught Square. On December 4, a filthy cold foggy day, Robert Graves came to lunch with me and I went back to Oxford with him. Stayed the night at the Randolph. William Nicholson and his wife were staying there. The train was an hour and a half late, and I didn't go to the Playhouse to see Glen in *The White Blackbird*.[1] He came to the hotel for an hour after. Saturday was fine. Glen to lunch, and stayed till 4.30 (sitting in my room, while a dancing-class went on outside). Spent week-end at Garsington. Yeats, E. Sackville-West,[2] Miss Sands[3] and Gilbert Spencer there.

David Cecil to lunch Sunday. Weather still cold. Pond frozen. Yeats pleasant, and less remote than usual.

Monday afternoon I came in here, Burton to tea. Glen dined with me at the club, and came back here after. On Tuesday we went to *Juno and the Paycock*[4] (which I saw with Roderick the

---

[1] By Lennox Robinson (1886–1958), Irish dramatist.
[2] Later fifth Lord Sackville, novelist, musician and dilettante (1901–65).
[3] Ethel Sands (1873–1962), American-born painter who lived in England and France. Friend of many writers and painters.
[4] By Sean O'Casey.

previous week—a fact I hid from Glen). Liked it even better the second time. This evening we went to *The Madras House*[1] and Glen came back here and stayed till 1.30, talking about his inability to read many books. Nothing could be more ideal than our present relationship, which coincides with my pleasure at being in improved surroundings (and he lives only three minutes from here). I am being compensated for much unhappiness in the past.

December 10

Dined with Alec Ross at the United University Club. Roderick there also. Wonderful wine (Steinberger 1900— Hock, '96 port, '58 brandy, etc.) and very agreeable conversation. Alec on the journalists of the Eighties and Nineties is always good (Besant,[2] Yates,[3] Buchanan,[4] etc.)—glimpses of the earlier Hardy and later Wilkie Collins.[5] Otherwise an uneventful day. I now rise at 10; at 11 I have a breakfast-lunch off a sole and coffee. Play the piano till 1.30 and write a few letters. Walk across the park 2–5. To-day I went to barber's in Curzon Street and then luxuriously bought in Grafton Street a £5 silver cigarette-case for Glen's twenty-first birthday (13.12.25). This *self*-indulgence I compensated for by sending £5 to a man I was in the army with and disliked and despised. (He wrote saying he was 'down and out'.) But the supreme luxury is to be safely detached from Turner and his gloomy house and heroic wife. My books are in order on fifteen shelves; my best pictures are hung in appropriate positions. My tiny kitchen is my own. And my bosom's best friend is only a few hundred yards away. (My ex-bosom friend is also only a few hundred yards away, though he is at present unaware of the fact.) It will take me some weeks to live myself into this new place, but I shall be able to use my mind detachedly then, I hope. And my landlord downstairs is sufficiently commonplace and complacent to be no trouble to me.

[1] By Harley Granville-Barker.
[2] Walter Besant (1836–1901), novelist. Knighted 1895.
[3] Edmund Yates (1831–94), journalist and novelist.
[4] Robert Buchanan (1841–1901), poet and novelist. Author of 'The Fleshly School of Poetry', an attack on Swinburne and the Pre-Raphaelites.
[5] Prolific novelist (1824–89). Author of *The Moonstone* and *The Woman in White*.

December 11

Another cold bright day. All the morning sunshine pours into my bedroom.

Alone till 6.45, when Glen came in and we went to see *Tess of the d'Urbervilles*,[1] after dining at the Reform. (Missed Act 1.) The play is a bad one. After O'Casey and Barker, with their sense of the theatre, T.H's amateur scenes fell quite flat. The play is a travesty of the novel. At Dorchester it seemed less absurd, owing to Mrs Bugler's sincere performance. It was an amateur play done by amateurs. To-night its defects were accentuated by the professional tricks of the actors, who over-acted for all they were worth.

Back here by 11.15, and Glen stayed till 1.45, sitting in my big chair, and being more charming than ever. He is an adorable youth, devoid of all the self-conscious behaviour of the ordinary young actor. Our happiness together seems so spontaneous and natural that there is nothing to be said about it.

I gave him his cigarette-case, as I shall not see him again till Monday (he has to be with his relations on his twenty-first birthday). So my new room is being blessed with happiness that fills it brimful with peace. I tell myself that this happiness has a quality unlike anything I have known before. Partly, I think, because I have learnt by past errors to behave with discretion. But he makes it easy by his simplicity and sincerity. And he has an instinctive capacity for avoiding misunderstandings. All this is irrelevant. There is nothing to be written except *Thank God for him*.

December 12

A peaceful sort of day. B. W. Huebsch[2] to lunch; we sat talking till 4.15 (in the club). I hadn't seen him since September 1920, but there seemed no gap of time; there never is with people one likes. H. is an unsuccessful publisher in New York— a Jew of the gentle artistic type; married and middle-aged.

---

[1] Hardy's own dramatisation.
[2] 1876–1964, a humane and charming publisher of great taste and integrity. Ran his own firm in New York from 1905 (in which he introduced James Joyce and D. H. Lawrence to America). In 1925 he became, and remained, a director of the Viking Press.

Walked back here in the early darkness. The Park hazy and strange with twinkling lights beyond the trees. Have been alone since 6 o'clock. Dined off the remains of my morning sole, and have been playing Schumann and reading *Jean Christophe* ever since. (Just the sort of evening I have often longed for at Tufton Street.) At present I am unable to do any writing here.

December 13

Wrote eleven lines last night ('The Power and the Glory') late, so I have broken the ice after all.

> *Let there be life*, said God. And what He wrought
> Went past in myriad marching lives, and brought
> This hour, this quiet room, and my small thought
> Holding invisible vastness in its hands.
>
> *Let there be God*, say I. And what I've done
> Goes onward like the splendour of the sun
> And rises up in rapture and is one
> With the white power of conscience that commands.
>
> *Let life be God* . . . What wail of fiend or wraith
> Dare mock my glorious angel where he stands
> To fill my dark with fire, my heart with faith?[1]

A cold hazy day: lunched with Emile Tas, at the Ritz! Ben Huebsch there too. Tas is a pleasant Dutchman, about thirty-five, who lives in New York (by trading in precious stones).

We talked about concerts most of the time. (They walked half-way back with me, and by 4.30 I was alone again, and have been in that enviable state ever since, except while I was dining solo at the Kensington Hotel restaurant—a quite good and inexpensive place less than ten minutes walk from here.) Am still enjoying *Jean Christophe*, which is far the most stimulating book I have read since I became acquainted with Proust in translation. It gives me courage and reminds me that I must learn to go my way alone as far as possible, if I am ever to be any good to the world.

[1] Published in the *London Mercury* April 1926, then in *The Heart's Journey*.

Back here I felt a craving to speak to Glen (who is dining with his family a few hundred yards away and having his health drunk on his birthday, no doubt). In fact I almost rang him up (on Speed's telephone). But I decided not to bother him, realising also that the craving was a more or less futile one, since I shall be with him for five days from December 18 to 23, unless something goes wrong with arrangements. Also he promised to 'look in' here between 5–7 this afternoon, but failed to do so; again, I didn't mind much, feeling so sure of him. The bigness of Rolland's book has made my diary-habit seem silly. But I am getting free of my former introspective scribblings, and I find these diaries useful to refer to afterwards.

December 14
Cold day, threatening snow. Feeling moderate, with a sore throat. Glen came in about 11, which cheered me more than anything else could have done. Was with me till 3.45. Lunched at the Reform and called at Chelsea for the car, but they refused to give it up unless I paid for the repairing etc.— £58. Not having a cheque, I had to leave it there, which annoyed me somewhat.

Mother and Burton came to tea; Mother stayed till 6. She was very pleased with my rooms, but had bad news. Uncle Hamo had a leg amputated on Saturday, above the knee; he'd got a clot of blood which caused gangrene.

Dined with Ben Huebsch at Garland's Hotel. He told me about the Untermeyers' marital troubles, which seem serious. I more or less arranged with him to publish my new book in America next summer. I don't think his firm is very impressive, but it will be nice to be dealing with a friend, instead of an inhuman 'corporation'.

December 15
Wintry weather. At noon Mr Wells and Mr Canfield (directors of Harper's) called by appointment to talk to me 'about Mr Hardy'. I foresaw that they wanted me to write an article about T.H. for their magazine, but it transpired that they had heard that I had been appointed as T.H's official biographer, which I hastened to deny. The question of T.H's

biography is one I've pondered often. No candid biography can leave out the unhappiness of his relationship with his first wife, and this is what he wishes to be glossed over. Having got rid of them I went to lunch with Aunt Mozelle at Jules, and did my duty till 5, bringing her back here. Glen came in about 6, and we were happy together till 9, when I left him at Clarence Gate (Regent's Park) after dinner at the Kensington Restaurant. He is a blessing. I shall see him again on Thursday, at Charter-house, where he is acting. And we'll go on to Weymouth on Friday (in the car, though I am rather doubtful about the weather, heavy snow being more than likely).

December 16

Weather milder. Bad cold in my head makes me feel stupid. Alone all day. I dined alone at the Kensington Restaurant and enjoyed *Jean Christophe* (have begun at the beginning, after reading some in Paris and half the last volume).

Deaf man from Whiteley's called this morning and put rubber tubing on the windows, which were very draughty (a very Pooterish entry).[1]

Rang up the Donaldsons and was told that Uncle Hamo is 'not so well'. I am afraid he may not recover from the operation. Life here is amazingly tranquil after the suppressed irritation of 54 Tufton Street. I am quite content to be alone all day, tinkling on the piano, and thinking my thoughts. Probably this is partly due to my happy experience with Glen. The happiness he has brought me is more soothing than anything I've ever known. I am surprised by my own emotional tranquillity.

Also I have felt lately a new sense of proportion as regards the trivial details of life (which used to harass me so incessantly). My life seems to be simpler in construction, and I realise how few are the details which are worth troubling about. This is an internal harmony which I have been striving for since 1918. And it has been showing itself in my poems for about a year. Or is it merely the complacency of middle age?

---

[1] Cf. *The Diary of a Nobody* by George and Weedon Grossmith (1892).

December 17 (Hotel, Godalming)

Left Campden Hill 2.30, and got here nicely. Weather quiet and mild with a red sun fully visible. Feeling better. After dinner I walked up to the School, and sat at the back of the hall, watching a silly farce in which Glen took a small part (as a hotel proprietor at Monte Carlo!). Very refreshing to see the boys enjoying the show. Went behind after and arranged to call for G. tomorrow morning. Thank God I'm not a Charterhouse master! Had never been to the School before, and have only just realised how impossible it is to connect it with Robert Graves (who will be one of its literary glories, when he is dead).

December 19 (Royal Hotel, Weymouth)

Left Godalming 10.15 yesterday. Lunched at Winchester. (Stopped at Petersfield to look at lead statue of William III, and went on by lanes to Tisted, Ropley, etc.) Glen drove the last ten miles. Left W. 3.30; through New Forest in dark. Tea Christchurch. Got to Bath Hotel about 7.

After dinner I was looking carelessly at the *Evening Standard*, and saw Uncle Hamo's death announced. He died in the early hours of Saturday morning.

We had come from Bournemouth by Blandford where we lunched. *Sunday morning* (the 20th) walked on shore after driving to Osmington Mills. Rather rainy. After lunch drove to Max Gate for tea. There 4.15–6. Quiet evening.

December 21

To Sherborne for lunch. Tea Max Gate. No rain to-day, after 11.30. Glen drove all day except back from Max Gate. Quiet evening. In spite of Uncle Hamo's death I have been very happy here. No one has ever been sweeter to me than G. T.H. was in good fettle; and our visits were perfect. Glen got on well. Can't write anything about such an experience as this.

December 23 (Garsington)

A sad end to a happy week. Left Weymouth yesterday in wet windy weather: called at Max Gate for T.H's laurel-wreath;

left there at noon. Got to Salisbury at 1.45, soaked and chilly.
I drove. G. seemed to enjoy the bad weather in the open car. He
is an ideal companion. Left S. at 3 and went by Amesbury,
Ludgershall and Chute, to Hungerford, in better weather. (G.
driving.) At Hungerford by 5; had tea, and left at 6. Snowstorm
going across the downs to Wantage. Got to Oxford at 8 (125
miles).

G. left by the 10.50 train this morning, and it was only then
that I began to feel sad about Uncle Hamo. Came out here,
borrowed a black suit off Philip Morrell, and was at the
Cathedral by 1.45. I placed T.H's wreath against the trestles on
which the coffin afterwards rested, and then hid myself in a back
seat, whence I could watch unobserved the arrival of the
relations.

Had difficulty in controlling my emotion, owing to the music,
but managed to hold out. After the service I joined the crowd
and drove in a car with Frances Donaldson, Eric P. and Mrs
Leonard to the cemetery, where C. H. Hamilton read the
service while we stood round on the crunching snow, in wintry
sunshine. It was a desolate business at the graveside.

To my great relief Mother did not come to Oxford. Had tea
with Frances Cameron and her husband and C. H. Hamilton
and his son and daughter, and saw them to the station.

At 5 I was back at the Randolph, packing my bag; it felt
strange to be there again with no Glen, and the family funeral
dividing us. Wrote to Mother and Gosse (and Glen) and then
drove out here with Philip Morrell.

Ottoline, Julian and two young men and a girl went off to a
county ball, and I spent the evening playing bridge with Philip
and the Woodroffes. A queer day.

Christmas Eve (Garsington)

Started at 10.30 in fine weather (cold; roads icy) and drove
to town; got to Campden Hill Square at 1. Not many letters
there, and none of them interesting. Packed some fresh clothes
and left at 2.30 with a sense of escape. Had hair cut and bought
some bottles of scent for presents here. Back here by 6 (by
Henley both ways). Turner and Delphine arrived about 6.30.
Gilbert Spencer also here. Played poker etc. after dinner for two

hours and won sixpence. Still unable to condense and reconsider the emotions of the past week.

Christmas Day

Weather milder. Played poker and *vingt-et-un* after dinner and won three shillings and sixpence. Went to bed exhausted.

Boxing Day

Mild day. Sunny morning. Ottoline, Turner and I went to Chilswell for tea, and called at Masefield's on way home. (J.M. not visible.) To village entertainment at Stadhampton after dinner. (Julian acting in waxworks as the Empress Eugénie.) Fetid atmosphere and excruciating cornet-solo and songs by scouts and guides! Home 9.15. Turner drove Glen and me in his car. He is the worst driver ever seen.

December 27

Read W. P. Ker's essay on Keats 11–12.[1] Walked alone after. Julian annoyed me at lunch by objecting to my going to the Graves's. Went there (Islip) 3.45–7.15. Mr and Mrs Lockett there (staying). Nice people.

R.G. read Laura Gottschalk's[2] poems which bore me. Children very nice, and both Robert and Nancy in good spirits— going to Egypt has enfranchised them. Very happy visit. Played bridge with Julian, Philip and Gilbert Spencer this evening, and lost one shilling and threepence. The only objection to staying here is that I am too little alone and am obliged to listen to a lot of conversation which I find tedious. Now, when I am free, I am too tired to read or write or reconstruct the day. Just as well, perhaps.

December 28

Mild and rainy. Drove Turner to Masefield's for lunch. Dropped him in Oxford after and went to Islip. There 4–6.45.

[1] In the *Collected Essays* (1925) of W. P. Ker (1855–1923), Professor of English Literature in the University of London.
[2] Better known as Laura Riding.

Drove Mary Neighbour back to Oxford. Played bridge after dinner. All square. J. Masefield was as usual. Kind, courteous, but not stimulating. He looks pink and plump.

December 29

Mild south-west wind, cloudy; ideal winter weather. To Oxford 11.30–1 with Julian. Before that the Turners departed in their car, which refused to start. Turner is quite incompetent about it.

Walked alone 4–6 (by Baldon). Turner has bought a piece of land in Westminster for £8300, and intends to build a theatre on it and make a fortune. As he hasn't £500 in the world this seems rather rash. (This came to nothing; he wisely withdrew.)

December 30

Berners to lunch.

December 31

Drove to Abingdon. Morrells' car broke down. Saw Spencer.

APPENDIX

THE TRIUMPHS OF OBLIVION

(versified by S.S. from the *Dictionary of National Biography*)

A MISER (1716–1794)

Young Daniel Dancer from his niggard sire
Inherited a fair-sized farm at Pinner;
Let the rich fields lie fallow; grudged a fire;
And chewed one hard-boiled dumpling for his dinner.
With bands of hay for boots, skimp-garbed in rags,
For fifty years he mouldered on a shelf,
And purchased one sour virtue with his bags
By being most a skinflint to himself.

A PHYSICIAN (1764–1831)

John Abernethy flourishes in days
Of Regency dyspepsia. Fashion fills
His ante-chamber, credulous of his craze
For systematic purgatives in pills.
A flimsy scientist, his popularity
Derives from bullying bedside jocularity.
Prince of Practitioners his patients name him;
And though they die, not one is heard to blame him.

Appendix

A CLOWN (1785-1843)

Dick Usher was a public servant who
Was born to cut the capers of caprice.
He steered from Westminster to Waterloo
A wash-tub drawn by four large gabbling geese.
His Astley Circus patrons to amuse,
He progressed in a carriage hauled by cats . . .
Let those who Life's Conundrum Book peruse
Regard his droll career and raise their hats.

A HANGMAN (1800-1879)

Calcraft was born at Baddow. He became
The Common hangman, and adorned his post
Full five-and-forty years; acquiring fame
While felons doomed to die gave up the ghost.
A man of blameless character, he saw
Life's melodrama through death's microscope.
The gallows gave him wages; and the Law
Seared on his hands two words—'*Abandon Hope*'.

GEORGE LILLO (1693-1739)

George Lillo, jeweller (of Dutch descent),
Turned playwright with didactical intent,
Urged the importance of the commonplace,
And used plain prose to dialogue Disgrace.
'Apprentice ruined by a courtesan,'
And 'Rustic maid seduced by scoundrel farmer';
Such were the plots which made this worthy man
The pioneer of modern melodrama.

ROGER PAYNE (1739-1797)

On olive-brown morocco, a design
Of elegant devices, gilt but plain;
Star, crescent, circlet, acorn, running vine,
Shone paramount, employed by Roger Payne.

Appendix

Contrast with this, Payne's raggèd outer-cover;
His squalid face, forever at a tankard;
Arrogant, improvident, cross-grained and cankered;
And (if you trust externals) you'll discover
That men whom you've disparaged for their looks
May earn your approbation by their books.

SAMUEL ROGERS (1763–1855)

Rogers, who primmed and pruned to well or worse
The desiccated laurel of his verse,
And breathed for ninety years (without a wife)
The literary atmosphere of life,
Respectably survives his bland meridian,
A man of taste whose talents were quotidian.

GEORGE WOMBWELL (1778–1850)

No one was once more famous at a Fair
Than Wombwell with his wizened wine-red skin.
From the capricious purchase of a pair
Of boa-constrictors his displays begin.
In later years his stock-in-trade includes
A score of lions and caravans twice twenty.
Though rich with anecdote his life eludes
Analysis. He died in peace and plenty.

FANNY UMPHELBY (1788–1852)

'Who was this Fanny Umphelby?' you ask . . .
She lived in Leatherhead and died at Bow;
Made Education a congenial task,
And taught mild infants all they ought to know.
Pensive she sits,—the Urbane's genteel disseminant,—
Nibbling her pencil in an arbour shady;
Authoress of that compendium, once pre-eminent,
Called 'The Child's Guide to Knowledge; by a Lady.'

Appendix

THOMAS HAYNES BAYLY (1797–1839)

'We met—'twas in a Crowd'; 'The Soldier's Tear';
'I'd be a Butterfly'; and, best of all,
'She wore a Wreath of Roses'; songs we hear
But seldom now; yet Bayly wrote them all.
The 1820 charmer, with high-waist,
Brown ringlets, ostrich-feathers, and gold locket,
Warbled them languishingly. Modern taste
Reacts from hers; and would, I fancy, shock it.

INDEX

Index

Index

Index

Index

Index

Index

Smyth, Ethel, 282
Snowden, Mrs, 133
Somerville, Mary, 271
Speed, Harold, 292-3, 302
Spencer, Gilbert, 246, 298, 305, 306, 307
Spencer, Stanley, 28
Spenser, Edmund, 82, 243
Squire, J. C., 134, 137, 138, 141, 160, 206, 225, 246, 294, 295
Stamfordham, Lord, 210
Steer, P. Wilson, 205
Stephen, Leslie, 220
Stephens, James, 62, 82
Stevenson, Helen, 233, 255
Stirling family, *55*
Strachey, Lytton, 41, 143, 291
Straus, H., *156*, 167
Strauss, Richard, 127, 136, 230, 251, 257, 297
Stravinsky, Igor, 194
Sturges, Judge, *156*, 225
Swinnerton, Frank, 209, 257
Swynnerton, Annie, 230-1
Synge, J. M., 139

Tas, Emile, 301
Taylor, Walter, 59, 180
Temple, Richmond, 39, 54, 129, 131, 133, 262
Tennyson, Alfred, 23, 240, 259, 277
Thomas, David, 196
Thomas, J. H., 210
Thompson, Myles, 24, 25
Thomson, James, 63
Thornycroft, Hamo, 47, 48, 144, 231, 293, 302, 303, 304
Tomkinson, Cyril, 43, 91, 141, 151, 154, *156*, 195, 209, 285, 297
Tomlinson, H. M., 131, 185, 186, 189, 190
Toole, J. L., 122
Toscanini, Arturo, 101, 109, 115
Toye, Francis, 38
Tree, Viola, 23, 24
Trenchard, Lord, 68
Trevelyan, Charles, 128, 129
Trevelyan, R. C., 289
Trevor, Captain, 103
Turner, Delphine, 37, *42*, *55*, 56, 59, 66, 67, 68, 75, 86, 87, 92, 93, 94, 125, 126, 133, 139, 163, 164, 169, 171, 176, 209, 237, 253, 260, 261,
262, 266, 267, 268, 269, 270, 271, 272, 280, 281, 284, 286-7, 289, 290, 305, 307
Turner, W. (of Oxford), 28
Turner, W. J., *passim*

Umphelby, Fanny, 311
Untermeyer, Louis and Jean, 46, 302
Usher, Dick, 310

Van Dresser, Marcia, 162
Vaughan, Henry, 84, 90, 191-2, 282
Vaughan Williams, Ralph, 167, 282
Vaux, Thomas Lord, 90
Verdi, Giuseppe, 101, 109, 111, 142, 150
Verhaeren, Emile, 221-2
Villiers, George, 282

Wagner, Richard, 37-8, 60, 101, 109, 111, 115, 124, 127, 150, 190, 196, 231, 237, 258
Wagstaff, Professor, 167, 176
Wakefield, Gilbert, 91, 208
Walpole, Horace, 81
War Poems, 56
Ward, Mrs Dudley, 103
Warrender, Lady Maud, 126, 162
Warwick, Lady, 128-9
Watson, Francis, 176
Watson, William, 63
Waugh, Alec, 156
Weelkes, Thomas, 155
Weguelin, Mrs, 135, 136
Weigall, Lady, 108
Wells, H. G., 29, 30, 41, 42, 43, 79, 127, 128, 129, 130, 131, 132, 133, 140, 141, 162, 209, 236, 242, 247, 294
Wells, Jane, 129, 130
Wemyss, Lady, 255
Wendela, *see* Boreel
Wesley, S. S., 155
Whibley, Charles, 182
Whichelo, C. J. M., 49
Whistler, J. A. M., 122
Whitworth, Geoffrey, 285
Whitworth, Mrs, 93, 176
Wiggin, Charles, 36
Wilde, Oscar, 58, 122
Wilson, Mrs Arthur, 108
Wilson, Romer, 254, 255, 272, 286
Windsor, Dean of, *see* Baillie

[319]

Index

Wolf, Hugo, 136
Wolsey, Cardinal, 49
Wombwell, George, 311
Wood, Derwent, 204
Wood, Richardson, 53, 95
Woolf, Leonard, 78
Woolf, Virginia, 78, 79, 131, 219, 220, 251, 258
Wordsworth, Dorothy, 202, 259, 260, 277
Wordsworth, William, 82, 87, 184, 218, 227, 277, 278
Worthington, Nigel, 27

Wright, Haidée, 296
Wycherley, William, 86
Wylde, Anzie, 36, 65, 97, 99, 101, 104, 105, 106, 107, 111, 113, 115, 116, 120, 121, 123, 125, 133, 136, 141, 142, 143, 145, 146, 147, 149, 150, 151, 153, 154, 161, 162, 219, 228, 229, 258, 259, 263

Yates, Edmund, 299
Yeats, W. B., 298
York, Duke of, 121